Internal Labor Markets

Internal Labor Markets

edited by Paul Osterman

The MIT Press
Cambridge, Massachusetts
London, England

This book was set in Palatino
by The MIT Press Computergraphics Department
and printed and bound by Halliday Lithograph
in the United States of America.

Library of Congress Cataloging in Publication Data

Main entry under title:
Internal labor markets.

   Bibliography: p.
   Includes index.
   1. Personnel management—Addresses, essays, lectures.
   2. Industrial relations—Addresses, essays, lectures.
   3. Labor supply—Addresses, essays, lectures.
   I. Osterman, Paul.
   HF5549.I574 1984   658.3′12   83–17531
   ISBN 0-262-15026-3

Contents

List of Contributors

Peter Cappelli, Assistant Professor of Labor and Industrial Relations, University of Illinois at Urbana

Peter Doeringer, Professor of Economics, Boston University

Bernard Elbaum, Assistant Professor of Economics, Boston University

Sanford Jacoby, Assistant Professor of Industrial Relations, University of California, Los Angeles

Rosabeth Moss Kanter, Professor of Sociology and Professor of Organization and Management, Yale University

Thomas Kochan, Professor of Industrial Relations, Massachusetts Institute of Technology

Marc Maurice, Maître de Recherche (section Sociologie), Centre National de la Recherche Scientifique, Laboratoire d'Economie et de Sociologie du Travail, Aix-en-Provence

Paul Osterman, Associate Professor of Economics, Boston University

Paul Ryan, Lecturer, Faculty of Economics and Politics, University of Cambridge

François Sellier, Professeur, Département d'Economie, Université de Nanterre, Paris

Jean-Jacques Silvestre, Directeur de Recherche at the Centre National de la Recherché Scientifique (section Sciences Economiques), Laboratoire d'Economie et de Sociologie du Travail, Aix-en-Provence

Preface

This book originated from two perceptions. First, I felt that the idea of internal labor markets was of continuing importance in our efforts to understand the distribution of economic rewards and security. Second, I felt that much of the interesting work in the area was scattered, and given the substantial interest in the topic, a book such as this could perform a useful service. I also felt it important to cut across academic disciplines. Therefore, although this book may be dominated by labor economists, it also contains essays by historians, sociologists, and industrial relations specialists.

All but one essay in this book is original. The one exception, the piece by Maurice, Sellier, and Silvestre, is appearing in English for the first time.

My friends assured me that putting together such a book would be a dreadful experience as each author proved to be a greater prima donna than the next. In fact everyone cooperated as well as I could have asked, and the experience proved a pleasure. The Boston University Institute for Employment Policy provided both support and a happy environment.

As I write this, I am spending my sabbatical working for the Commonwealth of Massachusetts implementing the new Job Training Partnership Act. I have found some of the material in this book useful at the level of policy as well as theory, and I hope others have a similar experience.

Internal Labor Markets

1   Introduction: The Nature and Importance of Internal Labor Markets

Paul Osterman

Most Americans spend the majority of their working years in the employ of a single enterprise. According to a recent calculation, the average worker today is holding a job that will last for eight years. Nearly 40 percent of men aged thirty and above hold jobs that will eventually last twenty years or longer. For women, who have difficulty gaining the most preferred (and hence stable) jobs in our society, 15 percent hold jobs that will last twenty years or longer (Hall 1982). Thus, contrary to the popular image of change and turnover, the work experience of most men and many women is best characterized as stable and continuous.

This long-term attachment to a single firm should direct our attention to understanding how work is organized inside companies. Evidently, as is true of much else in our lives, the policies and procedures of bureaucracies—in this case our employers—loom large. Lest this point seem obvious, it should be remembered that much of the economics profession directs its scholarly attention to understanding the labor market, that hypothetical bourse where employers bid against each other for the services of workers who in turn shop around for the employment that offers the greatest net advantage. In this world—which dominates not just theory but also much popular discussion about who gets ahead and why—bureaucracy, personnel policy, rules, and procedures play no role. Yet in reality we pass only briefly through the market and instead spend most of our lives inside the firm.

It has, of course, not gone unrecognized that internal employment practices of firms are worthy of sustained study. The sociology literature has examined *The Organization Man* (Whyte 1956), *The World of the Office Worker* (Crozier 1971), *Men and Women of the Corporation* (Kanter 1978), and other inhabitants of the large firm. A minority of economists has also taken up the topic, with the leading institutional economists of the 1950s first directing our attention to the "Balkanization of Labor Markets" (Kerr 1954) and the emergence of job clusters within firms (Dunlop 1966). More recently, these ideas were formalized around the concept of internal labor markets, and among institutionally oriented economists a surge of research emerged. Needless to say, students of industrial relations and personnel have long recognized the importance of employment practices within firms. However, with the emergence of human capital and other neoclassical maximizing models of the labor market, industrial relations and personnel specialists grew increasingly estranged from their sister discipline of labor economics. Only recently have attempts been made to bridge the gap.

The employment practices of which we speak are a set of administrative rules and procedures often denoted by the term "internal labor markets" (Doeringer and Piore 1971). The point of this term is that the pricing and allocational functions of the market take place within rather than outside of the establishment. The ideal type of such a market consists of a set of rules that limits hiring to certain occupations, or ports of entry, and reserves the remainder of the firm's jobs to those already employed. Rules and procedures govern who is eligible to move into given jobs and how the decision is made. Wage determination is similarly subject to formalized rules which often carefully spell out a set of relationships among all the jobs within a given family. Several such "families" may exist within one firm. Typically, each group has its own ladders, ports of entry, and wage system. However, some rules, particularly those covering procedural justice, are common across families. Rules concerning job rights and job security are established within these internal markets.

This book contains eight original studies on issues related to internal labor markets and the employment practices of large firms. Such studies are timely because of the recent surge of interest in the topic. In the past ten years a large number of scholars, from different disciplines and from different perspectives, have focused their attention on internal labor markets. The reasons why such an effort is deemed important are discussed in this chapter, but for now we can simply note that, despite the considerable progress in the field, much of the work has been scattered in a variety of hard to find journals, working papers, and the like. As a result people interested in the topic may be unaware of much of the interesting new material now available. This volume was conceived to fill this gap.

Why Study Internal Labor Markets?

There are a variety of practical reasons why understanding internal labor markets is of considerable interest. Take, for example, the current discussion of productivity and the concern that the industrial relations arrangements of other nations, notably Japan, give them a competitive advantage over the United States. One aspect of this is job assignment: in Japan workers in many enterprises are willing to accept reassignment to different jobs as the need dictates. In the United States the typical pattern is extreme, often legal, attachment to particular assignments (Cole 1979). Underlying this is not team spirit nor some other cultural attribute but rather a profound difference in the rules of the internal labor markets. In Japan wages are attached to individuals, and even if the person takes a less demanding or responsible job, the wage is maintained. In the United States wages are attached to jobs, and any reassignment would involve a change in income (Cole 1979). Hence the bureaucratic rules have a significant, real impact on the workings of the economy.

A related concern is the introduction of technological change. Resistance to such change is often cited as a major obstacle to economic renewal. Resistance, however, is by no means universal, and a significant consideration is internal rules on training opportunities and job security. Some firms have established rules that offer incumbent workers the chance to learn new skills and thus the assurance that innovation will not cost them their jobs. Other firms offer fewer safeguards. The ease with which change can be introduced depends in part on the particular arrangements at hand.

A third example concerns the periodic complaints of employers and public officials about shortages of skilled workers in key occupations. Recent examples include computer professionals, engineers, and welders. In such cases firms claim to be unable to hire in the outside market a sufficient number of workers to meet increases in product demand. Often closer examination of the complaints reveals that the problem lies either in the wage structure of the firms or in the nature of the internal training system. The wage structure may prevent firms from increasing wage offers to attract workers due to fear that rigid internal wage relationships will require a readjustment for the entire firm or a significant fraction thereof. An inadequate supply of internally trained workers can be the result of an internal promotion system that provides few inducements for trained employees to remain with the firm. In both instances what appear to be shortages in the external labor market are seen upon closer examination to result from difficulties in the internal market.

Some additional immediate relevance is lent to the topic by indications in recent years that the structure of internal labor markets has shifted in interesting and important ways. One significant impetus for change has been government regulation, notably, Equal Employment Opportunity programs. Both judges and administrative regulators have moved beyond simple hiring issues to examine promotion, wage, and other rules. A great many investigations have found these procedures to be biased against women and minorities. In part the response has been case-by-case remedies of particular situations. However, more generally, firms under review and those that fear legal action have responded by revising their rules on the allocation and compensation of labor. A common example is job posting and bidding programs. Under these schemes individuals in one job ladder (e.g., clerical) have the opportunity to learn of openings elsewhere in the firm and apply for them. Hence formerly dead-end ladders are opened up (Shaeffer and Lynton 1979). Of course many of these efforts are ineffective and exist only for display, but the evaluative evidence is that, on balance, equal opportunity programs have indeed changed the pattern of opportunity structures within firms (Osterman 1982).

A second recent development results from the difficult economy of the 1970s. One of the consequences of a well-developed internal labor market is that labor is transformed from a fully variable factor, which can be laid off and hired at will in response to economic fluctuations, to a quasi-fixed factor. The fixedness takes many forms, including rules on job assignments, procedural protections that make layoffs cumbersome, seniority provisions that limit the firm's discretion concerning who can be laid off, and a variety of other impediments that make it costly to vary the size of the labor force. The economic pressures of the 1970s, which both shrunk profit margins and also made long-range planning more difficult, forced many firms to find ways around the limitations imposed on them by internal labor markets. One common response has been a growing use of temporary help services and subcontractors. This is essentially a strategy that moves the work outside of the firm's internal market. The size of the labor force to which the firm is committed is reduced and uncertainty is shifted to other firms, which in all likelihood lack well-developed internal markets. Although this strategy is most common for clerical employees, it is also frequently used for professionals such as computer programmers and engineers.

A related response to the difficult economic circumstances of recent years has been the growing aggressiveness of nonunion, or "union-free," firms and the proliferation of personnel arrangements designed to maintain that status. It is important to emphasize that the concept of internal labor markets is in no sense limited to the union sector and that the construct provides a useful framework for examining employment arrangements throughout the economy. Many nonunion firms have fully developed internal labor market rules. Nonetheless, it is true that in the past the cutting edge in the development of formalized internal labor markets has been the union sector, with the nonunion firms following and imitating in order to avoid unionization. The significance of the recent developments is that the innovating firms in the economy, the firms that are establishing new patterns, are increasingly found in the nonunion sector, and this may have significant implications for future practices.

Internal Labor Markets and Economic Theory

In the textbook presentation of economic theory, and in more technically sophisticated but spiritually identical versions, institutions such as internal labor markets play no role. Wages and employment are set through the impersonal interaction of supply and demand. Particular institutional arrangements are simply mechanisms for registering and acting upon market forces. In the words of Robert Hall, "The central argument of good economics in general and the theory of human capital in particular [is] that economic forces determine institutions and not the other way around . . ." (Hall 1975). From this perspective the characteristics of an internal labor market are irrelevant: regardless of the particular rules in place, a given set of market forces will always dictate a specific outcome.

One way around this challenge is to examine more closely the standard economic view of production which has as its centerpiece the production function. The production function is simply a statement of how productive inputs, such as labor and capital, are combined to produce outputs. It is a set of blueprints or recipes. In part, the shape of this function is determined by technical considerations, by the laws of science and engineering. However, a moment of thought will show that work rules must also play a role. The amount of effort a worker is willing to put forward, the extent and quality of training made available, the degree of flexibility available for deploying labor, are among the considerations that must affect the relationship between the volumes of inputs and outputs. The work rules are an essential part and product of the internal labor market of the firm. Hence the internal labor market underlies the neoclassical production function in the same sense as does technology and as such has an independent claim for attention and a standing secure from the kind of attack cited earlier.

The most likely response to this point is that it is a short-run phenomenon. In the long run product market competition will force a convergence to the least cost form of production. Firms that fail to meet this standard will go bankrupt. As a practical matter this position is valid only in the very long run at best. A brief consideration of industries such as steel and automobiles shows how slowly work rules change in the face of long-term deterioration in competitive position. Furthermore the industrial relations literature contains numerous examples of customs that were solidified in the distant past and continue to exert influence upon present wage and staffing patterns (a good example of this is the discussion in Elbaum's chapter of how wage arrangements established at the turn of the century in the steel industry continue to influence modern patterns). At a more theoretical level, once we admit even a medium-term importance of internal labor markets in shaping outcomes, then these become significant because they change the pattern of factor payments and employment and hence must influence the nature of the final equilibrium.

Once we accept the importance of internal labor markets and look inside them it develops that in a number of important ways the nature of their operation poses difficulties for conventional analysis. Most generally, the internal labor market is a set of administered bureaucratic rules and procedures. Economic efficiency considerations are important in determining the nature of these procedures, but sociological and political factors are also significant. Sociological considerations are relevant because in most enterprises stable work groups develop and small group dynamics become important. A common example, at an informal level, concerns norms that often emerge to restrict output (Roy 1952). Customs concerning what constitutes a "fair day's work" are also commonly embedded in formal documents, either union contracts or, in nonunion environments, company handbooks.

Political considerations are also important in setting rules. The classic discussion of this is Ross's demonstration of how union politics affect the internal wage structure (Ross 1948). Wage differentials between occupations become important in the process of building political support within the membership both by maintaining certain customary differentials between skilled and unskilled work and by narrowing other differentials that might be sources of internal divisiveness. More recent econometric work demonstrates that internal wage structures differ systematically in union and nonunion settings (Freeman 1980).

Within the internal labor market there are no market supply and demand curves for given positions. Many, though not all, positions are filled from within and the number of eligible incumbents is limited. The upshot of these entitlements and the weight (though not absolute preference) given to seniority is that the distribution of occupational positions and rewards is disassociated to a significant extent from the human capital characteristics of the individuals involved.

The nature of the internal labor market also introduces a number of indeterminacies into conventional market analysis. For example, because people spend a great part of their working life in the employ of a single enterprise, there is no longer any requirement that wages be closely related to productivity at any particular point in time. Instead the dictum becomes that discounted lifetime (or employment time) wage equals the discounted lifetime productivity. Furthermore the distribution of wages over the period of employment may vary across enterprises. As a consequence of both of these considerations cross-sectional analysis of wage determination is likely to be difficult and to produce unreliable results.

An additional source of indeterminacy arises from the variety of adjustment responses available in the context of internal labor markets. In conventional analysis wages adjust to clear the market, and responses to shortages, technological change, and any other shocks are wage responses. This focus on wages permits model builders to produce clean predictions since they need only examine one dimension. However, the reality of the internal labor market is considerably more complicated. Doeringer and Piore (1971) identify eleven different instruments of adjustment including such tactics as subcontracting work, changing hiring standards, altering training procedures, and redesigning jobs.* Although they point out that these are not all equally likely under all

---

*Some of these mechanisms have been identified by earlier authors. See, for example, Reder's (1955) discussion of the manner in which firms adjust hiring standards in response to aggregate conditions.

circumstances, it does seem apparent that there is no valid expectation that wages will be the primary source of adjustment. If wages no longer move to clear the market, the predictions of standard models break down quite badly.

The thrust of the argument thus far has been that internal labor markets pose severe difficulties for standard treatments of the labor market. It does not follow, however, that economic analysis is rendered irrelevant or even of secondary importance. Some writers have argued that from a more general efficiency perspective internal labor markets represent maximizing solutions to difficult problems of management and control. Other analyses reject the universalism of this argument but view internal labor markets as the outcome of a complicated interplay between efficiency considerations and other forces. Finally, some scholars have argued that internal labor markets can only be understood from the perspective of class struggle. It is to these differing interpretations that we now turn.

The Rationale for Internal Labor Markets

Much of the recent literature on internal labor markets has focused on their rationale. In the nineteenth century and early part of the twentieth most labor markets resembled the neoclassical textbook model (Jacoby, chapter 2). There were few attachments between individuals and firms and hence turnover was very high, and job security nonexistent. Wages fluctuated with short-term shifts in economic conditions, individual wage bargaining was common, and industrial jurisprudence was limited or nonexistent. Over the course of the twentieth century these conditions changed, and the modern rules emerged. It is commonly felt that if we could understand why this happened, then we could better understand the role internal labor markets play today in organizing the labor market.

One line of argument, rooted more closely than others in neoclassical theory, contends that internal labor markets developed because they are efficient solutions to problems of management in complex environments (Williamson, et al. 1975). In large enterprises, the argument goes, perpetual monitoring of employee activity is difficult and costly. Furthermore it is very difficult to specify in advance the full range of worker tasks and the desired responses to particular situations that might arise. In addition workers who become very good at particular tasks may be tempted to take advantage of their monopoly position to extract special reward from the firm. Standard economic arrangements—short-term employment contracts and bargaining—are poorly suited to deal with these difficulties since, virtually by definition, they permit individual bargaining and encourage individualistic strategies.

In this view internal labor markets establish a set of rules and procedures that reduces the need for monitoring and the incentive to engage in personally advantageous but globally inefficient behavior. For example, wages are attached to jobs; hence individual bargaining is limited. Internal promotion encourages cooperative behavior since workers have a history that is observable prior to moving up the ladder. In union settings the union management of the grievance process helps condition individual complaints to the greater interests of the group.

On a point-by-point basis it is clearly possible to set forth productivity-maximizing advantages of any particular aspect of formalized internal labor markets. However, taken as a whole, this general approach seems unsatisfactory. It is equally easy to establish efficiency-limiting aspects of internal market procedures. For example, seniority provisions may prevent the most able from attaining jobs in which their talents are best used. More generally, the rules and procedures of internal markets considerably limit management discretion concerning deployment of their labor force. For proponents of the efficiency-based explanations to prevail, they must assume as a matter of faith, since no data are available on costs and benefits of different procedures, that the arrangement that dominates is by definition the most efficient. The theory is reduced to a tautology.

Although cost data on different procedures are not available, the historical record is accessible and also casts doubt upon the maximizing explanation. Two aspects of this record draw attention. First, in many instances employers exhibited strenuous, even bloody, resistance to the establishment of seniority systems, formalized wage setting procedures, and the like. The extent and nature of this resistance is difficult to rationalize in the language of the model. Second, the theory proposes no explanation of why the internal labor market emerged when it did. The firms that operated from the mid-nineteenth to mid-twentieth centuries presumably had the same problems of monitoring their labor forces, avoiding opportunistic behavior, and the like, yet they found different solutions. The discontinuous nature of the introduction of internal labor markets (which occurred largely during World War I and the Great Depression), the important role of union organization and of government intervention, and the absence of internal markets in other periods, taken together, cast severe doubt on the maximizing explanation. At the very best these models become post hoc rationales, not explanatory theories.

The class-based, or radical, explanation of internal labor markets shares a good deal with the maximizing story in that both emphasize the needs and motivations of employers and both focus on problems of control. The beginning of the radical story is to deny that purely technological considerations dictate any particular division of labor or job ladders. The same technology frequently permits broadly or narrowly defined jobs with no visible loss of output. More broadly, the choice of particular technology itself is often open to doubt, and in making this choice, firms consider the implications for monitoring and controlling the work force as well as more conventional issues.

The particular patterns that we observe in internal labor markets serve the management objectives of reducing skill levels, dividing the work force, and creating and legitimizing hierarchial control. The reduction of skills is important to management because skilled workers are in a more powerful bargaining position regarding work rules and wages. Even in cases where substantial worker knowledge is compatible with a least-cost production strategy, management will opt for another technology. The emergence of job ladders divides the labor force because the relatively privileged position of those within the ladders gives them an incentive to exclude others. A system of "haves" and "have nots" is created and tends to perpetuate itself. Finally job ladders legitimize hierarchy and top-down control, both because the system appears to flow from the dictates of impersonal technology and because even the limited opportunities for upward advancement that workers enjoy along the job ladders create the illusion of fair play.

Many of these arguments can be well documented and serve as important counterbalances to the more common technological determinism. A variety of industry case studies—in steel, machining, and more recently computer programming—suggest that management has been interested, as a conscious policy, in limiting employee power by abolishing skilled craft modes of production. It is an article of faith among managers that division of labor brings with it productivity advantages, and observation of the introduction of new technologies suggests that this faith is rarely if ever subjected to a serious test. Management seems to be instinctively hostile to broadly defined jobs with substantial worker power and discretion. Furthermore most discussion of job design is cloaked in a technological determinism that obfuscates the real available choices.

The great weakness of this analysis, however, is the insistence on a single pattern of causality. Although there are instances where the emergence of internal labor markets arguably represented a worsening in the economic position of craft workers there are numerous other examples where job ladders and industrial jurisprudence represented a significant improvement in the welfare of the labor force. Unionization and establishment of internal regulation in the core industries during the Great Depression is one example. More recent examples include the establishment of job ladders, formalized grievance systems, and collective bargaining among hospital workers, building service workers, and farm laborers. In all of these instances unionization is the decisive element, but there are nonunion firms in the same or related industries in which, out of fear of unionization, comparable systems were established. The point is that, while it is true that internal labor markets can be imposed from above as part of an antilabor strategy, they also can result from a struggle from below by workers for whom the system of job rights and regulation is a desired improvement.

The radical view of technological change is also flawed. It is true that in many instances the introduction of new technologies deskills craft workers. However, it is incorrect to argue, as do writers such as Braverman (1974), that capitalist technological change always leads to a deskilling process. Historically, a great deal of technical change involved replacing unskilled human labor used for lifting and carrying type jobs by machines, and the new machine operators certainly were more skilled and better off than the workers they replaced. In addition, new technologies can knit together previously subdivided tasks and create new and broader job content. Computers are especially powerful in this regard, and in many large white-collar firms the duties of filing clerks have been expanded by the increased access to information that computers afford (Feldberg and Glenn 1983, Osterman, chapter 6). Finally, new technologies create wholly new jobs involving the design, maintenance, and repair of the new technology. It is an empirical matter, not an issue of doctrine, whether these new jobs are more or less numerous than the ones they replace and also whether they are held by former employees or by new ones. This is especially true at the firm level where management may find the urge for minimizing labor costs more persuasive than that for control and hence may replace large numbers of relatively unskilled workers with fewer but higher-skilled employees assisted by a new technology. None of this is to deny that the deskilling argument is often correct, only that once again reality is more complex than a single-factor story.

The institutional perspective on the origins of the internal labor markets is a somewhat eclectic combination of various viewpoints. Four factors are emphasized: skill specificity, on-the-job training, custom, and unionization. Skill specificity refers to the fact that certain kinds of skills are applicable only in the enterprise where they are learned. A particular machine may be configured in a unique way, a computer program designed for a specific accounting system, or the production flow laid out in a manner unique to the firm. In this way firms can share the expense of training with workers and can protect their investment by insuring that the trained work force remains with the company. Job ladders provide an incentive to remain because wages may rise rapidly with seniority and because the worker accumulates job rights that would be lost if forced to start at the bottom of another ladder elsewhere. Second, most skills are learned informally on the job, and job ladders promote this process by creating gradations with relatively small steps and providing incumbent workers with job security. This ensures that they will be willing to train those below them without viewing them as a threat to their position.

Internal labor markets also develop from forces on the supply side. If a group of workers remains in the same firm for some time, then a set of expectations, or customs, will develop. These expectations, which can be enforced through noncooperation or even sabotage on the job, tend over time to become codified into a set of rules. The process of unionization speeds this up and formalizes it, and hence many internal labor markets emerge out of unionization drives. However, even in nonunion situations customary rules and procedures and the force of group expectations can lead to internal labor markets. An example close to home are the very structured rules and norms that govern hiring and promotion policies in academe.

Further insight can be gained by examining firms that never develop internal labor markets. What distinguishes these from others? Piore (1973) has argued that, in order to subdivide tasks sufficiently to create job ladders and in order to permit a stable labor force to remain over extended periods, a reliable portion of the product market must be captured by the firm. Those firms that do develop well-articulated internal labor markets do so by serving the stable portion of demand and by operating in markets with sufficiently large demand to permit division of labor. They leave the remainder of the market to other firms that are unable as a consequence to create stable job structures. This cannot be the whole story, however, because within many firms with stable product demand are groups of occupations, such as clerical work, which do not exhibit well-developed job ladders.

Taken together, the institutional explanation seems to touch on what most observers would agree are the major points, and thus an eclectic analysis may be the best that can emerge. The difficulty is that the explanation does not seem to be much more than a list of plausible factors. One set of items on the list—the role of skill specificity and on-the-job training—is drawn from the human capital literature which in turn is essentially an extension of the maximizing neoclassical models. The emphasis on custom and unionization flows from another tradition. In fact it is this latter tradition that represents what is distinctive about institutional analysis. Specifically, the two central perceptions are that it is important to study (and not treat as a black box) the internal workings of institutions such as firms or unions and that these cannot be understood without considering how the existence of informal work groups and formal bureaucracies alters standard behavioral assumptions.

No effective synthesis of these quite different perspectives on how the labor markets works is yet available, and taken as a whole, the institutional model is left in a somewhat uncomfortable ad hoc situation. The analyst is too free to fit together the pieces in any way that makes sense in a particular situation.

The Plan of the Book

The preceding material argued that internal labor markets are an important topic and that much remains to be understood about them. The subjects of the studies in this book were chosen because they address the most important outstanding questions. The first group of studies takes up the question of why internal labor markets exist in the first place and seek to resolve it through historical analysis of the evolution of internal labor markets in the twentieth century. The second group of four studies examines modern internal labor markets from two perspectives. They either explore topics that to date have not received adequate attention—for example, white-collar internal labor markets and the nature of training—or they explore recent changes in the organization of work within firms—the rise of the personnel function and the nature of work within the high-technology sector. The final two studies address the question of variation in job structure by considering the impact of social environment on internal labor markets. One examines matched pairs of firms in different countries, whereas the other takes up rural-urban differences.

The Origins of Internal Labor Markets

The neoclassical, radical, and institutional perspectives on internal labor markets have had an unsatisfactory aspect because of the abstract level of discussion. A variety of after-the-fact rationalizations have been developed and it is difficult to choose among them. The obvious resolution of this difficulty is to turn to historical analysis. The chapters by Jacoby and Elbaum do just this. Jacoby surveys the emergence of internal labor markets in twentieth-century American industry. It is the first available broad overview and as such is especially helpful in identifying the periods in which internal labor markets made the greatest inroads into business practices. Jacoby highlights the tension between employer preferences for the "drive" system of personnel management, with its disregard for jurisprudence and job rights, and union and government efforts to establish internal labor markets. Joining in this latter effort were personnel officials employed by firms who viewed themselves in competition with line officials over the proper principles for organizing labor.

Elbaum provides in-depth study of the emergence of job ladders and the development of the wage system in the steel industry. Elbaum first shows that job ladders emerged from conflict within the steel workers union between highly skilled craft workers and their helpers who demanded access to training and a chance to move into the craft positions. This is especially interesting because it refutes the most popular radical interpretation of job ladders in steel, an explanation that interpreted them as emerging from management efforts to control the work force and deskill the craft workers (Stone 1972). The remainder of the chapter takes up wage determination and shows the long-lasting impact of custom and union politics upon the wage structure. Early in the century the steel industry experienced considerable technological change, and the pattern of the change was uneven in its impact both on different occupational groups and different plants. This was because of the importance of piece rates in the payment schemes. What is especially interesting is that the wage distribution that emerged in this period—which in itself was the product of worker power and bargaining systems—persisted throughout the modern history of the steel industry and was only modified after World War II at considerable expense to the industry. Even today the peculiarities of the American steel wage structure—in contrast to that of other nations—can be traced to the turn of the century. Hence internal labor markets clearly have important consequences for wage determination.

Characteristics of Modern Employment Practices

As has been made clear, there are many unresolved issues concerning the origins of internal labor markets and the role of social structure in forming them. But what of modern employment systems themselves? What do they look like and how are they changing? Four chapters, those by Kochan and Cappelli, Kanter, Ryan, and Osterman, explore these questions. Each author takes up a topic that is important because it has been incompletely discussed in previous work or has been an area of change in recent years. Taken together, these chapters paint a picture of employment practices that is more varied and dynamic than has been generally realized.

The function within the firm that has primary responsibility for shaping employment practices is of course the personnel operation. However, personnel officials have not always had an easy time asserting their role. This is due to the natural tension between line managers, whose job is producing output at least cost, and the personnel staff, who often take a broader and longer view of the employment relation. Historically, the relative power of the two interest groups has shifted, as Kochan and Cappelli make clear and as also is apparent in the Jacoby study. In addition Kochan and Cappelli show that within the overall personnel function the relative power of the industrial relations staff—the officials concerned with union-management relations—and the human relations staff—who work directly with employees—has also varied over the course of this century. In recent years, however, the human resources function has become increasingly important.

The reasons for this new importance and the nature of modern practices are the themes of the chapter by Kochan and Cappelli. It is apparent that a complex set of factors—government regulation, more aggressive antiunion attitudes, and the changing character of the work force— lies behind the new status of human resources officials. Interestingly, the current situation appears to be unstable as firms seek to establish a stance with respect to unions, as unions search for responses to growing employer hostility, and as government reconsiders its activist role in the work place. Kochan and Cappelli analyze the nature of this instability and suggest some possible resolutions.

The external environment of firms also seems considerably more complex than in previous years. This is especially true of newer high-technology companies. These enterprises are often characterized by rapid growth, decentralization of function, strong emphasis on team-work, and a need to retain a highly technical staff. Furthermore they must find ways to encourage and maintain the incentive for innovation. The impact of these characteristics is the subject of Kanter's analysis of managerial career ladders in high-technology firms.

Kanter's chapter is especially interesting for two reasons. First, most work on internal labor markets has slighted managerial ladders, and hence this chapter helps fill an important gap. Second, many analysts look to the high-technology sector both as the source of growth in the American economy and as a new model for work organization. Indeed these firms exercise a powerful fascination among manpower specialists. Despite this, very little is known about the actual organization of work within these enterprises, and Kanter's study therefore fills an important gap.

Not only has the literature on internal labor markets tended to slight managers, it has also given short shrift to white-collar employees in general. This is unfortunate since white-collar workers are a majority of the work force, and their importance will continue to grow. In addition, once we turn to the topic, we are forced to recognize that a given firm may contain several different internal labor markets or employment systems and that these may differ in important ways. These concerns are the theme of the chapter by Osterman. He first sets forth a perspective for understanding the existence of multiple employment systems within one firm and then applies this to understanding the internal labor markets for four categories of white-collar employees: clerical workers, managers, computer programmers, and salespeople. Osterman also discusses how the nature of white-collar work has changed in recent years and relates these developments to alterations in the internal labor markets of these occupations.

One of the important functions of the internal labor market is to provide a system for training. Job ladders and the willingness of more skilled workers to train those below them are important in this regard. However, in recent years the perception has become widespread that the system is failing to train adequate numbers of skilled workers.

Examples of occupations in which serious shortages have occurred include computer programmers, welders, and skilled word-processing operators. Evidently, there is something about the nature of internal labor markets that creates or, at the minimum, fails to prevent shortages in certain kinds of occupations. The nature of the training process within firms and the possible sources of dysfunction form the subject of Ryan's study. Ryan explores the incentives that face firms with respect to training and how the nature of the wage structure and training system may interact to create shortages or inadequate training in certain kinds of jobs.

Community Structure and Culture

What is the impact of culture or social structure upon employment patterns within firms? Is it reasonable to expect that comparable firms in different countries, or different regions within the same country, will have similar practices? Until recently the commonly accepted answer to these questions drew from the industrial relations literature of the 1950s and 1960s. This line of thought generally assumed, either explicitly or implicitly, that what might be termed the American mainstream industrial model was the outcome toward which all maturing systems evolved. This view was argued most influentially in *Industrialism and Industrial Man* (1960) and came to be known as the convergence thesis.

Underlying this argument was the assumption that all industrial systems have to solve a common set of problems—discipline, maximizing output, distributing rewards, and planning—and technology and the nature of organizations dictate the optimal response. Because technology and organization are crucial, the problem and solution were seen as "industrialism," a term that transcends any particular political, social, or cultural setting. In this view all industrial systems will eventually look alike in their main features.

For our purposes this implies that the internal labor market model, both in terms of its rules and its structure, should be viewed as universal. Yet we have already seen that there are good grounds for skepticism of technological determinism. An additional challenge to the universalistic view is raised by careful comparative research. This kind of work develops new perspectives by identifying anomalies in the universal model, anomalies that are sufficiently numerous and stable to raise serious questions about what constitutes "exceptions" and "rules." Examples of such findings are the important role of culture and tradition in structuring internal labor markets in Japanese firms (Dore 1973) and the persistence of a strong informal sector in the midst of dynamic industrial settings (Berger 1979).

Two chapters in this book take a comparative approach, and in so doing, both undermine the universal model and enrich our understanding of modern employment systems. The first of these is the study by Maurice, Sellier, and Silvestre of firms in France and Germany. In this pathbreaking project six French and six German firms were matched by product, size, and technology. Hence these considerations were controlled in as close a natural experiment as is available in such work. The authors then observe that despite the close match the French and German firms differ systematically in several respects. The wage structure of French firms is more unequal than is true in Germany (with the relative wage of managers higher), and the staffing pattern also differs. The French firms have a larger proportion of low-level managers and officials. Because of the nature of the sample these differences cannot be explained by technology, nor can they be understood as the result of a neoclassical optimizing process since high wages should lead French firms to economize on the very group, managers, which they have relatively more of. There is no evidence that the productivity of French management is higher than that of their German counterparts; hence this consideration cannot explain away the finding.

In lieu of these traditional considerations the authors demonstrate how a set of socially specific factors shape internal employment systems. They emphasize the nature of the educational system, training procedures for skilled positions, national attitudes toward authority, and the history of working class attitudes. In raising these considerations they persuasively point toward a considerably more textured and subtle understanding of enterprise characteristics than is now available. Also at a time when the American literature is filled with discussions about borrowing or imitating foreign work systems, especially the Japanese, this chapter makes it clear that any particular practice is part of a whole cloth. It is by no means clear that it is possible to pick and choose successfully among specific practices while ignoring the circumstances from which they emerged and the constraints they place upon choices in other areas.

Employment systems may differ not only across countries but also across regions within one country. In recent years in the United States the most rapid growth of manufacturing employment has occurred not in the industrial heartland but in rural areas. Low wages are a portion of the explanation but research suggests that other considerations also weigh heavily. In particular, local culture and community structure seem important. Exploration of this theme is the goal of Doeringer's study.

Doeringer reports on research conducted in rural Maine. The striking feature of this area is the expansion of firms whose employment systems feature low wages, few benefits, and paternalistic personnel systems. Despite these characteristics the work force exhibits stability, discipline, and unusually hard work. In urban areas firms like these would expect high turnover and poor employee performance. Doeringer's chapter is directed to describing the personalistic employment system, explaining how it emerged and analyzing why is perpetuated. In the course of this he begins to delineate the role of community economic structure and social attitudes in shaping employment patterns in local firms.

Conclusion

Internal labor markets exert a strong pull on researchers because so many workers spend a large fraction of their careers within a single structured unit. Hence the distribution of economic well-being is closely tied to the operation of internal labor markets. Furthermore the existence of these institutions poses an intellectual challenge. An internal labor market represents a structured pattern of interaction or behavior that persists over time. How should such stability be explained? What role should be given to market forces, to custom and tradition, to political or economic power? How do these considerations interact, and how do internal labor markets change?

The chapters in this book bring us further toward understanding the purposes, functioning, and sources of variation in internal labor markets. The subjects were not chosen with any predetermined set of conclusions in mind, and the research styles and intellectual orientation of the scholars are sufficiently different that no unified perspective emerges. However, several tentative conclusions do seem possible.

First, at this stage it seems impossible to go confidently beyond a rather eclectic orientation toward understanding the origins and functions of internal labor markets. Without doubt internal labor markets perform the efficiency functions of conserving on supervision, assisting in the training process, and helping to keep skilled employees attached to the firm. However, unionization drives, intraunion politics, government intervention, national and community cultures, and work group norms also play important roles in explaining the emergence of these job systems. As yet no well-developed paradigm is available to knit these factors together. If we are to develop a more coherent understanding of internal labor markets then it seems important to focus on variety and change.

It seems apparent that there is considerably more variety in the nature of internal labor markets than has generally been recognized. The internal labor markets for different occupations, such as clerks and managers, differ considerably within the same firm. There is also industrial variation; for example, career lines for managers in high-technology firms may differ in significant ways from the lines for managers in older industries. Internal market rules for comparable industries also differ across national boundaries. Such variety both belies any simple understanding of the origins and functions of internal labor markets and poses a significant challenge to the analyst.

Finally, internal labor markets are more susceptible to change than has previously been recognized, and this change provides useful research opportunities. There has been a tendency in the literature to think of job systems as fairly static, changing only when major technological innovations became too pressing. However, as discussed earlier, this view is clearly incorrect. Furthermore dynamic considerations seem to be the area of greatest challenge. Institutional writings have always had a slightly descriptive quality, which in itself is fine, but there has also been a tendency to treat the rationalization of current arrangements (i.e., showing how the pieces fit together in a sensible way) as if such rationalization constituted theory building. The weakness of such an approach is highlighted when the institutions change and scholars are left with an incomplete understanding of why the change happened when it did and why it took a particular form. Some additional urgency is given to this by the widespread interest in employing public policy to encourage and channel such change, whether in the service of Equal Employment Opportunity efforts, work force retraining, or productivity enhancement programs. For all of these reasons then, we can expect the topic surveyed here to be one of continuing interest and fruitful research.

References

Berger, Susanne, and Piore, Michael J. *Dualism and Discontinuity*. New York: Cambridge University Press, 1979.

Cole, Robert. *Work, Mobility, and Participation: A Comparative Study of American and Japanese Industry*. Berkeley: University of California Press, 1979.

Crozier, Michel. *The World of the Office Worker*. Chicago: University of Chicago Press, 1971.

Braverman, Harry. *Labor and Monopoly Capital*. New York: Monthly Review Press, 1974.

Doeringer, Peter B., and Piore, Michael J. *Internal Labor Markets and Manpower Analysis*. Lexington, Mass.: D. C. Heath, 1971.

Dunlop, John. "Job Vacancy Measures and Economic Analysis." In *The Measurement and Interpretation of Job Vacancies*. New York: Columbia University Press, 1966.

Dore, Ronald. *British Factory, Japanese Factory*. Berkeley: University of California Press, 1973.

Freeman, Richard B. "Unionism and the Dispersion of Wages." *Industrial and Labor Relations Review* **34** (October 1980):3–23.

Hall, Robert E. Review of Jacob Mincer's *Schooling, Experience, and Earnings. Journal of Political Economy* **83** (1975):445.

Hall, Robert E. "The Importance of Lifetime Jobs in the U.S. Economy." *American Economic Review* **72** (September 1982):716–724.

Kanter, Rosabeth. *Men and Women of the Corporation*. New York: Basic Books, 1978.

Kerr, Clark. "The Balkanization of Labor Markets." In E. Wight Bakke, et al. *Labor Mobility and Economic Opportunity*. Cambridge: The MIT Press, 1954, pp. 92–110.

Kerr, Clark, Dunlop, John T., Harbison, Frederick, and Meyer, Charles A. *Industrialism and Industrial Man*. Cambridge: Harvard University Press, 1960.

Osterman, Paul. "Affirmative Action and Opportunity: The Impact of the Contract Compliance Program Upon the Employment of Female Workers." *Review of Economics and Statistics* (November 1982).

Piore, Michael J. "The Technological Foundations of Economic Dualism." Working Paper No. 110. Department of Economics, MIT, Cambridge, May 1973.

Reder, M. "The Theory of Occupational Wage Differentials." *American Economic Review* **45** (December 1955): 833–852.

Ross, Arthur M. *Trade Union Wage Policy*. Berkeley: University of California Press, 1948.

Roy, Donald. "Quota Restriction of Goldbricking in the Machine Shop." *American Sociological Review* **57** (1952):427–442.

Shaeffer, Ruth, and Lynton, Edith. *Corporate Experience in Improving Women's Job Opportunities*. New York: The Conference Board, 1979.

Stone, Katherine. "The Origins of the Job Structure in the Steel Industry." In David Gorden, et al., eds., *Labor Market Segmentation*. Lexington, Mass.: D. C. Heath, 1972.

Williamson, Oliver, Wacter, Michael, and Harris, Jeffrey. "Understanding the Employment Relation: The Analysis of Idiosyncratic Exchange." *Bell Journal of Economics* 6 (Spring 1975):250–280.

Whyte, William F. *The Organization Man*. New York: Simon and Schuster, 1956.

2   The Development of Internal Labor Markets in American Manufacturing Firms

Sanford M. Jacoby

To paraphrase D. H. Robertson, internal labor markets may be thought of as "islands of conscious power in an ocean of unconscious cooperation [much] like lumps of butter coagulating in a pail of buttermilk."[1] Little is known about the processes by which these lumps of butter were formed. Current theories about internal labor markets often have been tacked onto various historical generalizations without regard for the complexity of underlying causal and temporal sequences. This chapter analyzes the development of internal labor markets in American manufacturing firms from the perspective that their origins are part of a historic shift in the principles of employment. Emphasis is placed on unionization and personnel management as institutions that impelled and reflected the replacement of a market-oriented, arbitrary and impermanent employment system by one that was more bureaucratic, rule-bound, and secure.

The characteristic features of an internal labor market did not gradually take hold in an ever growing number of firms. Instead they were adopted during two periods of crisis for the older system of employment—World War I and the Great Depression. These were periods when the unions gained strength, when personnel managers were influential, and when the state intervened in the labor market. This uneven growth suggests that many firms did not immediately perceive the value of a bureaucratic system of employment. It also suggests that the internal labor market was an adaptation to new social norms of employment, especially those of trade unionism, rather than a simple response to growing organizational complexity.

The Foreman and the Drive System, 1870–1915

America's manufacturing industries underwent dramatic expansion in the late nineteenth and early twentieth centuries. Manufacturing employment nearly doubled between 1880 and 1900, and nearly doubled again between 1900 and 1920. This growth was accompanied by a trend toward larger establishments. New industries such as electrical machinery and motor vehicle manufacturing soon rivaled steel and textiles in establishment size.[2]

Both the scale and speed of manufacturing operations rose markedly after 1880, cutting the time involved in processing each unit of output. Behind the decline in production time was the widespread substitution of power machinery and handling equipment for human labor. Increased speed and volume of production allowed for a persistent reduction in unit costs, which permitted the channeling of internally generated cash flows into the acquisition of other firms that produced inputs or substitutes for the merging firm's products.[3]

The increased size and complexity of the manufacturing firm created numerous administrative difficulties. Until the 1880s most proprietors had been content to leave the management of production to their foremen and highly skilled workers. Where skill mattered, the foreman and his workers often knew more about technical matters than did the firm's owners.[4] But the rapid growth of industry put pressure on this decentralized system of production management. The flow of production was hindered by a lack of coordination between the various departments of a firm. Data on costs were not kept or were gathered irregularly, which made it difficult to compare the performance of various units. Greater coordination was required if production speed was to be increased.[5]

Between 1880 and 1920 the systematic management movement introduced new methods of production management to industry. Most of the movement's members were engineers; discussions of plant administration and cost accounting rarely were found outside of engineering publications during this period. Efficiency engineers introduced various administrative innovations that displaced traditional methods of production management. Early production control systems told the foreman which units to produce, the order in which operations were to be performed, and the method by which these operations were to be carried out. Standardized procedures, cost accounting, and detailed record-keeping facilitated the centralization of decision making. Thus the foreman's technical and administrative duties in production were gradually assumed by engineers and middle managers; the routine aspects of his duties were assigned to clerical personnel. This bureaucratization resulted in a steady increase in the ratio of administrative to production employees.[6]

Efficiency engineers, despite their forays into production management, left relatively untouched the other major area of a foreman's responsibilities, his employees. The overall lack of attention to employment matters in early management literature stemmed from two sources. There was first the engineers' belief that most employment and labor relations problems could be solved by a properly devised incentive wage. Second was the perception that there was nothing notably inefficient about the foreman's traditional employment methods. Robert F. Hoxie's 1914 survey of firms that had systematized their production processes found that they used no more advanced methods of employment management than nonsystematized firms. This prompted Hoxie to criticize the engineers for their "naive ignorance of social science" and indifference to the "human factor." Consequently the development of a bureaucratic system of employment lagged behind the systemization of other spheres of the firm.[7]

In contrast to the varying degrees of control that the foreman exercised over production, his authority in employment matters was more uniform across industries. In most firms the foreman was given free rein to manage the acquisition, payment, and supervision of labor. To the worker, the foreman was a despot—and not often benevolent—who made and interpreted employment policy as he saw fit. There were some checks on the foreman's power, but usually they emanated from the workers he supervised and not from the proprietor.

The foreman's control over employment began literally at factory gates. On mornings when the firm was hiring—a fact advertised by newspaper ads, signs, or word of mouth—a crowd gathered in front of the factory. The foreman stood at the head of the crowd and picked out those workers who appeared suitable or had managed to get near front. At one Philadelphia factory the foreman tossed apples to the throng; if a man caught an apple, he got the job. Foremen could be less arbitrary, hiring their friends or relatives of those already employed. Many relied on ethnic stereotypes to determine who would get a job or which job they would be offered. Workers often resorted to bribing the foreman with whiskey, cigars, or cash to get a job, a practice that one study found to be "exceedingly common" in Ohio's factories.[8]

Assignment to a job was determined in large part by favoritism or prejudice. The foreman often had little interest in or knowledge of an employee's previous work experience. If a newly hired employee proved unsatisfactory, he was easily replaced by someone else. Transfers from one department to another were rare. As one observer noted, "Foreman are apt to assume the attitude that 'if you do not work in my department you cannot work elsewhere,' and will do everything in their power to prevent dissatisfied workmen from being replaced." Intradepartmental promotions occurred, although definite lines for promotion were unheard of before 1910, except on skilled work.[9]

The foreman also had considerable power to determine the wages of the workers he hired. Whether piece- or daywork, the foreman could and did set widely varying rates for different individuals doing the same work. Because labor costs were monitored by management, the foreman had an incentive to hire individuals at the lowest rate possible. It was common practice for a foreman "to beat the applicant down from the wage he states he wishes to the lowest which the interviewer believes he can be induced to accept."[10] Variations in rates across departments were common because each foreman ran his shop autonomously. Employment and wage records were rarely kept before 1900; only the foreman knew with any accuracy how many workers were employed in his department and the rates they received. Foremen jealously guarded wage information, allowing them to play favorites by varying the day rate or assigning favored workers to jobs where piece rates were loose.[11]

A firm's owners expected the foreman to hold labor costs down despite or because of the latitude they gave him in determining rates. This meant paying a wage no greater than the going rate for a particular job. But it also meant striving to keep effort levels up to reduce unit costs. When the going rate rose, effort became the key variable to be manipulated by the foreman.[12]

Foremen relied on a combination of methods to maintain or increase effort levels that were collectively known as the "drive system": close supervision, abuse, profanity, and threats. Informal rules regulating work behavior such as rest periods were arbitrarily and harshly enforced. Workers constantly were urged to move faster and work harder. Sumner Slichter defined the drive system as "the policy of obtaining efficiency not by rewarding merit, not by seeking to interest men in their work . . . but by putting pressure on them to turn out a large output. The dominating note of the drive policy is to inspire the worker with awe and fear of the management, and having developed fear among them, to take advantage of it."[13]

The drive system depended, ultimately, on fear of unemployment to ensure obedience to the foreman. Workers were more submissive when the labor market slackened, and jobs were scarce, as was often the case before World War I. A tight market tended to undermine the foreman's authority, forcing him to rely more heavily on discharges to maintain discipline. The foreman was free to fire anyone he saw fit, and discharges were liberally meted out.[14]

The instability of employment had causes wider than high rates of dismissal. In its cyclical and seasonal forms unemployment regularly touched a large portion of the working class. Between 1854 and 1914 recessions or depressions occurred every three to four years with about twenty-five of these sixty years spent in contraction.[15] In Massachusetts the incidence of unemployment was high even during relatively prosperous periods such as from 1900 to 1906, when at least one out of every five of the state's manufacturing workers experienced some unemployment each year. Even Massachusetts' trade union members, a relatively skilled group, were not immune to job loss. An average of 29 percent of these workers experienced some unemployment each year between 1908 and 1916.[16]

Unemployment filtered widely through the labor force even during good years because of dismissals and seasonal instability. Employment tended to be most stable in those consumer goods industries that produced items unaffected by style changes. But in 1909 even the most stable industry—bread and bakery products—had monthly employment levels that varied by 7 percent. That same year, the industrial average fluctuated by 14 percent over the year, rising to 45 percent in the automobile industry.[17] The seasonal instability of employment perpetuated the drive system. Activity became frenzied during the busy season as firms rushed to fill orders. Capacity utilization rates and employment levels rose by magnitudes rarely encountered today.

However, the existence of widespread unemployment is in itself no indication of the impermanence of the employment relationship. If there had been an understanding between workers and their employers that they would be recalled when needed, periodic unemployment need not have severed the relationship. But few firms made systematic attempts to rehire their workers after layoffs. For example, statistics from a large metal-working plant whose records distinguished between new hires and rehires of workers who had been laid off on account of the depression that began late in 1907 reveal that only 8 percent of all new hires for the following three-year period were rehires of those who had been laid off during the depression. Average industrial rehire rates probably were much lower.[18]

Mechanisms to maintain the employment relationship during downturns also included guaranteed income or employment plans and work-sharing arrangements. Employment guarantee plans were in operation at only fifteen firms by 1920, although work-sharing was more prevalent. However, the bulk of these work-sharing plans were initiated by trade unions in cooperation with unionized employers. Employers in nonunion firms maintained that work-sharing was cumbersome and inefficient.[19]

Few workers had anything resembling equity in their jobs. When layoffs came, rare was the employer who ordered his foremen to reduce the work force systematically. Employment security was determined by the same arbitrary criteria as hiring. Bribes were a common means of ensuring job security. In some shops, "everyone has to pay some sort of tribute to his foreman. The tribute is usually in the form of money or service, but there are cases where the tribute is of a nature which cannot be mentioned in an open paper."[20]

Thus, prior to World War I, employment for most manufacturing workers was unstable, unpredictable, and inequitable. The worker's economic success and job satisfaction depended on a highly personal relationship with his foreman. There *was* an implicit system of employment here, although it wasn't bureaucratic. Foremen had many favors available for those whom they befriended or who bought their friendship. Personal ties and loyalty counted for much, although later reformers were horrified by the particularism and brutality that infused the drive system. Yet where employment practices first achieved a semblance of rational organization, stability, and equity, these features were not a managerial innovation but were imposed from below.

The Workers' Response

The institution of trade unions curbed the foreman's arbitrary exercise of prerogatives and gave the skilled worker considerable control over the terms of his employment. The trade union ensured that strict rules and equitable procedures would govern allocative and wage decisions.

In hiring, the closed or preferential shop enhanced the demand for union labor and restricted the foreman's discretion. It protected union members against discrimination and guaranteed that a given number of vacancies would be filled by them.[21] In wage determination, the union's approach entailed the so-called "standard rate" that all members were supposed to receive. This prevented wage inequities as well as the use of individualized compensation systems that could weaken the union. To prevent foremen from paying different rates for similar work, some unions demanded that rates be listed in a book to be made available to them.[22]

Rules regulating manning levels and working hours were intended to stabilize the demand for union labor. When cyclical unemployment threatened, the unions attempted to mitigate its impact through work-sharing and seniority layoffs, although work sharing was more prevalent. Seniority also was used to prevent favoritism and promote equity in the allocation of promotions. In the Chicago meat-packing industry the cattle butchers devised a detailed system of promotion lines governed by seniority. Foremen strongly opposed this practice, as John R. Commons observed, because they thought "that forced promotion takes a man away from work he does well."[23]

Finally, unions sought to regulate dismissals by requiring that a member be discharged only for just cause.[24] This requirement, together with the closed shop and seniority rules, undermined the fundamental assumption of the drive system—that employment was a relationship of indefinite duration terminable at the employer's will. The unions held the alternative concept that employment was a permanent relationship between the union—a set of workers—and the employer(s)—a set of jobs. The union behaved as if it owned a set of jobs continuing through time. Under the closed shop system only union men could fill these jobs; under work sharing, the jobs could not be dissolved. The unions' employment security mechanisms restricted the employer from turning to the open market to fill vacancies. Moreover the unions' allocative, wage, and dismissal practices embedded the employment relationship in a web of impersonal, equitable rules. These restrictions, when redefined as a permanent, rule-bound relationship between a set of incumbents and a set of jobs in a particular firm, would comprise an internal labor market.[25]

Few options were available to the less skilled, nonunion worker who was dissatisfied with his job or his foreman. Unskilled or nonunion workers had few rights; the only one that was consistently recognized was the right to quit. Thus despite some spectacular strikes, in most instances, the less skilled worker had no alternative in seeking higher wages or better conditions than to terminate employment. Quit rates were high long before World War I. They varied directly with skill;

annual separation rates for unskilled workers often surpassed 200 percent. "Exit" of the unorganized was an alternative to "voice."[26]

The Personnel Management Movement, 1890–1915

Prewar employers were satisfied with the profitability of the decentralized, drive system of employee management. Immigrant labor was abundant, which fostered an attitude of indifference to improving employment methods. But the drive system was not without costs. First, it entailed administrative costs that could be reduced by more bureaucratic methods of coordination. Elements of the engineers' approach to production management—orderly procedures, accurate records, and the departmentalization of routinized functions—came into play in the decade after 1900 when a few firms first established personnel departments. One such department was initiated by Goodyear Tire and Rubber in 1900; it performed essentially clerical functions. Most of these departments had a limited effect on employment policy since they were adjuncts of the firm's production division which was preoccupied with producing maximum output at top speed.[27]

The production manager's short-run, cost-minimizing orientation made him suspicious of any attempt by the personnel department to expand its ambit beyond the clerical. Production officials were wary of changes in employment methods since they led to few immediate or easily measured improvements in output or costs. Consequently critics of the drive system pointed to the personnel manager's low status and powerlessness as barriers to employment reform.

These early critics also pointed to a second set of costs generated by the foreman's crude employment methods: recurring labor unrest and erratic working habits. They worried about the relationship between private employment policies and such societal problems as unemployment and a drift to the political left. These problems had been apparent to nineteenth-century observers as well. What was new was the intensity of the critics' perception that social order was declining, that disorder was linked to private employment practices, and that order could be achieved by more scientific and humane methods of labor administration.

Many of these critics were middle-class professionals—social workers, settlement house workers, academics and ministers—who were applying their expertise toward solving the pressing social problems of the cities and industry. The social justice movement of the time was made up of individuals who were imbued with a humanitarian ethic of uplift and social reform that made them sympathetic to the immigrant working classes. Yet despite their good intentions their writings and programs contained distinct strains of social control, accommodation, and elitism. The reformers in this group technicalized and rationalized the problems of a rapidly industrializing society. The reforms they devised helped to strengthen existing institutions and steer social change from more radical paths.

Like the engineers, these reformers idealized scientific expertise and rational administration, but they were also deeply concerned with the nonadministrative costs of the drive system. Although they had a limited impact on most firms before World War I, their activities laid the foundations for the proliferation of personnel departments during the war. Industrial welfare work and labor market reform were two branches of the social justice movement that had direct links to wartime developments.

Welfare Work

One strand of welfare work may be traced to the period of labor unrest between 1877 and 1894, when employers sought to turn the loyalty of their skilled workers away from the unions through the use of quasi-pecuniary incentives such as profit-sharing, pension, and stock bonus plans. Another strand was rooted in the belief that the cause of labor unrest, social tension, and a perceived decline in the work ethic was the worker himself—the intemperate, slothful worker or the ignorant, immigrant worker prey to radical nostrums. To countermand this, firms experimented with a variety of programs ranging from thrift clubs, compulsory religion, and citizenship instruction to company housing, outings, magazines, and contests. The idea was to use the firm to recast the worker in a middle-class mold, thus making him sedulous, sober, and loyal.[28]

Many of those engaged in employee welfare work had backgrounds in social work, mission work, and the civic reform and settlement house movements. Welfare work was the private sector analogue to the "search for order" that these professionals then were conducting in American cities. Welfare workers believed that their moralistic paternalism would improve workers' lives and change some of industry's cruder aspects.[29]

Welfare work was viewed skeptically by some who thought that paternalistic attempts to uplift workers had an uncertain effect, at best, on productivity and loyalty. Welfare workers regularly encountered resistance from production managers and foremen who resented intrusions into their domain. To counter this, welfare work increasingly was justified by the engineers' criterion of efficiency. Welfare workers argued that conflicts with line management only could be alleviated by vesting their authority in a separate department free of interference from the line.[30]

By 1910 firms had begun to centralize their welfare programs in a single department with clearly defined responsibilities. A few of these departments were on a par with other major corporate divisions and included employment management responsibilities.[31] But in most firms the welfare department, like the personnel department, remained subordinate to the production division. The welfare worker in these firms, said one observer, "has not yet been assimilated in the operating organization. . . . He deals largely with matters outside the regular routine of industry operations, he has to do primarily with the men while *off* the job rather than *on* the job. . . ." Most welfare departments posed little real threat to the foreman's autonomy since they lacked both independent authority and a mandate to intervene in employment matters. The drive system could and did coexist with extra-work paternalism.[32]

Yet welfare work created a distinctive role. Labor management was becoming the province of the specialist, and labor-related policy was turning into a decision variable subject to rational administration. The creation of welfare departments marked the beginning of efforts to develop employment policies that weren't subordinate to the firm's short-run emphasis on production and that recognized the value of maintaining employee morale and loyalty.

Labor Market Reform

Personnel management was also heavily influenced by the vocational guidance movement. Vocational guidance had developed alongside vocational education to assist in directing the "manually minded" child to his appropriate niche in the labor market.[33] However, some educational and child-labor reformers believed that vocational guidance should be more than just an effort to fit children to particular curricula or jobs. They were concerned about the numerous immigrant youths who entered "blind alley" jobs with unstable futures and little chance for advancement. These reformers thought that schools could be better used to regulate the youth labor market by having counselors scrutinize the jobs that employers offered school leavers to ensure that decent, stable jobs were provided. Counselors were to encourage employers to educate and train their young workers, rationalize their hiring procedures, and promote from within.[34]

Leading this group was Meyer Bloomfield, a former settlement house worker who had introduced vocational guidance to the Boston schools in 1910. Bloomfield began to have doubts that the schools were "the most suitable agency to attempt the organization of the labor market for the young" and redirected his energies from the schools to industry.[35]

Bloomfield and his supporters thought that personnel managers should be the vehicle for introducing vocational methods to industry, which would ensure that young workers continued to receive guidance and training. They criticized the foreman's crude motivational methods and his failure to assign workers to jobs that matched their interests and abilities. They advocated the establishment of personnel departments that would change allocative practices through such techniques as scientific selection procedures, written job specifications, tryout transfers, and internal promotion plans. These techniques were supposed to decasualize employment and promote stable working habits by providing something akin to a career path for manual workers.[36]

Vocationalists thought that the transfer of allocative authority from foremen to personnel departments also would reduce the amount of youth and adult unemployment. Other labor market reformers in groups such as the American Association for Labor Legislation (AALL) were attracted to the idea of organizing the labor market through voluntary measures as an alternative to national labor exchanges and unemployment insurance. The AALL claimed that personnel departments could permanently reduce unemployment by making hiring more efficient, restricting dismissals, and administering transfers in lieu of layoffs.[37]

Liberal followers of Frederick W. Taylor, the noted efficiency engineer, became ardent advocates of this new approach to unemployment for it held the promise that a major social problem could be solved by the same efficient managerial techniques then being applied to production. This brought the engineers into the ranks of what was to become a national personnel management movement. During the 1914 depression groups formed in major cities to discuss unemployment problems and promote personnel management by local employers. The groups were organized by Bloomfield, the Taylor Society, and AALL members; they became the nucleus of the first national association of personnel managers, founded in 1918.[38]

Thus the disparate strands that would compose the personnel management movement began to come together in the years before America's entry into the war. Efficiency, the engineers' watchword, with its connotations of scientific method and bureaucratic order, infused the welfare work and vocational guidance movements at the same time that employment reform began to be taken seriously by the engineers. The roots of personnel management are to be found not only in the technical imperatives imposed by a firm's increased size and complexity—these created the empty slots in the managerial hierarchy—but also in the backgrounds of those who filled these slots. Personnel managers brought with them the same ideologies and techniques that were being used to solve social problems outside industry. Adapted to an industrial setting, such methods contained an implicit attack on the laissez faire principles governing employment. These professionals argued that industry had an obligation to restrain itself by making the employment relationship less arbitrary and more responsive to the worker's needs and thus to the needs of the firm.[39]

Supporters of personnel management had high hopes that the professionalization of employment management would humanize industry by injecting liberal values into the firm. Those who were most concerned with the issue of professionalism tended to be sympathetic to trade unionism. The precise relation of the personnel manager to the union rarely was specified, but these liberals envisioned some sort of joint control exercised by judicious managers and responsible, accommodative trade unions.[40] Others in the movement were ardent foes of the unions. They saw the need for reform and restraint, not as an opening wedge but as a way to ensure that the unions lost their attractiveness. Change was necessary, but it was always to be unilateral and designed to maintain employer control.[41]

In mitigating the drive system, personnel managers of either persuasion weakened the potential appeal of trade unions by preempting reforms that skilled workers had been pushing for themselves. For less skilled workers, the personnel management movement brought some of the benefits that the trade union had delivered to the more skilled, including allocation by rule, enhanced security, and rudimentary grievance mechanisms.

The Personnel Management Movement during World War I, 1916–1920

Employers were slow in coming to the realization that a change in employment methods could serve as a backfire against unionism. They were put off by the reformers' attitudes toward unions; they were skeptical that a relationship existed between morale and effort; moreover labor was cheap and abundant.

The foreman's drive system allowed firms the flexibility to adjust their forces to shifts in demand. It seemed an effective mode for holding worker expectations and unit costs in line. As Sumner Slichter noted in 1919, the drive system was profitable, given an elastic supply of immigrant labor and a short-run perspective on what he called "the interests of employers as a class." These conditions held until 1916. But the tightening of labor markets induced by the war created a host of problems that made employers more receptive to change.[42]

During the period from 1916 to 1920, unemployment rates fell to their lowest levels since 1890.[43] A serious consequence of tight labor markets was an erosion in effort norms and shop floor discipline. In the past, periodic downturns and a labor surplus, as reflected in high unemployment rates even during good times, could be relied on to maintain worker discipline and make the foreman a credible driver. But with the labor shortage caused by the war, the traditional forces for maintaining effort and discipline were at their weakest. The result was a deterioration in what Slichter called "capital's ability to compel production." When Guy Tripp of Westinghouse addressed a dinner in New York in 1920, he said that "effort" at Westinghouse had fallen off by 20 to 30 percent and that "this transcends in its vital importance all questions of strikes, wages, prices, and everything else."[44]

Despite Tripp's ordering of priorities, strikes were very much on employers' minds during this period. A wave of labor unrest swept the country between 1916 and 1921. The ratio of strikers to all workers during these six years remained constantly at a level achieved later during the more famous strike years of 1934 and 1937. Trade union membership nearly doubled between 1915 and 1920. Public sympathy for organized labor created pressure for change, as did heavy government intervention in the war labor market.[45]

The combination of these problems—labor shortages, slackened effort, and labor unrest—brought about an increase in quit rates, especially among unskilled, unorganized workers. But the wartime rise in quit rates was not unprecedented. Labor turnover in a relatively "good" prewar year such as 1913 approached wartime levels: the unemployment rate was about 35 percent higher, and turnover was 33 percent lower, in 1913 as compared to 1917–18. What made the war period unique was not the level of quits so much as a new concern for the implications of such a separation. These included the higher cost of replacing a separating worker, the belief that a propensity to quit was related to weak effort norms, and the realization that the same conditions that gave rise to quits today might lead to a strike tomorrow.[46]

Despite lingering skepticism about the wisdom of tampering with tradition, a substantial minority of industrial firms rapidly established personnel departments. Between 1915 and 1920 the proportion of large establishments (those employing more than 250 employees) with personnel departments rose from less than 7 to 25 percent.[47] The federal government helped to speed the creation of personnel departments by training hundreds of personnel managers in war emergency courses at various universities. Several war labor agencies promoted personnel management, believing that it would standardize employment conditions in war industries and thus reduce the likelihood of disputes. The government's Emergency Fleet Corporation was directly responsible for the creation of personnel departments in thirty-four private shipyards; the industry had none at the start of the war.[48]

There was, however, a sharp disjuncture between the ideal personnel department envisioned by the movement's proselytizers and the actual practices of most firms. Only a small number of departments, perhaps as few as fifty, approached the ideal. These were fully centralized departments whose mandate was on a par with the firm's other functional divisions. They controlled the formulation of all labor-related policy as well as its execution. An independent, powerful personnel department provided the authority needed to curb recalcitrant line officials and administer programs that required intrafirm coordination. But most personnel departments failed to establish either their independent authority or a full range of the employment policies that were considered "best practice" at the time.

Employment Reforms

The selection and assignment of new employees were the functions most commonly taken over by the new personnel departments. As presumed experts in human relations, personnel managers were supposed to be more skilled in choosing the "right man for the right job." The new procedure was to have foremen requisition workers from the personnel department when needed; they were not allowed to refuse the workers sent to them. Personnel departments were to maintain employment records and keep a list of applicants on file. In theory this was intended to create a reserve to be drawn upon when the demand for labor increased. In some open-shop firms these records were used to screen out union members or other undesirables. Other firms followed a policy of hiring an ethnically diverse group of workers to forestall unionization. The personnel manager, said Arthur H. Young, "is like unto a chef, in charge of the mixture at his particular plant."[49]

Yet the hiring techniques used by most personnel departments were quite rudimentary (see table 2.1). Only about a half kept employment records; maintaining a list of reserve applicants was said to be "seldom practiced." Much of the personnel manager's energy was spent trying to convince foremen of the virtues of centralized selection. Foremen resented their loss of authority. They blamed production problems on the personnel department's poor judgment in selecting workers. Personnel managers complained that they had a harder time selling their selection methods to foremen and line executives than to a firm's top managers.[50]

Personnel managers advocated the use of rules and procedures to curb the foreman's discretion in wage setting and create a more equitable wage structure. The first step in this process was to analyze the duties and requirements of every job in the firm, using methods similar to those employed by vocational guidance counselors. From the job analysis data the personnel department could classify jobs into groups and standardize wages within groups. This allowed the department to identify those rates that were out of line and thus might become a source of disputes. One of the first classification systems was introduced at Ford Motor Company in 1914; it reduced the number of basic wage rates at Ford from sixty-nine to eight.[51]

Several major wartime strikes were held over the issue of wage standardization. The unions involved, most notably the Machinists, demanded that firms standardize occupational nomenclature, classify jobs and standardize wages within classifications. This was intended to reduce the inequities produced by the foreman's rate-setting methods and weaken the individualizing tendency of incentive wage systems, which carried different rates for different workers. Various war labor agencies occasionally supported the unions as part of the government's

Table 2.1
Employment practices in industry, 1918–1923

	All firms[a]	Firms with personnel departments[b]
Records of hiring and firing	18%	50%
Use of selection tests	4	12
Job analysis	12	
Centralized wage determination	—	38
Periodic wage increases	24	
Plant promotion plan	15	
Promotion by formal ratings	12	
Vacancies posted	2	
Transfer plans	23	
Personnel department has a say in dismissals		36

a. Data from Leslie H. Allen, "The Workman's Home," *Transactions of the ASME* **40** (1918):217; Paul F. Gemmill, "Methods of Promoting Industrial Employees," *Industrial Management* **67** (April 1924):240, 243, 246; Roy W. Kelly, *Hiring the Worker* (Boston, 1918), p. 32. These data probably are biased upward by the overrepresentation of advanced firms in the surveys.
b. Data from "A Survey of Personnel Activities of Member Companies," National Association of Corporation Schools (NACS) *Bulletin* **7** (August 1920):347–348; Kelly, *Hiring the Worker*, p. 32.

wide-ranging efforts of head off labor disputes and shortages by standardizing wages both within and across industries and regions.[52]

Employers were wary of standardization since it carried the risk of politicizing wage determination by tying groups of workers together in a common wage band. They also worried that standardization would undermine the incentive effects of the new bonus wage systems. Consequently, despite the volumes written about job analysis and wage standardization, they were less popular in practice than a review of the literature would suggest (table 2.1). Wages often continued to be set by foremen or by time-study engineers.[53]

Personnel managers and employment reformers believed that an internal promotion system was an essential feature of a well-managed firm. There were several reasons for this belief. First, vocationalists in the personnel movement thought that a promotion plan provided an incentive for greater effort and commitment to work. They emphasized the need to provide career motivations for manual workers since this would "put the zest of the struggle and contest into their work, [and] the hope of better things tomorrow to take their minds off the difficulties of today."[54]

Second, these policies were supposed to develop skills systematically and to act as a screening device by which "the competent and persevering employee gradually rises to the top." Third, internal promotion plans were said to depress quits since they rewarded the worker for stability and gave him "hope that efficiency in his present job will win him something better." Finally, these policies were thought to "engender loyalty and esprit de corps" by reducing the foreman's discretion and making promotions subject to definite criteria. Loyalty would increase if workers were assured that good behavior and ability were going to be recognized and rewarded.[55]

A definite plan for promotion and a policy of filling vacancies from within normally accompanied each other. The incentive effects of a promotion plan were weakened if a firm turned to the external labor market to fill vacancies above entry level. And if vacancies *were* filled internally, a definite promotion and transfer plan eased the bureaucratic task of finding appropriate workers. If promotion lines were vague and centralized labor allocation was weak, as was often the case, promotion continued to be somewhat haphazard and hiring from within was only minimally enforced.[56]

Firms were reluctant to implement definite promotion plans because it was believed that they hindered allocative flexibility. A plant manager at a large manufacturing firm said, "Our business is not a progressive series of positions. Any good organization is always adjusting itself to new conditions. Lines of promotion are absurd." Other firms maintained that promotion plans created unrealistic expectations among incumbent workers that a particular job would be theirs when it became vacant— this hampered the firm if and when it preferred to hire someone else to fill the vacancy—and would create "softness" among workers by making advancement appear to be too automatic. Firms that had definite promotion plans considered it wise to view them as guidelines rather than definite commitments. Hence only a very few firms guaranteed their workers an internal hiring policy for vacancies above entry level. Internal promotion plans were not widespread (table 2.1) nor were merit wage increases in lieu of promotion.[57]

The absence or ineffectual enforcement of promotion policies meant that most promotions still were controlled by foremen, even in firms with personnel departments. Only 3 percent of firms surveyed in 1924 allowed their personnel department to have a say in promotions. A personnel manager at one firm complained, "Pull goes a long way in this company. It is a long, slow process trying to introduce modern personnel methods."[58]

Personnel managers made their deepest raids into the foreman's territory when they removed or restricted his discharge privileges. To justify this incursion, foremen were portrayed as autocratic, barbaric, and overworked. As noted, tight labor markets and rising unionization rates made unrestricted dismissals a liability to employers. Foremen at one Philadelphia firm were told, "Your system may have been good once, but it won't go now."[59]

There was tremendous variation in the extent to which personnel departments assumed control of dismissals. At many firms the foreman was only allowed to suspend a worker from his department. The worker could then go to the personnel department for a hearing and possible transfer to another department. For example, Standard Oil issued a list of offenses for which a foreman could dismiss a worker and guaranteed the right of appeal to the personnel department. Some progressive, nonunion firms instituted quasi-judicial arbitration boards to adjudicate disputed dismissals.[60]

The ethos of professional neutrality found practical expression in these new dismissal systems. The personnel department had to be somewhat independent of the rest of the firm if it was to mediate disputes between workers and their supervisors. Only through demonstrated neutrality would workers trust personnel departments to define and protect their rights. As a third force in the firm, the personnel department would function as both management and union. One personnel manager said that his "most important duty is just this one thing: to come in close contact with employees; to gain their confidence; to hear their troubles and adjust them; to be their champion and *at the same time* the guardian of the company's interest."[61]

Foremen and production officials were more resentful of this reform than any other. The unrestricted discharge was considered fundamental for maintaining effort on the shop floor. The fact that a worker could appeal a discharge to the personnel manager was said to undermine the foreman's authority, independence, and prerogative to establish his own rules. Personnel managers, on the other hand, argued that the use of rules and appeals procedures actually would increase the foreman's authority by allowing any conflict over rule enforcement to be deflected to the "higher-ups." But this left open the question of what would happen if the personnel department disagreed with the foreman's interpretation of the rules, which was precisely what worried critics of personnel management.[62]

A 1918 survey of forty firms found that the personnel department was involved in discharge decisions at about one-third of the firms surveyed, either to approve the foreman's choice (23 percent) or to make the determination independently (13 percent). Limits were imposed on the extent to which the personnel department could overrule the foreman in these firms; most personnel managers lacked the authority to reinstate an employee. Some skeptics claimed that at most firms, "a foreman may still be as petulant as ever about discharging."[63]

Another area where efforts were made to strengthen the bonds between firms and their incumbent employees was the so-called "new welfare work." This included such quasi-pecuniary programs as savings and stock ownership plans, group insurance, pensions, and paid vacations. These welfare programs began to supplant more paternalistic welfare work after the war and increased in popularity during the 1920s.[64]

The new welfare work relied on individual incentives that tied receipt of benefits to a worker's loyalty, punctuality, obedience, and seniority. Most of the programs had an eligibility rule known as the "continuous service provision"; an employee had to be continuously employed for a certain period before he was eligible to receive benefits. This provision was strictly enforced. A worker lost *all* of his accumulated seniority if a break occurred in his service record. This could be caused by a suspension, participation in a strike, or other forms of "disloyal" behavior. By tying hefty benefits to an unbroken service record, these programs increased the cost to the worker of a dismissal or quit. This had the effect of increasing employer control over the work force.[65]

The industries where the new welfare work was most prevalent tended to be those with little or no union organization. Employers said that the programs had a quieting effect on labor disturbances and contributed to loyalty and cooperation. The Studebaker Company introduced a program consisting of paid vacations, pensions, stock ownership, and life insurance in 1919. When a strike occurred in Detroit in 1920, the firm's body painters and trimmers refused to participate for fear they would lose their new benefits.[66] It is wise, however, not to make too much of these plans. Even by the late 1920s the new welfare plans reached no more than about one out of every seven industrial workers. Moreover employer expenditures on these programs were meager by current standards, averaging only 2 percent of compensation in 1927.[67]

Thus in a short span of time a visible minority of firms adopted policies that created a more equitable and secure employment relationship, one that encouraged workers to remain with the firm and be loyal to it. Yet old attitudes and practices continued to exert a strong hold on line officials and employers despite the efforts of personnel managers to convince them of the virtues of an alternative approach. This explains the limited scope of pre-1921 employment reforms; internal labor market arrangements affected only a minority of the work force. Even for this minority these arrangements were unevenly applied, either restricted to particular groups or ineffectually practiced, which suggests a less than wholehearted commitment to an enduring employment relationship. The persistence of the ideology that liberality undermined discipline, that foremen had to be upheld in disputes with workers, that labor was a commodity, made it difficult for personnel managers to expand their influence within or beyond the minority of firms that had initiated personnel departments by 1920.

The 1920s

By mid-1920 it was evident that the beliefs that had stymied the progress of personnel management were growing in intensity. An open-shop movement spread from state to state while the Red Scare hysteria gripped the nation. Hostility to progressive reform movements became widespread. A prominent personnel manager warned that, if labor markets softened, employers would "seize with avidity what they consider a long-deferred opportunity to put the screws down."[68]

A split appeared in the personnel management movement several months before the onset of the depression of 1921–22. A conservative faction launched a broad attack on their more liberal colleagues. It is not now clear whether they were motivated by a genuine disagreement with the liberals or by fears about their own futures. Yet they were able to articulate a program for the movement that was more in tune with the new mood of the times, a mood that was to prevail throughout the 1920s.

The most common charge leveled by the conservatives was that personnel managers had gone too far in blaming the foreman for industry's problems and stripping him of his authority. They argued that foremen should be given greater discretion to allocate, discipline, and discharge workers. The personnel department was to be an auxiliary to the production division rather than an independent department.

Under the new view the personnel manager would no longer be an impartial force for change within the firm; he would have to give up his professional pretensions. The new model of personnel management promised to restore allocational flexibility and preserve authority relations on the shop floor at a time when calls for "a return to business principles" and a reassertion of discipline were on the increase. Those personnel managers who adopted this model presumably would stand the greatest chance of weathering the oncoming depression.[69]

The depression demonstrated that a personnel department was not essential to the maintenance of morale, effort, or stability. Unemployment rates in manufacturing reached over 20 percent in 1921. With this came a decline in strikes and turnover as well as a sharp increase in labor productivity.[70] Many firms cut back or completely eliminated their personnel departments during the depression. Personnel departments that survived the depression lost their status as independent units and were integrated into manufacturing or production divisions. A 1927 study found that "many personnel departments, even those extensively organized, are . . . 'mere fronts.' The term is especially applicable where such departments are definitely ordered not to interfere with 'production' and where the personnel staff is given to understand that its function is not an integral part of the administration."[71]

Although these moves were touted as cost-cutting necessities, they had more to do with the desire to restore discipline. In 1928, after the dust had long settled, one well-placed observer commented that "more personnel men lost their jobs because they were given and used too much authority, because they usurped the prerogatives of line organizations and consequently interfered with normal disciplinary procedure, than because of business depression." Personnel management faded from public attention amid the quiescent labor atmosphere of the 1920s. Although new personnel departments appeared after the depression, the proportion of large firms with these departments grew more slowly than before, rising from 25 percent in 1920 to 34 percent in 1929.[72]

The manufacturing labor market during the 1920s was a buyer's market characterized by stagnant employment and relatively high employment. Manufacturing employment did not grow at all between 1919 and 1929; average annual unemployment rates in manufacturing were higher between 1923 and 1927 than for any other five-year period since 1900, excluding depression years. In twenty out of twenty-six manufacturing industries, average hourly wage rates declined between

1920 and 1929.[73] These factors were responsible for the decade's downward trend in quit rates and, ultimately, for the slow growth of employment reform.[74]

After the depression personnel departments conformed to the new model of decentralized management, which left the foreman with considerable power. Many departments now lacked the requisite authority to ensure compliance with intraplant allocative and pay rules. However, firms with personnel departments still were relatively attractive places to work during the 1920s, unlike firms that did not initiate personnel departments or failed to replace those that had been discontinued during the depression.[75]

The decentralization of authority made it difficult to operate or expand programs that required the foreman's cooperation. The proportion of firms with definite promotion plans remained constant throughout the decade and may have even declined slightly from predepression levels. The foreman's resurgence was most noticeable in the area of hiring and dismissals. Fewer firms reported using centralized selection methods in 1929 than in 1918. The proportion of firms that allowed their personnel departments to have a say, either final or advisory, in discharge decisions also declined between 1918 and 1929. Liberals in the personnel management movement were bitter about this shift away from professionalism and reform. They castigated advocates of the new model for "turning the clock back a considerable distance in regard to the development of centralization in the selection and training of workers as well as in safeguarding discharges, because of their blind zeal in defending what they called the foreman's 'rights.' "[76]

Wage determination again became the foreman's prerogative as individualized incentive wages became more popular during the decade. A 1928 survey of firms belonging to the open-shop National Metal Trades Association found that over 90 percent relied exclusively on either time study or an individual's past performance in setting wage rates. The proportion of manufacturing workers on incentive pay rose from 44 percent in 1922 to 71 percent in 1932. One result of this failure to continue wartime experiments in wage standardization was a widening of occupational wage differentials. An International Labor Organization study noted that skill differentials were wider in the United States than in other industrialized nations. This failure no doubt contributed to the urgency with which organized workers later sought to reform pay structures and attach wages to jobs rather than individuals.[77]

Despite the efforts made to retain workers during the war period, most firms did little to ensure the continuity of employment during the severe depression of 1920 to 1922. A few firms like International Harvester and McElwain Shoe paid dismissal wages and engaged in relief activities such as work sharing. But studies by the AALL and the Russell Sage Foundation turned up few instances of work sharing, systematic transfers, or dismissal compensation, which were termed "unusual relief arrangements." The ten giant firms that made up the Special Conference Committee issued a statement in favor of layoffs based on merit rather than seniority.[78]

However, after the depression there appeared to be a greater adherence to seniority as an allocative criterion. During the brief recession of 1927, 40 percent of the firms surveyed by the Conference Board reported that seniority was a primary factor in determining layoffs. This reflected some concern with the permanence of employment but the commitment to seniority was still weak. Sixty percent of the surveyed firms gave no preference to senior workers when rehiring; 14 percent erased all accumulated seniority if a laid-off worker was rehired. Even in those firms where seniority was a primary factor in layoffs, there were few definite rules as to when it applied. At many firms, seniority only became more important than efficiency or ability after the worker had been with the firm for more than five, and in some cases more than ten or twelve, years. That is, use of seniority as the governing factor in layoffs was itself a seniority benefit.[79]

The shallow commitment to employment security and the decentralization of allocative authority suggest that drive methods still were prevalent. In the automobile industry during the 1920s, the most commonly cited worker grievances were speed-ups, accidents, and foreman favoritism. In the mid-1920s, when the Lynds visited open-shop Muncie, Indiana, they found considerable pessimism among the town's working-class families concerning employment security and promotional opportunities.[80]

There were, however, some firms that adopted advanced employment methods during the 1920s. C. Canby Balderston studied a group of firms with "pioneer" personnel programs, by which he meant the existence of a personnel department, the provision of benefits to enhance employee security, formal wage plans, and mechanisms for maintaining the stability of employment.[81]

Balderston's "pioneer" firms shared certain characteristics. During its earlier phase of expansion, personnel management had shown no obvious relation to particular industrial characteristics such as technological sophistication or profitability. Most wartime industries had been buoyed by high demand and hefty cost-plus contracts. But during the 1920s some industries declined (e.g., metals, textiles, railroads) while more dynamic "new" industries (e.g., chemical and petroleum products, electrical manufacturing, public utilities) took the lead as a result of age, innovation, and mergers. Balderston's firms came from industries that had relatively high and stable profit levels during the 1920s, which assured these firms of sufficient funds to finance personnel programs.[82]

This is not to say that profitability, which was correlated with technical sophistication, was the only determinative factor. Balderston's "pioneer" firms also came from industries with relatively stable seasonal and cyclical product demand. The assurance of a continuous derived demand for labor permitted a firm to plan employment policies based on a presumption of a continuing employment relationship. Firms in industries that weren't on the technological cutting edge but were relatively stable, such as producers of consumer nondurables, were the decade's heaviest users of various employment stabilization techniques and constituted the tiny group that guaranteed their employees a minimum amount of employment or pay per year.[83] Medium-sized, "low" technology but stable firms like Dennison Manufacturing or Hills Brothers offered their workers greater job security than firms that were larger and possessed more market power but were less stable (e.g., auto producers) or less profitable (e.g., textile mills), or both (e.g., steel mills).[84]

Finally, Balderston's firms showed a tendency to be privately owned or tightly controlled. This allowed such well-known liberal employers as Henry S. Dennison, Morris Leeds, and William P. Hapgood to gain the control necessary to exercise their preferences over those of more conservative managers and shareholders.[85]

Most manufacturing workers continued to be employed by firms that had neither unions nor personnel departments. Autocratic methods, arbitrary practices, and employment insecurity persisted at these firms, encouraged by the waning of wartime sense of urgency. On the other hand, about 20 percent of the industrial work force in 1929 was employed by firms that had personnel departments.[86] Some of these firms expanded the liberal employment policies introduced during the war. In others there was evidence that the commitment to reform had weakened, and this slowed the pace of change. Yet an extrapolation of employment policy trends would have been a misleading guide to future developments.

The Great Depression, 1930–1940

Industrial employment policy faced an uncertain future during the first three years of the Great Depression. Some personnel departments and many welfare programs were discontinued as they became a drain on scarce corporate funds or lost their incentive value. Although large firms did not initially cut wage rates as they had done during the 1920–1922 depression, smaller firms were quick to make cuts. By 1932 major firms like General Motors and U.S. Steel had joined in. Early in 1933 William H. Leiserson gloomily wrote that the "depression has undone fifteen years or so of good personnel work," and he warned that "labor is going to look to legislation and not to personnel management for a solution of the unemployment problem."[87]

Contrary to Leiserson's pessimism, the passage of the National Industrial Recovery Act in 1933 set in motion a chain of events that stimulated employment reform. The primary effect of the act was to rejuvenate the labor movement, which in turn led firms to establish new or beefed-up personnel departments. These firms, including many pioneers of the 1920s, viewed the threat posed by unionism as temporary and manageable. They thought that the impulse to unionize could be squelched if they moved quickly to adopt or expand policies that promoted employment security and equity. One employer noted in 1934 that "any labor disturbance or unrest" at his firm would be viewed as evidence that management had failed to "fairly administer the company's labor policies."[88]

Most of the employment reforms introduced after 1933 were not new. The trend during the 1920s toward weak personnel departments and a decentralization of allocative authority was reversed as foremen came under the authority of strengthened personnel departments. The ten giant corporations that made up the Special Conference Committee reported in 1933 that the threat of unionization had "added measurably to the task of personnel managers and to the importance of their functions within organizations."[89] As during World War I, there was a dramatic expansion between 1933 and 1935 in the proportion of industrial firms with personnel departments, especially large firms (table 2.2).

Table 2.2
Employment practices in industry, 1929–1963

	1929	1935–36	1939–40	1946–48	1957–63
Personnel department (L)	34%	46%		61%	
1,000–5,000 employees	39	62		73	
5,000+	55	81		88	
Employee rulebooks (A)		13	16%	30	43% (L)
Centralized selection (A)	32	40	42	63	
Dismissal					
Foreman sole authority (A)		55		24	
Personnel department involved (A)		7	17	31	
(L)	24	38			
Allocation, wages					
Centralized transfer and promotion (L)	24	42			
Promotion charts (A)			19	25	28
Merit rating		11	16	31	
	14 (L)	16 (L)			42 (L)
Job evaluation (A)				55	72
Seniority, security					
Layoff results in loss of all seniority (A)	14	3		1	0.5 (L)
Seniority rules (A)			50	83	
Pension plans (A)	2	6	8	23	73 (L)
Number of wage or employment guarantee plans	35	79	138	196	

Sources: 1929: National Industrial Conference board (NICB), *Layoff and Its Prevention* (New York, 1930), p. 56; NICB, *Industrial Relations Programs in Small Plants* (New York, 1929), pp. 16, 20; NICB, *Industrial Relations: Administration of Policies and Programs* (New York, 1931), p. 54. 1935: NICB, *What Employers Are Doing for Employees* (New York, 1936), pp. 23, 33, 60–65; NICB, *Personnel Practices Governing Factory and Office Administration* (New York, 1937), pp. 73–74, 78. 1940: NICB, "Personnel Policies in Factory and Office," Studies in Personnel Policy No. 23 (1940), p. 15; NICB, "Personnel Activities in American Business," Studies in Personnel Policy No. 20 (1940), pp. 19–29. 1946–48: NICB, "Personnel Practices in Factory and Office," Studies in Personnel Policy No. 88 (1948), p. 13; NICB, "Personnel Activities in American Business (Revised)," Studies in Personnel Policy No. 86 (1947), pp. 16–36; W. D. Scott, R. C. Clothier, and W. R. Spriegel, *Personnel Management* (New York, 1961), p. 583. 1957–63: ibid., p. 583; NICB, "Personnel Practices in Factory and Office: Manufacturing," Studies in Personnel Policy No. 194 (1964), pp. 17, 52, 111, 139. Data on employment guarantee plans from Office of War Mobilization and Reconversion and Office of Temporary Controls, *Guaranteed Wages: Report to the President by the Advisory Board* (Washington, 1947), p. 293.
Note: A = proportion of all industrial firms; L = proportion of industrial firms with more than 250 employees.

To bolster employee morale and prevent any union or Labor Board charges of discrimination, allocative procedures were centralized and made subject to definite rules and procedures.[90] Especially at larger firms the personnel department became more heavily involved in hiring and dismissal decisions (table 2.2). Firms now were more careful to ensure due process in dismissal decisions and promulgated rules that detailed the offenses for which an employee might be dismissed. Large firms rushed to adopt foremen-training programs in which supervisors were instructed to improve relations on the shop floor so as to prevent "misunderstandings or incipient unrest."[91]

Promotion methods changed as the authority to promote and transfer employees again was vested in the personnel department. Merit ratings plans for wage earners, which substituted definite criteria for foremen discretion, also were more widely implemented between 1933 and 1935, especially in larger firms (table 2.2). But despite the centralization and formalization of allocative procedures, promotion plans and job ladders remained uncommon before 1940. In part, this was due to continued opposition by line managers to any loss of allocative authority and flexibility. A 1939 study found that definite promotion lines were "rare" and that firms "which usually have been the leaders in industrial relations progress have not been greatly concerned with this aspect of employment management relations."[92]

Wage determination was another area where foremen were being displaced by personnel managers. Several large firms adopted job classification and evaluation plans during the early 1930s.[93] These methods, which first had been tried during the war, were intended to enhance a firm's control over its rate structure and to improve employee relations. By attaching wage rates to jobs rather than individuals, wage determination was made more impersonal, fair and consistent. But job evaluation methods did not become widespread until after 1935, when the threat of unionization had grown more intense.

A major change in personnel policies during the mid-1930s as compared to preceding periods was the greater emphasis placed on providing employment security to the work force. Job security was the primary concern of workers after 1933, according to Roper polls taken during the depression.[94] By 1935 a minority of large firms had instituted various measures to regulate force reductions and assure their workers of future job security. First, there was renewed interest among managers in the employment stabilization techniques espoused by labor market reformers before World War I.[95] Second, a growing, albeit small, number of firms went so far as to guarantee annual employment or income to their employees (table 2.2). Third, nearly 70 percent of a group of nonunion firms surveyed in 1938 reported that seniority was a factor in layoff decisions.[96] Also workers were being allowed to retain their seniority for longer periods after layoff (table 2.2), which suggested a greater commitment to an enduring employment relationship.

But in the area of job security, as in other realms of employment, the expansion of internal labor market arrangements after 1930 was too little or too late to stem wholly the tide of unionization. For example, a majority of firms in 1935 still allowed their foremen to exercise full discretion in deciding layoffs (table 2.2). A magazine reported that at U.S. Steel in 1936, "steel workers are filled with stories of money lost to foremen after a better-than-usual pay, and never repaid or expected, of minor officials who have small business interests that the men patronize in the hope of getting more work."[97] Some firms used the depression as an excuse to get rid of long-service workers, yet fewer than 10 percent of all firms in 1935 provided dismissal compensation or pensions to ease the pain of job loss.[98]

Unions also grew more concerned with security after 1930; the proportion of union contracts that contained layoff provisions rose sharply after 1930.[99] However, unions typically pressed for more rigid protections than even liberal employers were willing to grant. In 1938, 69 percent of a group of unionized firms made seniority the governing criterion for layoffs; the corresponding figure for nonunion firms was only 8 percent.[100] The rigidity of the unions' approach to security and other allocative procedures reflected a pervasive distrust of management, which the expansion of personnel departments was unable to overcome. Too many firms moved too slowly during the 1920s and early 1930s in the direction that personnel managers had charted during the war. As one prominent personnel manager said in 1937,

A number of so-called progressive employers have, over a period of twenty years, voluntarily done a great many of these things to their lasting credit. The point is that not enough employers have done it. It has often been said that it is 10 percent that are holding back. It may be more accurate to say it has been the 10 percent who have taken the lead. It would not take very long to list the companies in these United States who have taken the lead and have been progressive and done these things voluntarily, and done them in the hope and expectation that we would have been saved some of these developments of the past three years.[101]

At some small or slow-moving firms unionization preceded the establishment of a personnel department. In these firms unions were directly responsible for a rapid expansion of rules, job security measures, and centralized and standardized allocative procedures.[102] But a more common sequence after 1935 was the organization of firms that already had implemented a range of internal labor market policies. Here, unions adapted to the status quo and used preexisting employment policies as a basis for formulating new demands, sometimes even incorporating the firm's personnel procedures into the collective agreement. Developments in the unionized sector were closely watched and often imitated by firms that had managed to avoid unionization.

The spread of labor unions had similar effects on these three types of firms. It elevated the status and authority of the personnel function within the firm and accelerated the implementation of internal labor market arrangements after 1935 (table 2.2). Moreover various innovations now emanated from the unionized sector, especially those related to job security. Unions became the moving force behind the adoption of employment or wage guarantee plans; two-thirds of the firms offering these plans in 1946 were unionized.[103] Nonunion firms responded to union initiatives in the area of job security by formalizing their force reduction procedures—the proportion of nonunion firms with definite layoff procedures rose from 50 percent in 1938 to 80 percent in 1950—and by promising in employee handbooks that they would provide continuous and stable employment.[104] Other union-sector innovations included job posting and job ladders, which ensured that firms filled vacancies from within, as well as a wider use of seniority criteria in layoff, rehire, wage, and promotion decisions.[105]

Managers in unionized firms were not opposed to seniority per se. As noted, some firms had used it as an allocative criterion before the depression. But few had adopted the rigid and all-encompassing approach that the unions now demanded. Production officials were concerned that this would hinder the firm's flexibility in making allocative and pay decisions. These conflicts were muted, however, by the fact that unions now were firmly entrenched and by the reascendance of the personnel department. Some personnel managers willingly implemented seniority systems which, by centralizing allocative authority, had the effect of increasing their own power.

Nonunion firms also relied more heavily on seniority after 1935. A 1950 study of seniority reported that "a great number of nonunionized firms are constantly aware of the implied threat of unionization if their personnel procedures are mishandled. Their attitude is that as long as they keep their house in order, they can remain unorganized.''[106] In addition to threat effects the existence of a personnel department made it more likely that a nonunion firm would rely on seniority rules.[107]

But seniority was more narrowly and flexibly applied in nonunion firms, where there was a stronger emphasis on merit and managerial discretion in allocative and pay decisions. At the end of World War II, for example, a unionized firm was roughly seven times more likely to promote strictly on the basis of seniority than a nonunion firm.[108] However, allocative, pay, and disciplinary procedures in nonunion firms were only slightly less rule bound than those in the union sector. Formalized procedures promoted supervisorial fairness and consistency, thus serving as a partial substitute for the grievance procedures found almost exclusively in unionized firms.[109]

Innovations in employment policy did not flow exclusively from the labor movement after 1935. Techniques such as job evaluation and merit rating grew popular partly as a result of attempts by personnel departments to maintain their control of employment decisions (table 2.2). The prospect of having to bargain over wage differentials led a large number of firms to preemptively adopt job evaluation plans after 1935. According to one study, half of the plans in existence in 1946 had been implemented before 1941, usually without any union involvement in the process of creating a rational rate structure.[110] Similarly, the post-1935 growth of merit rating for pay and allocative decisions was due to management's realization that it needed a defensible alternative to any union demands for making those decisions strictly on the basis of seniority.[111]

Other managerial innovations arose out of competition with unions to secure employee loyalty. Pecuniary welfare or "fringe" benefits for wage earners expanded rapidly between 1935 and 1940, including paid vacations, health and life insurance, and pension plans. The proportion of firms with these programs in 1940 far exceeded levels reached a decade earlier.[112] Managements in unionized firms refused to bargain over these benefits and stressed to employees that unions had not been responsible for them. Also steady growth occurred in the number of firms with programs designed to prevent grievances and improve "human relations," including foreman training and sophisticated attitude surveys.[113]

There was even a resurgence of pre-1921 conceptions of personnel management as an impartial, third force within the firm. Although it was difficult for personnel managers to maintain this image in unionized firms, other personnel managers had more leeway to present themselves as guarantors of the employee's rights. Personnel managers again became interested in establishing a professional basis for personnel management. It was hoped that this would reinforce claims to neutrality and bolster the personnel manager's status within the managerial hierarchy.[114]

Government and World War II

Government intervention in the labor market was an important spur to the growth of internal labor markets after 1935. The government's unprecedented attempts to ensure labor peace and economic security diffused throughout industry new legal and social standards of fairness in employment. The wage stabilization and labor mobilization programs of World War II required that firms adopt particular employment techniques to facilitate the operation of a "command" labor market. Also the large number of regulations that emanated from Washington furthered an existing trend toward centralization and formalization in employment.

Government's major prewar impact on personnel policies was felt through the National Labor Relations Board. Although it was bitterly attacked by employers, the Board forced slow-moving firms to pay close attention to their employment practices lest they be accused of discriminating against union members.[115] This led to a wider use of uniform procedures in such areas as hiring, transfer, promotion, layoff, and dismissal. Personnel departments sharply reduced the foreman's authority to make employment decisions, both by a "reign of rules" and by directly taking over many of his allocative and disciplinary duties.

The centralization of the personnel function was further increased by the complex rules and data-gathering requirements of unemployment insurance, social security, and minimum wage laws. For example, the Fair Labor Standards Act (FLSA) demanded that records be kept of the wages and hours of every employee in a firm.[116] These laws also had direct effects on employment policy. The merit-rating provisions of most state unemployment insurance laws and the overtime provisions of the FLSA provided an incentive for firms to stabilize employment and eliminate erratic production patterns.[117] Also social security pensions and unemployment insurance established economywide standards for protection against the insecurity of old age and unemployment. Rather than eliminating demands that employers provide this security, these laws stimulated private pension and dismissal compensation plans that raised an employee above what now was viewed as a minimum level of protection.[118]

The advent of war brought another round of expansion in the number of personnel departments, especially at small and medium-sized firms (table 2.2). These departments provided the expertise needed to cope with an array of government regulations and a stronger labor movement. Also hiring and dismissal became more centralized as these firms sought to conserve scarce war labor (table 2.2).

Government closely regulated allocative and wage payment practices in the private sector during the war. The War Manpower Commission (WMC) was created in 1942 to ensure sufficient labor both for defense production and the armed services.[119] Shortly after its inception the WMC asked all firms to prepare "manning table" plans to aid in the orderly deployment of labor. The plans outlined a firm's current and projected manpower needs. Firms were asked to describe their jobs and workers using occupational nomenclature taken from the recently compiled Dictionary of Occupational Titles. This forced firms that had not already done so to conduct extensive job analyses and create a rational structure of well-defined but rigid job titles. Also the plans showed training paths and promotion sequences between jobs, which aided in justifying deferments for skilled workers and trainees.[120]

The wage stabilization program administered by the War Labor Board (WLB) similarly encouraged the use of a variety of internal labor market techniques. The WLB, like its predecessor during World War I, pushed for the implementation of job and wage classification plans to reduce the likelihood of wage disputes and ease the administrative task of stabilizing wages. Job evaluation plans sometimes were required by the WLB to justify wage increases intended to remove inequities, although now the plans had to be jointly devised with union representatives.[121] This hastened the practice of tying rates to job titles through evaluation plans (table 2.2). Also, because the WLB permitted wage increases for merit, promotion, or seniority, firms were stimulated to implement formal policies to support rate increase requests for these purposes.[122] As a result merit rating and internal promotion plans, as well as seniority-based wage systems, spread throughout industry after 1940. Finally, many firms expanded their provision of welfare benefits because of the WLB's practice of allowing them to adopt without its approval various "fringe" benefits.[123]

Wages, promotion, and tenure were more tightly woven together as a result of the activities of personnel managers, unions, and government. Job evaluation was linked to promotion ladders, and seniority principles were strengthened. Job and relative wage structures grew more rigid, and tenure became a more important determinant of a worker's status.

The process of internal labor market formation had its most deleterious effects on the once-powerful foreman, who now was subjected to sharp pressures from above and below. Personnel managers crimped his prerogatives and took responsibilities away from him. Union grievance procedures and collective bargaining stripped him of much of his authority. Foremen now were described as management's "forgotten" or "marginal" men, terms that symbolized industry's forty year transition from the drive system to the modern internal labor market.[124]

Conclusion

A number of major points arise from this discussion of the historical development of employment practices in the manufacturing sector. The first concerns the erratic growth of internal labor markets in large firms, most of which occurred during World War I and the Great Depression. The bulk of the innovations that comprise the internal labor market were available by 1915, if not earlier, yet large firms implemented them only when prodded by various external forces, chiefly the threat of unionization. Labor scarcity and government regulation of the labor market also were forces that initiated internal labor market growth during World War I and reinforced established practices during World War II.

Growth patterns were different at small and medium-sized firms, most of which did not adopt internal labor market arrangements until after the mid-1930s. These firms acted only when the threat of unionization was more immediate, although some did not reform their employment practices until after they had been organized. Also these firms waited until clear patterns and standards had been established, either by their larger counterparts during the 1930s or by pressure from the government during World War II.

The erratic growth of the internal labor market reflected the low priority that most manufacturing firms assigned to employment policy. Closely related to this was the dominant position in management held by a firm's production division. Line managers, some of whom began their careers as foremen, perceived the policies proposed by personnel departments as bureaucratic encumbrances and a threat to operating efficiency. Fair treatment, job protection, and assurances of a continuing employment relationship were considered inessential to the firm's mission, which was to produce at least cost with the greatest degree of allocative flexibility. For line managers, a worker either "cut the mustard" or he was out; incentive plans were sufficient to motivate even the least-skilled worker. Unions could best be dealt with by a combination of decent pay, careful hiring, and coercion, if needed.

With the benefit of hindsight vision we may observe that internal labor market arrangements often enhanced efficiency through their effect on turnover and morale, or by stimulating programs to upgrade the work force. But this result wasn't always apparent to a firm's top managers, who were skeptical that these arrangements would lower costs. These attitudes, and the close relationship between external forces and internal labor market growth, suggest that efficiency incentives alone were not strong or obvious enough to generate an internal labor market.

Personnel managers can be viewed as having acted as mere conduits for union threat effects. Some of their ideas were borrowed from the unions; their influence often rested on the imminence of labor unrest. But industrial relations might have taken a very different course had this managerial specialty never developed.

The initiation of a personnel function introduced competition within management between the goals of the personnel department and the objectives of other divisions of a firm. For example, this forced managements to become more aware of the trade-off between allocative flexibility and employee morale, a choice that was less apparent when employment policy was subordinated to production objectives. Personnel management's roots, its semiprofessional status, and its ties to outside institutions like the universities all added legitimacy to the new values that it introduced into management. In the absence of these effects internal labor markets would have developed more slowly, and unions would have been both more popular and adversarial.

Unions, by giving voice to employee preferences for a more secure and equitable employment relationship, were a major force behind the proliferation of internal labor markets. The periods of rapid internal labor market growth were closely associated with increases in union bargaining power. This suggests that workers had strong interests in the characteristic bureaucratic features of the internal labor market. Often it was the unions, not management, that pushed most strongly for job ladders, wage classification, allocative rules, and guarantees of an enduring employment relationship.

But the differences between unions and management were not unbridgeable because of extensive imitation and adaptation by both sides. In establishing internal labor markets in large firms, personnel managers borrowed from the employment procedures and principles that the unions had built up since 1870. When unions organized a firm after 1930, they often had to adapt to the status quo established by personnel managers. Moreover unions and personnel managers had a mutual interest in restraining foremen, in order and stability, and in the use of formal rules and procedures. Although most managements never fully accepted unions, they came to accept many of their goals; this provided a basis for accommodation and bargaining over the shape of the internal labor market in unionized firms.

Until some years after World War II nonunion firms closely watched and imitated developments in the unionized sector. Personnel management in these firms has proved that it can provide and maintain the same internal labor market and other protections as are found in the unionized sector. But, if union threat effects rather than efficiency incentives were a prime force behind the adoption of internal labor market practices, would not continued dwindling of the labor movement produce a return to older and less benign employment practices?

There are several reasons to believe that this would not occur. First, as in the past, the government continues to set standards that create or reinforce internal labor markets. Hiring and allocative practices are highly regulated; wage minima, pensions, and workplace safety are protected; social welfare and macroeconomic policies provide incentives for stable, long-term employment relations; and there even is an emerging judicial line of thought that questions an employer's right to dismiss an employee at will.[125] The number of government rules has increased markedly during the last twenty years and, as during the 1935 to 1945 period, this has centralized and rigidified the administration of employment.[126]

Second, past experience and the continued professionalization of management have changed managerial attitudes and beliefs. Most managements no longer are skeptical that internal labor market practices reduce costs. In part, this is due to a wider acceptance of the motivational tenets of personnel management—that a satisfied, fairly treated, and secure work force is more productive. Also firms have adapted their training and administrative techniques to the existence of an internal labor market; these sunk costs prevent any quick transition to an alternative employment system.

Third, workers today have higher standards than their forbears, because the achievements of previous generations have created "customs" or shared norms of fair treatment in employment. Workers now expect a "good" employer to treat them equitably, make allocative decisions by rule, reward seniority, and provide advancement opportunities and employment security.[127] These expectations put pressure on government to maintain its activities and impose constraints on employer personnel policies. Firms without internal labor markets, in an economy where most firms have them, must recruit their workers from strata of the labor force that have lower expectations and standards. These tend to be the least-skilled and least-educated workers, such as immigrants.

Thus the practices that comprise the internal labor market have become what Robert Solow has termed "social conventions or principles of appropriate behavior."[128] They are embedded in a structure of law, managerial principles, and employee expectations. Unions played a most important role in creating this structure, but they no longer are the main prop to its continued existence. Yet there are sectors of industry where the unions did not reach, where the law is not enforced, and where managements and workers have low expectations of each other. Here one is unlikely to find internal labor market arrangements.

Notes

The author would like to acknowledge the comments of Daniel J. B. Mitchell, Paul Osterman, and Lloyd Ulman. The UCLA Institute of Industrial Relations provided financial support for this research.

1. D. H. Robertson, *Control of Industry* quoted in R. H. Coase, "The Nature of the Firm" *Economica* **4** (1937):388.

2. Stanley Lebergott, *Manpower in Economic Growth: The American Record Since 1800* (New York, 1964), p. 510; Daniel Nelson, *Managers and Workers: Origins of the New Factory System in the United States, 1880–1920* (Madison, 1975), pp. 7–9; Victor S. Clark, *History of Manufactures in the United States*, Vol. 3 (Washington, D.C., 1929), pp. 160–164.

3. Alfred D. Chandler, Jr., *The Visible Hand: The Managerial Revolution in American Business* (Cambridge, 1977), pp. 280–281, 338–339, 365.

4. Nelson, *Managers and Workers*, pp. 36–42; Dan Clawson, *Bureaucracy and the Labor Process* (New York, 1980), pp. 75–83; David Montgomery, "Workers'

Control of Machine Production in the Nineteenth Century," *Labor History* **17** (Fall 1976):486–492.

5. David Brody, *Steelworkers in America: The Nonunion Era* (New York, 1969), p. 19; Joseph A. Litterer, "Systematic Management: The Search for Order and Integration," *Business History Review* **35** (Winter 1961):469–474.

6. Henry Metcalfe, "The Shop-Order System of Accounts," *Transactions of the American Society of Mechanical Engineers* (ASME) **7** (1886); F. E. Webner, "Obtaining Actual Knowledge of the Cost of Production," *The Engineering Magazine* **36** (October 1908); Frederick W. Taylor, *Shop Management* (New York, 1911), pp. 110–122; Horace L. Arnold, *The Complete Cost Keeper* (New York, 1912); Marc J. Epstein, *The Effect of Scientific Management on the Development of Standard Cost Systems* (New York, 1978); Joseph A. Litterer, "Systematic Management: Design for Organizational Recoupling in American Manufacturing Firms," *Business History Review* **37** (Winter 1963):376–389; Reinhard Bendix, *Work and Authority in Industry* (New York, 1956), pp. 211–218.

7. Frederick W. Taylor, "A Piece Rate System: Being a Step toward Partial Solution of the Labor Problem," *Transactions of the ASME* **16** (1895):860–895; C. Bertrand Thompson, "Wages and Wage Systems as Incentives" in Thompson (ed.), *Scientific Management: A Collection of the More Significant Articles Describing the Taylor System of Management* (Cambridge, 1914), pp. 684–705; Robert F. Hoxie, *Scientific Management and Labor* (New York, 1915), pp. 31–32, 120–121.

8. Joseph H. Willits, "Steadying Employment," *The Annals* **65** (May 1916):72; H. Keith Trask, "The Problem of the Minor Executive," *The Engineering Magazine* **38** (January 1910):501; C. J. Morrison, "Short-Sighted Methods in Dealing with Labor," *The Engineering Magazine* **46** (January 1914):568; Fred H. Rindge, Jr., "From Boss to Foreman," *Industrial Management* **53** (July 1917):508–509.

9. Brody, *Steelworkers*, p. 120; Charles Fouhy, "Relations between the Employment Manager and the Foreman," *Industrial Management* **58** (October 1919):336; T. J. Zimmerman, "How They Hold Their Men," *System* **16** (August 1910):150–152.

10. Sumner H. Slichter, *The Turnover of Factory Labor* (New York, 1921), p. 319.

11. Willits, "Steadying Employment," p. 72; John P. Frey and John R. Commons, "Conciliation in the Stove Industry," U.S. Bureau of Labor Statistics Bulletin No. 62 (Washington, 1906), p. 128; Commission of Inquiry, Interchurch World Movement, *Report on the Steel Strike of 1919* (New York, 1920), p. 139.

12. Driving occurred under daywork, where the effort wage was indeterminate, as well as on the new incentive wage systems, which were calculated to reduce unit labor costs as output rose. But it also was prevalent on piecework, partly in response to workers' restriction of output. Lloyd Ulman, *The Rise of the National Trade Union* (Cambridge, 1955), pp. 549–551.

13. Slichter, *Turnover of Factory Labor*, p. 202; Ernest M. Hopkins, "A Functionalized Employment Department as a Factor in Industrial Efficiency," *The Annals* **61** (September 1915):117.

14. Discharges accounted for 16 percent of all separations between 1910 and 1918. Paul F. Brissenden and Emil Frankel, *Labor Turnover in Industry* (New York, 1922), pp. 80–81.

15. Robert A. Gordon, *Business Fluctuations*, 2d ed. (New York, 1961), p. 251.

16. Alexander Keyssar, "Men Out of Work: A Social History of Unemployment in Massachusetts, 1870–1916," Unpublished doctoral dissertation in History of American Civilization, Harvard University, Cambridge, 1977, pp. 73–79.

17. U.S. Bureau of the Census, *Census of Manufactures: 1909*, Part I (Washington, 1912), pp. 27–54.

18. Slichter, *Turnover of Factory Labor*, p. 126. The fact that the plant compiled data on rehires at a time when few others bothered to do so suggests that the data are not representative. Currently between 60 and 65 percent of workers on temporary layoffs are rehired by their original employers. Kim Clark and Lawrence Summers, "Labor Market Dynamics and Unemployment: A Reconsideration," *Brookings Papers on Economic Activity* 1 (1979):49.

19. Office of War Mobilization and Reconversion and Office of Temporary Controls, *Guaranteed Wages: Report to the President by the Advisory Board* (Washington, 1947), pp. 290, 295; New York City Mayor's Committee on Unemployment, *How to Meet Hard Times* (New York, 1917), p. 24; Louis Levine, *The Women's Garment Workers* (New York, 1924), pp. 279–283.

20. Morrison, "Short-Sighted Methods," p. 568; Keyssar, op. cit., 153.

21. Sumner H. Slichter, *Union Policies and Industrial Management* (Washington, 1941), p. 63; U.S. Industrial Commission, *Report on the Relations and Conditions of Capital and Labor*, Vol. 7 (Washington, D.C., 1901), pp. 603, 620; Sanford M. Jacoby and Daniel J. B. Mitchell, "Development of Contractual Features of the Union-Management Relationship," in Industrial Relations Research Association, *Proceedings of the 1982 Spring Meetings, April 28–30, Milwaukee* (Madison, 1982), p. 515.

22. David A. McCabe, *The Standard Rate in American Trade Unions* (Baltimore, 1912), pp. 101, 111, 226–232; John R. Commons, "Labor's Attitude toward Efficiency," *American Economic Review* 1 (September 1911):469; Ulman, *Rise of National Trade Union*, pp. 483–484; Frey and Commons, "Conciliation in the Stove Industry," pp. 128, 157.

23. Slichter, *Union Policies*, p. 117; Dan Mater, "The Development and Operation of the Railroad Seniority System," *Journal of Business* 13 (October 1940) and 14 (January 1941); George Barnett, *The Printers* (Cambridge, 1919), pp. 209–240; John R. Commons, "Labor Conditions in Meat Packing and the Recent Strike," *Quarterly Journal of Economics* 19 (November 1904):17.

24. Sanford Jacoby, "The Duration of Indefinite Employment Contracts in the United States and England: An Historical Analysis," *Comparative Labor Law* 5 (Winter 1982):121–125.

25. Frederic Meyers, "The Analytic Meaning of Seniority," Industrial Relations Research Association, *Proceedings of the 1966 Winter Meeting* (Madison, 1966),

p. 4; Clark Kerr, "The Balkanization of Labor Markets," in E. Wight Bakke (ed.), *Labor Mobility and Economic Opportunity* (Cambridge, 1954).

26. Brissenden and Frankel, *Labor Turnover*, p. 91; Slichter, *Turnover of Factory Labor*, pp. 30–33, 55–69; Sanford M. Jacoby, "Industrial Labor Mobility in Historical Perspective," *Industrial Relations* 22 (Spring 1983a):261–282.

27. Henry Eilbirt, "The Development of Personnel Management in the United States," *Business History Review* 33 (Autumn 1959):346; Fred W. Climer, "Cutting Labor Cost in Seasonal Business," *Manufacturing Industries* 13 (May 1927).

28. Stuart Brandes, *American Welfare Capitalism, 1880–1940* (Chicago, 1976); Robert Ozanne, *A Century of Labor Management Relations at McCormick and International Harvester* (Madison, 1967), pp. 32–40; Stephen J. Scheinberg, "The Development of Corporation Labor Policy, 1900–1940," Unpublished doctoral dissertation in History, University of Wisconsin, Madison, 1967, pp. 21–75. This section relies on Sanford Jacoby, "The Early Years of Personnel Management in the United States, 1900–1930," Unpublished paper, 1982, pp. 8–11.

29. Arthur Mann, *Yankee Reformers in the Urban Age* (Cambridge, 1954), pp. 84–85; A. F. Davis, *Spearheads for Reform: The Social Settlements and the Progressive Movement, 1890–1914* (New York, 1967), pp. 185–186. Mary B. Gilson, *What's Past Is Prologue* (New York, 1940), p. ix.

30. Daniel Nelson and Stuart Campbell, "Taylorism versus Welfare Work in American Industry," *Business History Review* 46 (Spring 1972):5; Ozanne, *A Century of Labor Management Relations*, pp. 34–35; Robert Clothier, "The Function of the Employment Department," U.S. Bureau of Labor Statistics Bulletin No. 196 (Washington, D.C., 1916), p. 9; Harold Ley, "Employee Welfare Work That Pays," *American Industries* 22 (March 1922):33.

31. Charles U. Carpenter, "The Working of a Labor Department in Industrial Establishments," *The Engineering Magazine* 25 (April 1903); Louis A. Boettiger, *Employee Welfare Work* (New York, 1923), p. 128.

32. Slichter, *Turnover of Factory Labor*, pp. 431–434.

33. John M. Brewer, *History of Vocational Guidance: Origins and Early Development* (New York, 1942); Frank Parsons, *Choosing a Vocation* (Boston, 1909); Sol Cohen, "The Industrial Education Movement, 1907–1917," *American Quarterly* 20 (Spring 1968); John M. Brewer, *The Vocational Guidance Movement* (New York, 1918), p. 289; Jacoby, "Early Years of Personnel Management," pp. 11–14.

34. Meyer Bloomfield, *The Vocational Guidance of Youth* (Boston, 1915); Owen Lovejoy, "Vocational Guidance and Child Labor," U.S. Bureau of Education Bulletin No. 14 (Washington, D.C., 1914), pp. 13–15; Sophonisba P. Breckinridge, "Guidance by the Development of Placement and Follow-Up Work," U.S. Bureau of Education Bulletin No. 14 (Washington, D.C., 1914), pp. 62–63.

35. Meyer Bloomfield, "The School and the Start of Life" in Bloomfield (ed.), *Readings in Vocational Guidance* (Boston, 1915), pp. 679–720; Meyer Bloomfield, "Introduction" in Roy W. Kelly, *Hiring the Worker* (Boston, 1918), p. 2.

36. Meyer Bloomfield in U.S. Commission on Industrial Relations, *Final Report and Testimony*, Vol. 1 (Washington, D.C., 1916), p. 393; Meyer Bloomfield, "The New Profession of Handling Men," *The Annals* **61** (September 1915); Kelly, *Hiring the Worker*, pp. 131–136; Henry Metcalf in National Association of Corporation Schools (NACS), *Third Annual Proceedings* (1915), pp. 348–410; NACS, *Fourth Annual Proceedings* (1916), p. 297.

37. Meyer Bloomfield, "General Discussion," *American Labor Legislation Review* **4** (May 1914):350–352; John B. Andrews, "A Practical Program for the Prevention of Unemployment in America," *American Labor Legislation Review* **5** (November 1915):585–587.

38. Richard A. Feiss, "Scientific Management Applied to the Steadying of Employment and Its Effect in an Industrial Establishment," *The Annals* **61** (September 1915):103–111; Herman Feldman, "The New Emphasis in the Problem of Reducing Unemployment," *Bulletin of the Taylor Society* **7** (October 1922): 176–177; Malcolm C. Rorty, "Broader Aspects of the Employment Problem," *Industrial Management* **52** (February 1917):723; *Personnel* **1** (April 1919): 7.

39. These developments were part of a broader effort then underway to professionalize management by teaching it in university schools of business administration. See Jacoby, "Early Years of Personnel Management," pp. 6–7.

40. Meyer Bloomfield, "Comments" in U.S. Bureau of Labor Statistics Bulletin No. 196 (Washington, D.C., 1916), p. 73; Boyd Fisher to Walter V. Bingham, February 12, 1919, Box 4, Bingham Papers, Carnegie-Mellon University, Pittsburgh; Ordway Tead and Henry C. Metcalf, *Personnel Administration* (New York, 1920), pp. 9–10.

41. Sanford M. Jacoby, "The Origins of Internal Labor Markets in American Manufacturing Firms, 1910–1940," Unpublished doctoral dissertation in Economics, University of California, Berkeley, 1981, p. 253; Sumner H. Slichter, "Review of Personnel Relations in Industry," *Administration* **2** (August 1921):261–263.

42. Slichter, ibid., 262; Slichter *Turnover of Factory Labor*, pp. 432, 426–427.

43. Lebergott, *Manpower in Economic Growth*, p. 512; Paul H. Douglas, *Real Wages in the United States, 1890–1926* (New York, 1930), p. 445.

44. Sumner H. Slichter, "Industrial Morale," *Quarterly Journal of Economics*, (November 1920), reprinted in *Potentials of the American Economy: Selected Essays of Sumner H. Slichter* (Cambridge, 1961), p. 169; Guy Tripp in *Iron Trade Review* **66** (January 19, 1920):369; John W. Kendrick, *Productivity Trends in the United States* (Princeton, 1961), p. 136; Paul H. Douglas, "Personnel Problems and the Business Cycle," *Administration* **4** (July 1922):17–18.

45. Alexander M. Bing, *Wartime Strikes and Their Adjustment* (New York, 1921), pp. 28–30, 291–296; Jeremy Brecher, *Strike!* (Greenwich, 1972), pp. 133–180; David Montgomery, "The New Unionism and the Transformation of Workers' Consciousness in America, 1909–1922," *Journal of Social History* **7** (Summer 1974):514.

46. For a detailed discussion of labor turnover during this period, see Jacoby, "Industrial Labor Mobility."

47. These figures are estimates. Robert F. Lovett, "Tendencies in Personnel Practice, "Bureau of Personnel Research, Carnegie Institute of Technology, *Service Bulletin* 5 (February 1923):11–12; Edward D. Jones, "Employment Management," Federal Board for Vocational Education Bulletin No. 50 (Washington, 1920), p. 15; Jacoby, "Early Years of Personnel Management," pp. 15–16.

48. Paul H. Douglas, "War Time Courses in Employment Management," *School and Society* 9 (June 7, 1919):692; Meyer Jacobstein, "Government Courses for Training Employment Managers," U.S. Bureau of Labor Statistics Bulletin No. 247 (Washington, D.C., 1918), p. 19; Paul H. Douglas and F. E. Wolfe, "Labor Administration in the Shipbuilding Industry during War Time II," *Journal of Political Economy* 27 (March 1919):376–377.

49. Kelly, *Hiring the Worker*, pp. 57–100; National Association of Employment Managers, *Proceedings* (Cleveland, 1919), p. 35; C. J. Shower, "Pontiac Centralizes Its Employment of Labor," *Automotive Industries* 39 (July 11, 1918); Arthur H. Young, "Harmonizing the Man and His Job," *Iron Trade Review* 60 (February 5, 1917):427.

50. Paul H. Douglas, "Plant Administration of Labor," *Journal of Political Economy* 27 (March 1919):551; "Relations of Employment Office and Foremen" in Industrial Relations Association of America (IRAA), *Proceedings* (Chicago, 1920), Part 2, pp. 559–563; D. R. Kennedy, "Training the Foreman of Industry," *Industrial Management* 59 (January 1920):68.

51. J. D. Hackett, "Job Analysis as Aid to Production," *Iron Trade Review* 67 (September 9, 1920):722–724; Hugh L. Clary, "The Zoning of Jobs," *Industrial Management* 61 (May 1921):324–326; John Lee, The So-Called Profit Sharing System in the Ford Plant," *The Annals* 65 (May 1916):300. The personnel manager at Clothcraft Shops, a pioneer in wage standardization, wrote, "we carefully went over our rates, wages, and salaries quarterly, always with the idea of relativity of rates in our plant in mind. That nebulous thing known as the 'market rate' did not govern us." Gilson, *What's Past Is Prologue*, p. 75.

52. See the discussion of the 1918 Bridgeport machinists' strike in Jacoby, "Origins of Internal Labor Markets," pp. 438–441; Richard H. Rice, "Discussion of Employee Representation Plans," National Association of Corporation Training. *Bulletin* 8 (August 1921):346–363; Bing, *Wartime Strikes and Their Adjustment*, pp. 195–206.

53. Wage standardization by the government was "almost everywhere resisted by employers." Bing, *Wartime Strikes and Their Adjustment*, p. 199; "Report of the Special Conference Committee," July 15, 1920, Industrial Service Department Committee Minutes, YMCA Historical Library, New York.

54. Slichter, *Turnover of Factory Labor*, pp. 189, 356; Meyer Bloomfield, *Labor and Compensation* (New York, 1918), pp. 308–309; Franklyn Meine, "Promotions of Factory Employees" in Daniel Bloomfield (ed.), *Problems in Personnel Management* (New York, 1923).

55. Meine, ibid., pp. 280–281; Phillip J. Reilly, "Planning Promotion for Employees and the Effect in Reducing Labor Turnover," *The Annals* **71** (May 1917):136–139.

56. "Survey Methods of Promotion," *Industrial Relations* **7** (April 2, 1921):619–624; B. S. Beach, "Filling Vacancies from within the Ranks," *Industrial Management* **67** (February 1924):90.

57. National Association of Employment Managers, *Proceedings* (Cleveland, 1919), p. 62; *Industrial Relations* **15** (May 26, 1923):1544; National Association of Corporation Training, "Methods of Transfer and Promotion in Business Organizations," Confidential Report No. 6 (October 1920), pp. 3, 4, 7–12; Paul F. Gemmill, "Methods of Promoting Industrial Employees," *Industrial Management* **67** (April 1924), p. 238.

58. Gemmill, "Methods of Promoting Industrial Employees," p. 246; Slichter, *Potentials of the American Economy*, p. 178; Fouhy, "Relations between the Employment Manager and the Foreman," p. 336.

59. Merlin M. Taylor, "We Can't Get Men to Stay," *Factory* **20** (February 1918):231; Charles M. Horton, "Under New Management—Judging Men," *Industrial Management* **55** (March 1918):226; National Association of Corporation Schools *Bulletin* **7** (April 1920):179–182.

60. "Standard Oil's New Labor Democracy," NACS *Bulletin* **5** (June 1918): 207–209; John R. Commons, *Industrial Government* (New York, 1921), chap. 5; Joseph T. Gilman, "Analyses of Reasons for Leaving and Their Use," U.S. Bureau of Labor Statistics Bulletin No. 227 (Washington, 1917), p. 135.

61. Edwin S. Blodgett, "I Quit—I No Like Job," *Factory* **21** (March 1919):473–474, emphasis added.

62. Jones, "Employment Management," pp. 19–20; Meyer Bloomfield, "Employment Management Department," *Industrial Management* **52** (January 1917):557.

63. Kelly, *Hiring the Worker*, p. 32; Commission of Inquiry, *Report on Steel Strike*, pp. 210–211.

64. Sumner H. Slichter, "The Current Labor Policies of American Industries," *Quarterly Journal of Economics* (May 1929); reprinted in Slichter, *Potentials of the American Economy*, pp. 184–212.

65. "Reduction of Absence and Tardiness," Industrial Relations Section, Princeton University (December 1927), p. 15; National Industrial Conference Board, *Industrial Pensions in the United States* (New York, 1925), pp. 13–15, 62–65.

66. Ibid., pp. 25–28; James P. Adams, "A Common Sense Attack on Labor Turnover," *Industrial Management* **62** (November 1921):302.

67. "Report on Profit Sharing and Stock Ownership" in YMCA, *Industrial Conference on Human Relations and Betterment in Industry* (New York, 1924), p. 21; "Reduction of Absence and Tardiness," p. 2; Adams, "A Common Sense Attack," p. 301; Jacoby, "Origins of Internal Labor Markets," pp. 476–479.

68. Allen M. Wakstein, "The Origins of the Open-Shop Movement, 1919–1920," *Journal of American History* 51 (December 1964):460–475; Robert K. Murray, *Red Scare: A Study in National Hysteria* (Minneapolis, 1955); Dudley R. Kennedy, "The Future of Industrial Relations," *Industrial Management* 59 (March 1920):558; Jacoby, "Early Years of Personnel Management," pp. 18–20.

69. National Associationn of Corporation Schools, *Eighth Annual Proceedings* (1920), pp. 97–101; Industrial Relations Association of America, *Proceedings* (Chicago, 1920), Part 1, p. 81; Charles Piez, "Trends in Management; What Is the Business Outlook Today?" *Factory* 26 (January 1, 1921):32; E. S. Cowdrick, "What Are We Going to Do with the Boss?" *Industrial Management* 60 (August 1920):195.

70. Douglas, *Real Wages*, p. 445; Douglas, "Plant Administration," pp. 18–23.

71. William L. Chenery, "Personnel Relations Tested," *The Survey* (May 21, 1921), pp. 236–237; Lovett, "Tendencies," p. 13; J. David Houser, *What the Employer Thinks* (Cambridge, 1927), pp. 74, 116.

72. W. J. Donald, "The Newer Conception of Personnel Functions," *Factory and Industrial Management* 75 (March 1928): 514–515; National Industrial Conference Board, *Industrial Relations Programs in Small Plants* (New York, 1929), p. 20.

73. Lebergott, *Manpower in Economic Growth*, pp. 521, 514; Douglas, *Real Wages*, p. 445; National Industrial Conference Board, *Wages in the United States* (New York, 1931), p. 19; Irving Bernstein, *The Lean Years* (Boston, 1960), p. 67. Real wages hardly decline, however, due to the steady drop in consumer and wholesale prices. Clarence D. Long, "The Illusion of Money Wage Rigidity," *Review of Economics and Statistics* 42 (May 1960), pp. 150–151.

74. See Jacoby, "Industrial Labor Mobility," for a detailed discussion of these points.

75. "The Personnel Content of Management," *American Management Review* 12 (April 1923), pp. 3–6; Sam A. Lewisohn, "Management's Part in Personnel Administration," *Personnel Administration* 9 (August 1922):3–4; T. G. Portmore, "Selecting Employees to Meet the Needs of the Foreman," *American Management Review* 12 (April 1924):3–5; Leo Wolman and Gustave Peck, "Labor in the Social Structure" in President's Research Committee, *Recent Social Trends in the United States* (New York, 1933), p. 830.

76. See table 2.2, infra; Gilson, *What's Past Is Prologue*, p. 101.

77. Florence A. Thorne to Morris L. Cooke, Box 66, Cooke Papers, Franklin D. Roosevelt Presidential Library, Hyde Park, New York; M. J. Jucius, "The Use of Wage Incentives," *Journal of Business* 5 (January 1932):6; Bernstein, *Lean Years*, p. 67; Robert Ozanne, *Wages in Practice and Theory* (Madison, 1968), pp. 144–155.

78. Leah H. Feder, *Unemployment Relief During Periods of Depression* (New York, 1936), p. 313; "Unemployment Survey, 1920–1921," *American Labor*

Legislation Review 11 (September 1921):210–213; "Report of the Special Conference Committee: Supplement," March 1921, Industrial Service Department Committee Minutes, YMCA Historical Library, New York.

79. National Industrial Conference Board, *Layoff and Its Prevention* (New York, 1930), pp. 38–39, 56.

80. Roger E. Keeran, "Communist Influence in the Automobile Industry, 1920–1933," *Labor History* 20 (Spring 1979):216; Robert S. and Helen M. Lynd, *Middletown: A Study in Modern American Culture* (New York, 1929), pp. 66–78.

81. C. Canby Balderston, *Executive Guidance of Industrial Relations* (Philadelphia, 1935), pp. 224–240.

82. Sanford M. Jacoby, "Union—Management Cooperation in the United States: Lessons from the 1920s," *Industrial and Labor Relations Review* 37 (October 1983b); David S. Landes, *The Unbound Prometheus* (Cambridge, 1969), pp. 359–385.

83. These techniques included product diversification, sales planning, production for stock, training workers for transfers, and working repairs in with production. See Herman Feldman, *The Regularization of Employment* (New York, 1925); S. A. Lewisohn, E. G. Draper, J. R. Commons, and Don D. Lescohier, *Can Business Prevent Unemployment?* (New York, 1925).

84. Less stable firms could have eased the burden of instability by paying unemployment insurance, but few nonunion employers did this. They offered higher wages, but observers felt that compensating differentials were "inadequate" so that "the primary burden of instability of employment falls upon the worker and his family." Finally, they could have tried to stabilize employment and reduce seasonal fluctuations. But for a variety of reasons the seasonal instability of employment actually increased after 1923 in durable and semidurable manufacturing industries. National Industrial Conference Board, *Layoff and Its Prevention*, p. 67; Alvin Hansen and Paul A. Samuelson, "Economic Analysis of Guaranteed Wages" in *Guaranteed Wages*, p. 425; Simon Kuznets, *Seasonal Variations in Industry and Trade* (New York, 1933), pp. 211, 311, 355–361.

85. Balderston, *Executive Guidance*, pp. 224–240.

86. National Industrial Conference Board, *Industrial Relations Programs*, pp. 2, 20.

87. Bernstein, *Lean Years*, pp. 314, 476–478; Joseph Shister, *Economics of the Labor Market* (New York, 1949), pp. 437–442; National Industrial Conference Board, *Effect of the Depression on Industrial Relations Programs* (New York, 1934), p. 12; William M. Leiserson, "Personnel Problems Raised by the Current Economic Crisis," *The Management Review* 22 (April 1933):114.

88. Industrial Relations Counselors (IRC), "Memorandum to Clients No. 2" (September 1934), p. 5.

89. U.S. Senate, Committee on Education and Labor, "Hearings before the Subcommittee on Violations of Free Speech and Rights of Labor," 76th Cong. (1939), Part 45, p. 16831.

90. Lewis L. Lorwin and A. Wubnig, *Labor Relations Boards* (Washington, D.C., 1935).

91. IRC, "Memorandum No. 2," p. 4; IRC, "Memorandum to Clients No. 24" (June 1936); American Management Association (AMA), "Management's Industrial Relations Problems," Personnel Series (PS) No. 22 (1936), p. 22.

92. NICB, "Plans for Rating Employees," Studies in Personnel Policy (SPP) No. 8 (1938); Helen Baker, "Company Plans for Employee Promotions," Industrial Relations Section, Princeton University, Report No. 58 (Princeton, 1939), p. 8.

93. NICB, "Job Evaluation," SPP No. 25 (1940), pp. 10–38; C. Canby Balderston, "Wage Setting Based on Job Analysis and Evaluation," IRC Monograph No. 4 (New York, 1940); AMA, "Compensation Problems and Training Techniques Today," PS No. 24 (1936), pp. 4–6.

94. Elmo Roper, "What American Labor Wants," *The American Mercury* (February 1944):181.

95. "Company Plans for the Regularization of Plant Operation and Employment," Industrial Relations Section, Princeton University (Princeton, 1933), p. 13; NICB, "Assuring Employment or Income to Wage Earners," SPP No. 7 (1938).

96. NICB, "Curtailment, Layoff Policy and Seniority," SPP No. 5 (1938), p. 8.

97. "The U.S. Steel Corporation: Part III," *Fortune* (May 1936): 141.

98. The proportion of the manufacturing labor force over 45 years of age declined from 30 percent in 1930 to 26 percent in 1940. Jacoby, "Industrial Labor Mobility"; NICB, *What Employers Are Doing*, pp. 32–33.

99. Sumner Slichter, *Union Policies and Industrial Management* (Washington, D.C., 1941), pp. 104–107.

100. NICB, "Curtailment . . . ," p. 8.

101. T. G. Spates, "An Analysis of Industrial Relations Trends," AMA Personnel Series No. 25 (1937), p. 24.

102. George S. Gibb, *The Saco-Lowell Shops* (Cambridge, 1950), pp. 345, 805.

103. *Guaranteed Wages*, p. 297.

104. NICB, "Curtailment . . . ," p. 9; NICB, "Seniority Systems in Nonunionized Companies," SPP No. 110 (1950), p. 11. NICB, "Written Statements of Personnel Policy," SPP No. 79 (1947), pp. 17–26.

105. NICB, "Selecting, Training and Upgrading," SPP No. 37 (1941), p. 8; Clint Golden, "Making the Collective Agreement Work," in *Addresses on Industrial Relations*, University of Michigan, Bureau of Industrial Relations, Bulletin No.

9 (Ann Arbor, 1939), p. 72; Frederick Harbison, "Seniority in Mass Production Industries," *Journal of Political Economy* (December 1940), pp. 851–864.

106. NICB, "Seniority Systems . . . ," p. 13.

107. H. Ellsworth Steele, William Myles, and S. McIntyre, "Personnel Practices in the South," *Industrial and Labor Relations Review* 9 (January 1956):250.

108. "Survey of Contracts under Taft-Hartley Act," Bureau of National Affairs, *Labor Relations Reference Manual* 22 (1948):3–7; NICB, "Seniority Systems . . . ," p. 5.

109. Steele, et al., "Personnel Practices," p. 250.

110. AMA, "Putting Job Rating to Work," PS No. 49 (1941), pp. 26–28; Helen Baker and John M. True, "The Operation of Job Evaluations Plans," Industrial Relations Section, Princeton University, Report No. 74 (Princeton, 1947), p. 13.

111. Sumner Slichter, "Layoff Policy" in *Addresses on Industrial Relations*, p. 87; NICB, "Employee Rating," SPP No. 39 (1942), p. 16.

112. NICB, *What Employers Are Doing* . . . , p. 26; NICB, "Personnel Activities . . . ," pp. 19–29.

113. Helen Baker, "The Industrial Relations Executive and Collective Bargaining." *Society for the Advancement of Management Journal* 4 (July 1939):107; Harold F. North, "The Personnel Man's Functional Relationships," AMA Personnel Series No. 45 (1940), pp. 19–21; AMA, "Principles and Methods of Industrial Training," PS No. 47 (1941); J. T. Burke, "Sensing Employee Attitudes" in *Addresses on Industrial Relations*, pp. 25–30; Arthur Kornhauser, "Psychological Studies of Employee Attitudes" in S. D. Hoslett (ed.), *Human Factors in Management* (New York, 1946).

114. C. A. Drake, "Developing Professional Standards for Personnel Executives," *Personnel*, 19 (March 1943), pp. 646–655; North, "Functional Relationships," p. 25; H. G. Heneman, Jr., "Qualifying the Professional Industrial Relations Worker," *Personnel*, 24 (November 1948), pp. 220–224; William V. Owen, "Decentralize Personnel Work," *Personnel Journal*, 19 (June 1940), pp. 65–68.

115. R. R. Brooks, *Unions of Their Own Choosing* (New Haven, 1939); Joseph Rosenfarb, *The National Labor Policy and How It Works* (New York, 1940), pp. 36–61; R. L. Greenman, *The Worker, the Foreman and the Wagner Act* (New York, 1939), pp. 9–113.

116. NICB, "Selected Interpretations of the Fair Labor Standards Act," Management Research Memorandum No. 8 (1942).

117. NICB, "Reducing Fluctuation in Employment," SPP No. 27 (1940), pp. 5–12; NICB, "Annual Wage and Employment Guarantee Plans," SPP No. 76 (1946), p. 9.

118. NICB, "Company Pension Plans and the Social Security Act," SPP No. 16 (1939), p. 25; NICB, "Dismissal Compensation," SPP No. 50 (1943), p. 3.

119. Paul A. C. Koistinen, "Mobilizing the World War II Economy," *Pacific Historical Review* **42** (November 1973):451–460; Joel Seidman, *American Labor from Defense to Reconversion* (Chicago, 1953).

120. NICB, "Time Schedules for Job Training," SPP No. 55 (1943); Carroll L. Shartle, "New Defense Personnel Techniques," *Occupations* **19** (March 1941):403–408; AMA, "Operating under Manpower Controls," PS No. 64 (1943), pp. 5–7, 29–42.

121. Carroll L. Daugherty, "A Review of War Labor Board Experience," AMA Personnel Series No. 77 (1944), pp. 3–10; *The Termination Report of the National War Labor Board*, Vol. 1 (Washington, D.C., 1947), pp. 226–273; NICB, "Principles and Applications of Job Evaluation," SPP No. 62 (1944), pp. 12–26.

122. *Termination Report*, pp. 274–289; G. L. Bergen, "War's Lessons in Personnel Administration," AMA Personnel Series No. 94 (1945), pp. 39–40.

123. *Termination Report*, pp. 380–385. Popular demands and new tax incentives for pension plans also triggered the post-1940 growth of welfare benefits. Jacoby and Mitchell, "Development of Contractual Features," p. 516; Adrian De Wind, "Federal Regulation of Pension Plans" in NICB, "Designing a Company Pension Plan," SPP No. 67 (1944), pp. 10–13.

124. Thomas H. Patten, *The Foreman: Forgotten Man of Management* (New York, 1969); Donald E. Wray, "Marginal Men of Industry: The Foremen," *American Journal of Sociology* (January 1949):298–301.

125. Theodore A. Olsen, "Wrongful Discharge Claims Raised by At Will Employees," *Labor Law Journal* **32** (May 1981):265–297.

126. "Personnel Widens Its Franchise," *Business Week* (February 26, 1979):120–121.

127. Philip Selznick, *Law, Society and Industrial Justice* (New York, 1969), pp. 185–211.

128. Robert M. Solow, "On Theories of Unemployment," *American Economic Review*, **83** (March 1980), p. 3. Also see George A. Akerlof, "A Theory of Social Custom, of Which Employment May Be One Consequence," *Quarterly Journal of Economics* **94** (June 1980):749–775.

3

The Making and Shaping of Job and Pay Structures in the Iron and Steel Industry

Bernard Elbaum

This chapter is concerned with the origins, rationale, and consequences of internal labor markets in the U.S. iron and steel industry. The consequences considered mainly pertain to the industry wage structure but have more general implications for the theoretical understanding of internal labor markets. The main period examined is that of the late nineteenth and early twentieth centuries, when internal labor markets were first established in the United States. Some attention is also paid to the determination of wage structure after World war II and to the comparative experience of the British industry.

Internal Labor Markets and Wage Structure

Alternative Approaches

Three basic approaches have been taken toward internal labor markets: neoclassical, radical, and institutional. The essential features of these approaches are well known and have already been reviewed in the introduction to this book. However, their distinctive implications for wage structure determination have been little noted and only loosely specified.

From the neoclassical viewpoint internal labor markets promote economic efficiency and are explained by enterprise-specific human capital, which may take such forms as on-the-job training or the screening of workers of differing ability by direct observation of job performance. With workers employed in the same enterprise for the span of their careers, the expected present value of wage earnings along internal job ladders must agree with prevailing competitive standards. Occupational wage rates are indeterminate but bounded by the size of investments in enterprise-specific human capital. Occupational wage rates must at least equal prevailing wages for workers with comparable general training, net of search and screening costs, and can be no more than the sum of prevailing wages and the additional value productivity of incumbent workers in the enterprise. Worker risk preferences, if added to the model, further constrain wage structure.

Since both the firm and its employees prefer any nonzero share of the returns to enterprise-specific human capital to labor turnover, they may also bargain over wage rates. The neoclassical literature minimizes the effect on wages of this pure bargaining indeterminacy, but handles it in different ways. Parsons (1972, 1120–1143), for example, considers wage bargaining to arise normally between an employer and individual employee and contends that settlements over shares of training benefits realistically fall within a narrow range.

On the other hand, Williamson, Wachter, and Harris (1975, 250–277) consider bargaining to arise normally between an employer and work group. In this situation of small numbers exchange, they argue, devising effective employment contracts is problematic. Managers, being only human, exhibit "bounded rationality," which means they have a limited capability for acquiring, handling, and communicating requisite information about ever-changing conditions. For their part, work groups with specific skills can opportunistically obstruct contractual agreement or enforcement by collectively withholding or distorting relevant information.

According to Williamson, Wachter, and Harris, internal labor markets overcome these problems of effective contracting by establishing enterprisewide regulation. In their words, "the internal labor market achieves a fundamental transformation by shifting to a system where wage rates attach mainly to jobs rather than workers," a shift that discourages small group bargaining, and frequently replaces it with job evaluation. Furthermore, "internal promotion ladders encourage a positive worker attitude toward on-the-job training, and enable the firm to reward cooperative behavior." The resulting wage structure, they conclude, "reflects objective long-term job values rather than current bargaining exigencies" (Williamson, Wachter, and Harris 1975, 269–276). However, just why internal labor markets should necessarily yield this result is not clear. The Williamson-Wachter-Harris argument only appears to support the comparatively noncontroversial conclusion that, in light of managerial limitations and work group bargaining leverage, internal labor markets may be less costly than alternative enterprise policies.

Similarly, the radical perspective maintains internal labor markets are functional for the firm because they promote employee identification with enterprise goals and effective managerial control over work standards. Stone (1974, 61–97) contends that U.S. iron and steel firms, with these ends in mind, unilaterally imposed highly differentiated job and pay ladders around the turn of the century, although revolutionary technological change had by then rendered occupational skill distinctions "virtually meaningless." By contrast, Edwards, Reich, and Gordon (1982) allow that internal labor markets were often instigated by unions, under compromise arrangements negotiated between union leadership and management. But whatever their origins, in the radical view, internal labor markets generally embody a new "bureaucratic" form of management control over workers, with little or no basis in technology. In fact managerial goals of consolidating control over the work process have biased technological change in the direction of narrow job content and low skill levels.

This portrayal of internal labor markets as an institutional product of class conflict gives radical analysis a Marxian flavor. However, its conclusions are more closely akin to those of revisionist historiography, which also maintains the character of major U.S. institutions has, in general, been shaped successfully by corporate management in order to foster worker cooptation and conservatism (see Kolko 1976, Bowles and Gintis 1975). By implication, occupational wage inequality is largely an artificial construct, constrained by managerial calculation of the costs and returns to pay differentiation. However, the radical literature has paid little explicit attention to wage structure determination or, in particular, to why wage structure varies among job ladders, within firms and across industries.

From the institutional viewpoint, unlike the previous two, job and pay structures within internal labor markets are significantly affected by ongoing bargaining between the firm and workers or their organizations. The rationale of internal labor markets reflects the customary, quasi-legal legitimacy attached to workers' desires for security and advancement, which is backed up by the ability of work groups to inflict damage upon the enterprise if prevailing norms are violated (Doeringer and Piore 1971, 13–40; Piore 1973, 377–384).

Within the spirit of the institutional approach, the rigidity of customary rules should afford latitude for deviation from competitive outcomes. However, in Doeringer and Piore's treatment, as in neoclassical analysis, indeterminacy in wage structure is bounded by the extent of enterprise-specific human capital (Doeringer and Piore 1971, pp. 74–78). This contrasts with an older, related approach taken by Raimon (1953), who views wage indeterminacy as the result of the prevalence throughout the labor market of minimal training requirements and of entry barriers for semiskilled employment posed by internal promotion practices. In Raimon's eyes, market wage rates for unskilled laborers and skilled craft occupations set the bounds of indeterminacy for the wage structure of semiskilled job grades. However, Raimon does not explain why barriers to labor market competition should be so effective or, in particular, why firms throughout the economy should refrain from poaching semiskilled workers employed elsewhere at relatively low occupational wage rates.

Questions for Analysis

These alternative approaches raise a number of questions: (1) What roles were respectively played in establishing internal labor markets by efficiency considerations, management initiative, and pressures from the work force? (2) To what extent is wage structure based on genuine differences in job content and skill requirements? In particular, is internal wage structure best characterized as reflecting "objective long-term job values," management aims of controlling workers, or the ongoing effects of bargaining between firms, and workers and their organizations? Is the observed range of indeterminacy in wage structure better explained by enterprise-specific human capital and worker-risk preferences, or by institutional rigidities? (3) Why have iron and steel firms, like many others, *invariably* filled all job vacancies, other than certain "port of entry" positions, by internal promotion?

Historic Origins of Internal Labor Markets in the Iron and Steel Industry

The story of how internal labor markets were first established in the iron and steel industry has never been documented. However, the available evidence points to the latter nineteenth century as the key period.

At the end of the third quarter of the nineteenth century, the bulk of the iron industry was characterized by interplant mobility of labor. Within the industry's unionized sector labor mobility was maintained as a matter of official union policy. Only fragmentary information is available on the nonunion sector. However, at least one nonunion firm, the Cambria Iron Company, was already following a policy of filling vacancies by internal promotion. In 1866 Cambria had introduced internal promotion, along with a program which anticipated the welfare policies of many large corporations during the 1920s, after a strike in its plant ended in local defeat and organizational ruin for the unions (Bennett 1977, 15–16, 180).

By the late 1880s national union rules had been changed to uphold internal promotion, which thereby became general practice in the industry. Although no pertinent union records for the intervening years can be found, the change in union rules seems best interpreted as a response to pressure from underhands for seniority promotion rights to skilled jobs, within an industry context that was rendering exclusive union organization increasingly vulnerable. These institutional influences on union policy appear to have outweighed whatever import enterprise-specific human capital had for iron and steel job structures. In the United States the union rule change is best documented for the puddling process, where technology was relatively homogeneous and stagnant and no evident change occurred in the comparative technical advantage of internal promotion.

Early Industry Context and Union Structure

The union concerned, the Amalgamated Association of Iron, Steel and Tin Workers, was formed in 1876 through merger of three distinct craft unions representing puddlers, rollers and heaters, and roll hands, respectively. The immediate spur to merger came from strike defeats which showed that disunity among these trades was debilitating (Bennett 1977, 42–48; Robinson 1920, 10–18).

Of the unions that merged, the two representing the puddlers and the rollers and heaters were comprised solely of an industry work force elite of inside contractors. The third merging union—the Roll Hands—was based among a variety of process hands working in and about the rolling mills. Although less elite, Roll Hand membership still was confined to higher ranking production workers. The puddlers' union, the Sons of Vulcan, was the largest at the time of the merger. In early years puddlers controlled top union offices and were the dominant group in the Amalgamated.

The initial structure of the Amalgamated reflected the technological, market, and organizational contexts then dominant in the industry.

Until the last quarter of the nineteenth century, the principal product of the iron and steel industry was wrought iron, which has a lower carbon content and less strength, hardness, and durability than steel. Wrought iron manufacture was labor-intensive and carried on by small-scale, batch methods within hundreds of firms amid a highly competitive industrial structure. Steel was manufactured by related methods, at so high a cost that it was a specialty item.

Wrought iron production involved three interrelated processes. In the towering, cylindrical stack of the blast furnace, oxygen impurities in the ores were removed by blowing a hot blast of air through a burden of coke, ore, and flux, yielding an intermediate product known as pig iron. In puddling furnaces, a second refining process removed carbon impurities from the pig iron through a combination of heat and manual manipulation. Finally, in the rolling mill, the metal pieces were shaped and finished by passing them through grooved, cylindrical, metal rolls that operated something like a giant clothes wringer.

Puddling was the iron industry's most labor-intensive process. It depended so much on manual work in production and handling that a group of puddling furnaces was required to supply one rolling mill adequately. Puddlers were therefore the largest homogeneous group of craftsmen in wrought iron establishments.

With the aid of one or two helpers, the puddler had to prepare the furnace by lining it with ore, throw a pig iron charge of some 400 to 600 pounds into the furnace, stir the molten metal with a hoe-shaped tool, or "rabble," that entered through a furnace porthole, form the metal into pasty balls as its purity and hence its melting point rose, and remove the balls of metal with tongs when refining was complete. Puddling work demanded extremely arduous manual labor amid simultaneous exposure to intense heat. The success of operations depended on the strength, manual skill, and practical metallurgical know-how of the puddler, who gauged furnace temperature and chemical composition through personal judgment and was directly responsible for the rate and quality of output.

Rollers and heaters occupied analogous strategic positions in rolling mill operations. The roller directed the operations of the entire rolling crew. His most important responsibilities were supervisory; typically, he would work with the crew only when there were difficulties in getting the mill going. When things went well, the roller had little to do; he was valued highly for knowing what to do when things went wrong.

The heater was in charge of one or more heating furnaces where metal pieces were heated in readiness for rolling. His job likewise consisted mainly of supervising helpers, but required considerable practical knowledge of the heat treatment of metals, which could only be gained by long experience.

As inside contractors, puddlers, rollers, and heaters were responsible for hiring, firing, and directing their own crew, were paid a tonnage wage rate based on crew output, and paid other crew members time rates of wages out of their own tonnage earnings. Usually, puddlers and heaters would hire and direct one or two helpers, while rollers might be in charge of a mill crew of fifteen or more. These managerial and pay arrangements gave contractors a monetary incentive to drive underhands in order to receive a portion of profit accruing to supervision of operations and labor. Serving at once as strategically positioned workers and piece-rate foremen, contracting operatives occupied an intermediate stratum between capital and labor.

Firms found contracting arrangements advantageous for several reasons. At a time when firms were comparatively small and management methods rudimentary, contracting allowed entrepreneurs to reduce overheads by delegating organizational and supervisory responsibilities. Payment by output also simplified cost accounting and allowed entrepreneurs to transfer some risk (Pollard 1965). Transfer of managerial authority was further convenient because of inherent difficulties in supervising men who occupied strategic positions at bottlenecks in the production process and possessed scarce skills and know-how. Finally, in adopting contracting arrangements, U.S. iron and steel entrepreneurs were following the tried and tested example of their British counterparts and of firms in many nineteenth-century British and U.S. industries (Nelson 1975).

Union Membership and Promotion Policy

Initially, the Amalgamated maintained the exclusiveness of its predecessors and was open only to leading hands and higher ranks of helpers. However, between the 1860s and 1890s a number of conflicts erupted between helpers and unionists, as helpers demanded access to skilled jobs, uniform tonnage rates of pay, and equal rights of unionization. The response from the craft unions was slow and limited. In general, a more liberal union leadership found itself constrained by rigidly conservative rank-and-file attitudes.

Conflict over internal promotion rights began as early as 1866, when differences between heaters and helpers over rights to certain jobs contributed to strike defeat at the Cambria Iron Works. In the same year helpers stayed at work during a Cambria puddlers' strike which also proved unsuccessful (Bennett 1977, 15).

At that time the Sons of Vulcan excluded helpers from membership. Starting in the late 1860s and continuing through the early 1870s, the Sons of Vulcan amended its rules to allow helpers a form of secondary membership status. By the new rules, helpers' union locals were subordinate to local "forges" of the Sons of Vulcan, met separately under craft worker superintendence, paid half the normal per capita assessment to the union protective fund, and received half the normal per capita strike benefits (*Vulcan Record* 1868).

However, Chicago helpers spurned the Sons of Vulcan's offer of second-class membership and organized on their own, with ambitions of forming an autonomous national union of helpers. In May 1873 they went on strike, demanding that a recently hired boiler (a type of puddler) be discharged and replaced by promoting a helper. According to the account in the *Vulcan Record*, helpers also demanded control over promotion rights, so that in the future, "no stranger shall be employed while one of them was qualified to fill the position, and that they themselves should be the judge of their member's qualification." The Sons of Vulcan viewed these demands as contrary to its own laws in a very serious matter:

If successful through our aid, it [the helpers' strike demands] would have been a dangerous precedent and might be attempted as a principle which would in effect drive all men out of the business who found it necessary to move to any other place, or compel him to accept a situation behind the last helper in the mill and again go through the same routine he had previously done when he learned the business; this to be repeated every time he moved to a new locality (*Vulcan Record* 1873)

Confronted by helpers' wishes for internal promotion rights, craft unionists at first attempted to maintain their interplant mobility and prerogatives over access to skilled jobs. The Chicago helpers' strike was defeated with the help of strikebreakers supplied by the Sons of Vulcan. But the defeat proved costly to the union cause, as the defeated Chicago helpers retaliated by taking the jobs of striking puddlers in Knightsville, Indiana (*Vulcan Record* 1873).

By the late 1880s union rules had changed to uphold internal promotion by seniority. No pertinent union records from the intervening years appear to have survived. But the attitudes of the Amalgamated leadership and membership on this issue can be gauged from their statements and behavior.

The Amalgamated leadership publicly justified restrictions on access to training for skilled jobs in terms of the need for promotion opportunities to maintain the underhands' morale:

The ranks of skilled workmen are filled by men who fill the minor positions; hence, we endeavor to prevent men from learning the skilled positions before they have served in the minor ones. If they are permitted to learn the skilled jobs, it would necessarily mean that those holding the minor positions would have no opportunity for improvement (Quoted in Robinson 1920, 131).

Despite these sentiments, in significant instances union regulations regarding job access were honored only in the breach. In 1888, amid contraction and unemployment in the iron industry, the Amalgamated leadership moved to break a strike by puddlers' helpers—all of them Amalgamated members—who were demanding dismissal of a puddler recently hired from outside the firm and promotion of a helper, in accordance with nominal union rules (Bennett 1977, 54–56).

An ambivalence toward craft exclusiveness within the Amalgamated was also manifest in ongoing union reform of membership regulations. The issue of admission of underhands to Amalgamated membership was handled piecemeal. Year by year ever more occupations were added to a long, complex list of eligibility, until 1889 when, except for laborers, all those working in and about mills were declared fully eligible for membership, with laborers to be admitted at the discretion of the local lodge.

In the 1880s liberalization of Amalgamated membership rules was prompted in part by jurisdictional competition with the Knights of Labor. The importance of organizing everyone in and around steel mills was raised in convention proceedings as early as 1882 by Amalgamated Secretary-Treasurer William Martin (Bennett 1977, 54). In 1888, to counteract the inroads of the Knights of Labor, Secretary Martin advised all Amalgamated locals to "take in every man in the mills outside common labor, and him too, if necessary," and he chided the locals for being "aristocratic" and "narrow":

Be liberal and admit to membership the men whom the Knights of Labor are planning to reduce wages. . . . We mean the unskilled workman. . . . Yes even the daily laborer. We have nothing to lose and all to gain by the admission of these men. Failing to get that, they naturally seek and get in the Knights of Labor (Robinson 1920, 50).

Martin's formal motion to extend membership eligibility to all working in and about the mills was ratified in 1889 over the recommendation of the Amalgamated's Committee on Constitution and Bylaws. The effects of liberalization on membership, if difficult to gauge precisely, appear to have been limited. Skilled craftsmen still were protective of their control over the Amalgamated in 1889, and fearful lest unskilled workers acquire numerical predominance. John Fitch (1911, 89, 97–98), a leading contemporary expert on conditions of employment in the steel industry, judged that the Amalgamated was, to the last, a top-heavy organization.

Amalgamated concern with restiveness among the lower ranks of the work force, and the consequent changes in union rules, must be seen in light of the revolutionary transformation of the iron and steel industry after 1860 by innovations that led to mass production of steel. The first and most radical innovation was the Bessemer process. In Bessemer converters, hot air was blown through molten pig iron, and carbon impurities were rapidly removed through ensuing violent chemical reactions. Over a few decades, in stages, the Bessemer process cheapened steel production costs sufficiently to allow replacement of wrought iron with steel for most uses.

The Bessemer process gave the industry an initial impetus toward concentration which subsequently was carried along much further by forces of oligopolistic competition, until the U.S. industry was dominated by large, multiplant firms (Temin 1964). With the growth in the size of investments, production operations, and enterprises, more systematic management methods were developed to facilitate the coordinated planning required for economies of high throughput production (Chandler 1977, 258–267). Contracting arrangements correspondingly became less advantageous. The bargaining leverage that the union derived from its members' autonomy and responsibility provided further incentive for firms to take initiatives to eliminate contracting (Bennett 1977, 48–50; Brody 1960, 52; British Iron Trade Association 1902, 58).[1]

Bessemer steelmaking also instigated a chain reaction of technological change which ramified throughout industry production processes. Improved controls over heat and chemistry involved introduction of technical instrumentation and analysis of samples by chemists. Furnaces and mills became more mechanized, and machines and railway cars handled the transportation of metal between processes. The new methods were at once material saving and labor saving. "By the turn of the century, there were not a dozen men on the floor of a mill rolling 3,000 tons a day, or as much as a Pittsburgh mill of 1850 rolled in a year" (Temin 1964, 165).

The incidence of technologically induced change in job content was uneven. Puddlers' jobs remained much the same but became increasingly obsolete. On the other hand, in heavy rolling mills, key operatives acquired the added responsibility of obtaining a massive output from expensive equipment, within a vertically integrated, large-batch, production process. Although the importance of their know-how was reduced by mechanization and instrumentation, and their autonomy by the elimination of contracting, in general, rollers and heaters retained strategic occupational positions at technological bottlenecks. Furthermore in sheet, tin, and hoop mills, which rolled products of thinner gauge, the basic operations were still manual rather than mechanical. In these so-called "hand mills," the skill and know-how of operatives remained central to production activity. The most pervasive effect of technology on job content was the elimination of most of the unskilled, heavy laboring jobs in which the bulk of the work force had been employed. Increasingly, the work force was composed of machine-tenders and ancillary and maintenance, rather than production, workers.

These changes in technology and market organization increased the leverage employers could exert in conflict with the Amalgamated. In particular, they made it easier to continue production in the absence of senior operatives so long as supervisors and other crew members remained at work. British experience provides supporting and contrasting illustration of the importance of this shift in the balance of bargaining power for union policy and organization.

In Britain mass union organization was first established among less skilled workers during the late 1880s. Within the iron and steel industry, the conservatism of the Amalgamated Malleable Ironworkers—the contractors' union—led to the emergence of rival organizations, chief among which was the British Steel Smelters Association. Founded in 1886, the Smelters organized at first among key process workers in open-hearth steelmaking, a process which was then beginning to supplant Bessemer technology in Britain. At their founding convention the Smelters debated "the apprentice question," which involved the merits of intraplant promotion as opposed to interplant craft mobility. Responding to pressure from lower ranks, the Smelters opted for internal promotion, and an industrial, rather than a craft, organizing approach (Pugh 1951, 90).[2]

The Smelters also favored elimination of contracting, direct employment and payment of operatives by the firm, and tonnage wage payment for unionized operatives as a group, with the old contracting rate split among them in agreed proportions. The Smelters dealt the contracting system a final blow in a series of conflicts with the Ironworkers by demonstrating the greater capability for stopping or maintaining production, as needed, when the two unions alternately struck the Hawarden Bridge plant in 1911. The Smelters' superior strength in this conflict derived from their more extensive, though still exclusive organization. Once they consolidated an organizational base among key operatives, the Smelters went on to organize downward, eventually recruiting common laborers and growing to become the predominant union in the industry (Pugh 1951, 157–166).

Several critical differences between the U.S. and British contexts appear to explain these divergent courses of national union development. In the United States union survival was in general more problematic. Dual unionism was vehemently opposed by the American Federation of Labor and never took root. Change in U.S. iron and steel industry technology and organization also was more dramatic. While in the United States newly emergent oligopolistic firms took independent action to eliminate the contracting system and trade union organization, in Britain, decisive managerial action was constrained by small firm size and lack of employer unity (Elbaum and Wilkinson 1979, 229; Holt 1977, 5–35).

In the end, Amalgamated attempts to adapt proved too little too late. In 1892 defeat in the infamous and bloody Homestead lockout drove the Amalgamated from heavy steelmaking. Afterwards, the Amalgamated remained a potent force only in the less mechanized departments of sheet, tin, wrought iron, hoop, and tube production. Another strike defeat in 1901 further weakened the Amalgamated, and a subsequent lockout in 1909, along with internal union divisions, all but destroyed its organization.

Yet the Amalgamated left behind a heritage that long outlasted its defeat. By managerial discretion, internal promotion practices, established under its rules, were maintained in the United States for decades afterwards, throughout the nonunion era. And as we shall see, the wage structure established during the Amalgamated era also had a long enduring influence.

The Impact of Bargaining on Industry Wage Structure

Wage Determination during the Early Union Era

During the early union era bargaining had an important impact on industry wage structure which was conditioned by the incidence of union organization, the distinctive technological and market conditions in various sections of the industry, and the prevalence throughout the industry of internal labor markets.

Iron and steel wage agreements linked tonnage rates to product prices through a sliding scale. Under the standard scale agreement, contractors' gross earnings depended on the price level, the schedule of tonnage wage rates, and productivity.[3]

In puddling, falling product prices were roughly offset by renegotiated tonnage rate schedules, and technology was comparatively stagnant.[4] As a result puddlers experienced increased employment insecurity and static earnings.

Among the puddling work force wage structure was a matter of controversy. At first, standard rate agreements only set the total wage bill and allowed variation in the division of tonnage earnings between puddlers and helpers. However, helpers voiced discontent over their exclusion from collective agreements as early as 1870, when they petitioned for a uniform tonnage rate of one-third the furnace make for a single helper and a split of one-half the furnace make between two helpers. At that time the Sons of Vulcan saw uniformity as both desirable and unattainable, and the subsequent union convention merely "suggested" these rates as standards (*Vulcan Record* 1871). Only in 1891, despite continued opposition from a few craft dominated branches, did the Amalgamated formally establish a slightly higher standard rate of one-third the puddlers' rate, plus 5 percent on top of this figure (or 36.7 percent of the puddlers' rate).

Circumstances in rolling mills occasioned greater disparity in economic fortunes. Rolling mill technology was relatively heterogeneous and dynamic. In contrast to the experience of puddlers, by 1892 rollers and heaters enjoyed earnings which the Amalgamated vice-president John Sheehan during the union's annual convention termed "abnormal" and beyond "the wildest dreams of early scale constructors" (quoted in Bennett 1977, 38).

Rollers and heaters obtained their high earnings through mechanisms of piece-rate bargaining. In general, administration of piece rates poses problems which have long been discussed in industrial relations literature. Even in the absence of a union, frequent rate cuts tend to demoralize workers and destroy the efficacy of incentives. In addition, it is difficult for management to determine the appropriate work load and incentive rate. Work groups tend to share a cohesive set of social norms protective of group work standards, knowledge, and earnings. Rate setting is especially difficult on new technology, where managerial experience is limited, and worker productivity may tend to rise, because of "learning effects," after a certain "running-in period" (see Brown 1973).

For these reasons, as technical change accrues, piece-rate earnings are likely to display an upward ratchet effect, leading to "wage drift." The results of rolling mill bargaining display just such a ratchet effect, reinforced by the presence of contracting arrangements and an exclusive and powerful national union.

Returns from a wage survey, conducted for the Carnegie Corporation by the former union secretary-treasurer William Martin, permit a detailed look at part of the U.S. industry wage structure in 1891 to 1893.[5] The returns strikingly show the effects of Amalgamated attempts to maintain rigid, standard tonnage rates in a manner akin to a discriminating monopolist. For example, in six of the bar mills surveyed, the union managed to maintain virtually the same tonnage rates for rollers and heaters. Accordingly, as tonnage output varied, shift earnings varied proportionately, ranging from $10.27 to $18.13 for rollers and from $5.60 to $8.63 for heaters. These earnings were in the upper spectrum among plants surveyed in 1891, but they were not unusual. Although there were some differences in tonnage rates, ten of the fourteen bar mills surveyed had earnings in a comparable range. Plate and structural mills had a similar earnings distribution. Across Bessemer steel plants producing outputs of 175 to 300 tons, tonnage rate reductions compensated only in part for output increases, and each of the three key occupations earned roughly from $5.60 to $8.10.

Aside from output, the Carnegie Corporation survey shows earnings to be affected by a variety of influences, including union presence, the size and type of rolling train, and managerial practice, particularly with respect to contracting. Contracting rollers and heaters almost invariably had far greater earnings than those receiving fixed day wages or salaries. In general, the union had less success maintaining standard tonnage rates in more technologically dynamic departments.

Occupational wage inequality within plants was positively correlated with the earnings of rollers and heaters. Other production workers organized by the union were also paid on tonnage wage rates, and their earnings, like those of rollers and heaters, varied with plant output. However, nonunion workers remained on time rates of wages, which were less sensitive to plant productivity. For example, two Pittsburgh area firms, Oliver Iron and Steel and Jones and Laughlin Company, followed a general practice of paying common laborers $1.35 per day, irrespective of mill output. Under these circumstances piece-rate bargaining led the earnings of union operatives to run away from those of the day wage work force (Carnegie Corporation 1891–93).

The tendency for union tonnage wage earnings to drift upward with plant technical improvement played an important role in management-labor conflict. It was cited by the industry journal *Iron Age* and the Carnegie Corporation as the chief reason for the Homestead lockout. For its part, the union justified high and variable tonnage earnings in terms of its right to share in the fruits of technical progress (*Iron Age* 23 June 1892, 1227; Brody 1960, 53–54; Bemis 1894, 379–389).

The high earnings of rollers and heaters also caused dissension within the work force which contributed to union defeat. A recent detailed study of two Pennsylvania steel towns concluded that the degree of success in melding craft cooperation was a key factor in the Amalgamated's local success or failure. Repeated union defeat in Cambria in the 1860s, and defeat in Johnstown in 1893, came when crafts broke ranks during critical strikes. In the latter case the conservative, well-paid rollers and heaters decided against joining in an uphill struggle for union survival (Bennett 1977, especially p. 42). This pattern of defeat foreshadowed that of the great national steel strike of 1919 when disunity helped undermine a bid to reestablish unionism in the industry, and "the skilled steelworkers were the soft flank in the strikers' ranks" (Brody 1960, 261).

The essential features of U.S. developments in wage bargaining were paralleled in Britain, though at an early date characteristic differences in national bargaining structure emerged. In the United States problems of survival led the national union to seek to establish centralized authority over wage settlements and a policy of standard tonnage rates. In Britain, on the other hand, the terms of national agreements were principally confined to sliding-scale schedules and disputes procedures; tonnage rates were determined largely autonomously by small group bargaining at the workplace. However, even in the United States a two-tiered structure of bargaining developed in more dynamic departments, with sliding scales fixed at the national level and tonnage rates at the workplace level (Elbaum 1982, 165–168; Robinson 1920, 148).

The prevalence of internal labor markets throughout the industry supported these bargaining arrangements in several ways. Internal promotion by seniority on plant job ladders broadened the range of feasible wage structures by providing insulation from competitive labor market pressure. Except for job opportunities at newly opened establishments, the opportunity wage for senior process workers was the entry wage for common laborers. With interplant mobility virtually foreclosed, and *industry-specific* job skills, bargaining could have an impact on relative occupational wages without causing shifts in employment patterns, as firms, like prospective employees, mainly concerned themselves with the expected career earnings offered and the implied average establishment wage. Amid high and rising wage differentials, internal promotion helped senior operatives gain the support of nonunion underhands, and the partial incidence of union organization in turn softened the cost impact for employers of high union wage earnings.

In brief, rather than replacing small group bargaining, or introducing a system of collective regulation that was rational by the efficiency standards of competitive theory, internal labor markets afforded greater leeway for bargaining impact on wage structure by erecting barriers to labor market competition. Contrary to Raimon (1953), even the wages of maintenance craftsmen with interindustry mobility provided no upper bound for wage structure, as key process workers were paid more than the skilled craftsmen. The only salient constraints on wage structure were those impinging on the entry level rate, expected career earnings, and enterprise profitability.

The Evolution of Wage Structure between 1892 and 1910

After the union's successive defeats, U.S. steel firms made periodic cuts in tonnage rates and thereby narrowed occupational pay differentials. Despite these tonnage rate reductions, piece-rate bargaining over plant productivity gains continued to influence earnings, as can be illustrated by observing divergent patterns in wage structure among the industry's various production departments.

Between 1890 and 1903, according to establishment data reported for a significant fraction of industry employment, earnings increases in iron and steel occupations generally ranged from 20 to over 40 percent. Yet in blast furnaces, increases were only 12 to 18 percent.

Puddling operatives fared even worse. Puddlers received a mere 4.7 percent increase; their helpers 12.5 percent. On the other hand, rollers and hookers within the same wrought iron establishments received earnings increases of some 47 percent (U.S. Commissioner of Labor 1904).

In 1910 virtually comprehensive data show that earnings inequality among iron and steel workers remained marked. Across production departments, occupational wage differentials varied in rough correlation with average departmental pay—an indicator of the expected career wage along distinct job ladders within the establishment. At the bottom of the pay distribution, in blast furnaces, the pay spread between the highest paid operative occupation and common labor was 1.4:1, and average pay was just 12 percent greater than the common labor rate. At the opposite end of the spectrum, in bar mills, the pay spread was 6:1, and average pay was 70 percent more than the common labor rate. In sheet mills and tinplate mills, among adult men, hourly pay spreads and average pay were still greater than in bar mills (U.S. Bureau of Labor 1911–13, v. 1).

Puddling, steelmaking, and heavy rolling departments fell between the extremes of blast furnaces, and the hand mills. In general, there were large interplant differentials in pay within occupations, though as in 1891 to 1893, interplant differentials were much greater for the higher-paid incentive wage occupations than for common labor and other low-paid, day wage occupations (U.S. Bureau of Labor 1911–13, v. 1).

In hand mills the high wages of key operatives reflected a premium paid for scarce skills as well as piece-rate bargaining dynamics. The U.S. sheet and tinplate industry expanded rapidly after passage of the McKinley tariff in 1892, and U.S. wages were high enough to attract emigration of skilled workers from South Wales. These were also the last bastions of Amalgamated strength. Even in nonunion mills the Amalgamated scale was still respected informally as late as 1910, when U.S. Steel, as part of its final campaign to stamp out the Amalgamated, increased wages to more than the union rate (Brody 1960, 73; U.S. Bureau of Labor 1911–13, v. 3, 133–134). Although the union tonnage rate schedule was reduced several times before 1910 under employer pressure, steadily increasing productivity more than compensated for these reductions, and the earnings of elite operatives increased enough for occupational pay differentials to be narrowed only fractionally (U.S. Bureau of Labor 1911–13, v. 3, 229–258). Under the union scale the earnings of individual operatives continued to vary between plants with the level of output.

In blast furnaces, on the other hand, low average wages and narrow occupational pay differentials are explained by minimal skill requirements and an historic absence of contracting arrangements, tonnage wage payment, union organization, and opportunities for piece-rate bargaining. In puddling, despite entrenched union organization, relative wages suffered over time because of stagnant market demand and productivity. In heavy steelmaking, productivity growth was most rapid, but skill requirements were moderate and union organization was never firmly established (Elbaum 1982, 187–196).

Again, the British industry provides a useful comparative reference point. As a rule occupational wage differentials have been considerably greater in the United States than in Britain, a fact conventionally attributed to an historic scarcity of skilled labor in the United States (Habakkuk 1962, Phelps Brown 1968). But in 1910, in several iron and steel production departments, particularly open-hearth steelmaking and blast furnaces, occupational pay differentials were wider in Britain (Great Britain Board of Trade 1911; Adams 1958, 72).[6] In puddling, U.S. pay differentials were historically greater than British, but the difference was eliminated by 1910. Among departments for which comparable data are available, U.S. pay differentials exceed British only in tinplate mills. The relative positions of production department by average pay also differs substantially between the two countries, with open-hearth furnaces at the top of the British pay distribution and blast furnaces at a much higher position than in the United States. Yet similar basic technology was employed in the two industries, and detailed job descriptions indicate that key process workers generally performed much the same tasks. The main producing units of the industry—blast furnaces, open-hearth furnaces, and rolling mills—apparently required fairly rigidly fixed complements of crew workers to perform well-defined individual job duties (Elbaum 1982, 111–208; U.S. Bureau of Labor 1911–13, v. 1; Great Britain Board of Trade 1911; Great Britain Industrial Health Resources Board 1920).

How is this comparative wage pattern to be explained? A relative scarcity of skilled labor did in fact contribute to greater occupational pay differentials in U.S. hand mill and puddling departments. However, in hand mills, U.S. differentials were in short order magnified by piece-rate bargaining dynamics, whereas over time in puddling, U.S. differentials were reduced more than British by stagnant productivity and by upward pressure on the wages for helpers and unskilled labor. In blast furnaces and steelmaking, unions were much better established in Britain than in the United States, and pay differentials grew to exceed U.S. levels by virtue of the greater ongoing influence in Britain of contracting and of piece-rate bargaining (Elbaum 1982, 111–208).

Neither radical nor neoclassical theory provides an adequate framework for comprehending this wage structure. Were job and pay structures, as radicals maintain, unrelated to technological differences in job content and designed in accordance with managerial aims of controlling workers, pay differentials within departments should have been neither so narrow as to dampen promotion incentives nor so wide as to add prohibitively to average wage costs. Yet in U.S. blast furnaces wage differentials were slight and average pay only marginally greater than the going rate for laborers, whereas in other departments steel management absorbed much greater levels of wages. By substantially affecting the average pay positions of entire departmental job ladders, the impact of bargaining on wage structure also far exceeded the bounds of indeterminacy set, from a neoclassical perspective, by enterprise-specific human capital.

Wage Structure and Job Evaluation in the Modern Day Steel Industry

The mechanisms and results of changes in wage structure after 1910 are indicative of a significant ongoing impact of bargaining and of historical continuity in steel industry wage structure throughout this century.

For the U.S. nonunion era, from 1910 to 1937, the influence of informal bargaining pressures can only be demonstrated indirectly. During this period occupational wage differentials in the U.S. steel industry were compressed substantially. On the other hand, management continued to voice concern over problems of incentive administration (Stone 1974). Although management had a freer hand to fashion wage structure according to its own design, no systematic design was evidently implemented. U.S. wage structure was rather the province of individual shop foremen, who had to contend with local tradition and the effects of incentive administration on the morale of strategically placed workers. Throughout this period steel firms adhered rigidly to internal promotion practices, along with a pattern of wage, as well as price, leadership (Daugherty, de Chazeau, and Stratton 1937, 904; Dunlop 1949, 34–46).

This is, *prima facie*, a sign of inoperative market-policing mechanisms. Interplant wage dispersion also remained large, although published descriptions and the attitudes of the parties indicate job content was generally comparable throughout the industry.

Systematic wage study and job evaluation was introduced by collective bargaining agreement in 1947, within the context of an industry besieged by numerous unresolved grievances over wage rate inequities. The language of the 1937 U.S. Steel Corporation agreement allowed the union to file grievances over wage inequities but ruled out arbitration of inequity disputes. Grievances alleging unequal pay for equal work soon became an overwhelming portion of all company grievance cases. Inequity grievances also piled up in other companies after their unionization. Because inequity grievances were not arbitrable under steel agreements, when unresolved, they went before regional offices of the War Labor Board (Stieber 1959, 175–231).

In 1944 the War Labor Board assumed jurisdiction of steel industry disputes in which conciliation appeared to be of no avail. After denying the union's main demand for an across-the-board wage increase, the War Labor Board directed that the union and the companies negotiate the elimination of intraplant wage inequities within a cost limit of 5¢ per employee hour for any one company.

An earlier union-management commission established at U.S. Steel by the 1942 agreement had failed to reach settlement of wage inequities after the union rejected a complex job evaluation plan that involved no net cost increase for the company and numerous occupational wage reductions. In 1943, with the breakup of this commission, a number of companies founded a group for cooperative study of the inequities problem. The plan developed by this group, as amended by negotiations, became known as the Cooperative Wage Study (CWS).

The CWS plan departed from the principles of existing job evaluation plans, which were employed in major steel companies as well as in other industries. Existing plans usually put a weight of 50 percent or more on skill factors in wage determination. The CWS plan put a weight of over 50 percent on responsibility and just 24 percent on skill factors. The CWS weights were derived from an evaluation of 2,565 versions of 140 benchmark jobs in the steel industry. Points were assigned to factors so as to minimize deviations from the existing industrywide structure of average occupational wage earnings. Jobs were then placed in some thirty classes on the basis of the factor point evaluations. Each job class received a standard rate of base pay. Incentive premia were not standardized under CWS but were to be fixed as a percentage of base rates.

At U.S. Steel the union accepted the CWS plan with modifications that improved the pay position of maintenance crafts somewhat, set the cost of the inequities program at 3.63¢ per employee hour for each U.S. Steel subsidiary company, and required identical wage scales within each geographical district "to the greatest degree practicable." However, uniformity in company implementation costs and district wage rates turned out to be mutually incompatible. To avoid further bargaining difficulties, U.S. Steel in the end agreed to a corporationwide plan with an estimated average cost of 5.18¢ per employee hour.

The most dramatic effect of CWS was on interplant wage structure. The magnitude of its effect in this regard can be observed by calculating the intraoccupational dispersion of earnings for selected occupations. In table 3.1 figures for ten occupations from three departments were calculated for 1929 and 1962, years when wage data covering large portions of industry employment were collected and presented by the U.S. Bureau of Labor Statistics in similar form.

Table 3.1 shows that by 1962 intraoccupational wage dispersion was a third to a half of the 1929 values. That this narrowing in intraoccupational pay dispersion was primarily the result of CWS is confirmed by descriptive accounts of its impact on steel industry wage structure.

The Steelworkers union proved much more conservative regarding changes in occupational wage structure. After 1937 only slight compression in occupational pay differentials occurred in the U.S. industry until 1970, when flat rate cost-of-living increases became an important part of compensation. The spread in base pay between the highest and lowest U.S. job classes went from 2.1:1 in 1948 to 1955 to 2:1 in 1956, 1.9:1 in 1970, and 1.5:1 in 1978 (U.S. Department of Labor 1974, 1980). This trend in occupational pay structure appears to reflect union internal political dynamics. With many high-paid members it was difficult for the Steelworkers to obtain internal agreement on a policy of occupational pay compression. The shift in the distributional consequences of Steelworker settlements after 1970 appears to reflect a general tendency for pay compression to become more politically acceptable under inflationary conditions, when it can occur through the mechanism of a standard form of cost-of-living increase (Knowles and Robertson 1951, 109–127).

In brief, since 1937 collective bargaining processes have settled the timing of changes in wage structure and established simple formulas

Table 3.1
The intraoccupational dispersion of earnings in the United States

	Coefficients of variation		Standard deviations of ln (earnings)	
	1929	1962	1929	1962
Blast furnaces				
Keepers	0.186	0.079	0.216	0.082
Stock unloaders (stockers)	0.283	0.078	0.318	0.077
Keepers' helpers	0.223	0.104	0.278	0.107
Larrymen	0.205	0.082	0.260	0.086
Open-hearth furnaces				
Melter, 1st helper	0.184	0.081	0.192	0.084
Melter, 2nd helper	0.186	0.065	0.202	0.069
Ladle craneman	0.179	0.082	0.183	0.084
Blooming mills				
Heater	0.183	0.099	0.206	0.101
Roller	0.222	0.101	0.229	0.107
Bottom maker	0.275	0.091	0.294	0.091

Sources: U.S. Bureau of Labor Statistics, *Bulletin* Nos. 513 and 1358, "Wages and Hours in the Iron and Steel Industry," and "Industry Wage Survey, Basic Iron and Steel."
Note: The 1929 and 1962 figures are calculated from distributions of earnings per hour which classify individuals into cells at intervals of from 5 to 20 cents per hour. The error caused by omission of within cell earnings variation generally is of the order of a few percent; if half the individuals in each cell were assumed to receive earnings at either cell extreme, the figures presented would generally have to be adjusted up by a few percent and by at most 10 percent.

to govern them. There is no good reason to believe the formulas of CWS or flat rate cost-of-living increases have conformed closely to the unseen, myriad supply and demand relations for steel industry occupations. On the contrary, the basic principles and relative wage outcomes of CWS were matters in which bargaining influence was evident, and the cost-of-living clauses adopted in steel were much like those of other, very different industries.

Comparison with Britain reinforces these conclusions. In Britain no systematic plan for wage study and job evaluation was ever introduced. The British Iron and Steel Federation, which had as members the various employers' associations in the industry, did undertake a study of the possibility of rationalizing industry wage structure in the early 1960s. However, the group established to study industry wage structure found that any scheme of uniform job evaluation was likely to increase costs, much as it did when introduced in the United States. Of particular concern was the elimination, by leveling up, of existing, tacitly accepted, regional differentials. It was concluded that the likelihood of a cost increase condemned any uniform industry job evaluation plan from the start (British Iron and Steel Federation 3 April 1963). Substantial compression of occupational pay differentials occurred in Britain chiefly after 1940, when flat rate cost-of-living increases were adopted.

Furthermore, as shown by tables 3.2 and 3.3, despite the intervening pay movements just described the same basic disparities between U.S. and British wage structure are evident in 1957 as in 1910. In rolling mills, U.S. and British occupational pay spreads are similar, but in blast furnaces or open-hearth steelmaking, British pay spreads exceed U.S.

It could conceivably be argued that this disparity in pay structure reflects an impact of custom and bargaining which was confined to one of the two countries. However, this line of argument confronts several difficulties. Wider international comparison at this date points to additional disparities, also documented by these two tables. In Belgium, unlike other continental European countries, occupational pay spreads are comparable in magnitude to British. However, in Italy, a relatively less developed country where wide pay differentials might be expected, differentials are in fact far narrower than in either the United States or Britain. International disparities in pay structure appear to be commonplace, rather than exceptional, and to be evident whether the United States or Britain is compared to other countries.

Moreover, in Britain the ongoing influence on wage structure of piece-rate bargaining can be documented in detail. Similarly, in the

Table 3.2
Index of comparative average weekly earnings (laborers' average earnings = 100)

	U.S.	U.K.	Sweden	Belgium	Germany	Holland	France[a]
Laborer	100	100	100	100	100	100	100
Fitter (on days)	145	142	111	141	143	115	145
Fitter's mate (on shifts)	115	152	98	—	126	98	122
Loco driver	140	157	104	157	137	114	115
Ingot-stripper crane driver	160	172	106	200	142	108	141
Blast furnace keeper	139	192	120	195	158	129	140
Fitter (rolling mill on shifts)	141	196	109	—	135	130	196
Electricians (rolling mill on shifts)	141	196	111	—	148	145	—
Furnace-bricklayer (on shifts)	161	201	118	169	154	119	145
Head roller (slabber or cogging mill)	192	220	115	196	175	140	151
1st hand melter	205	301	123	293	159	136	158

Source: British Iron and Steel Federation, "A Comparative Study of Wages Structure," 1957. Overtime, exceptional benefits, and social benefits excluded.

The data sources cited by BISF are average figures from U.S. Steel Corporation, the British Iron and Steel Trades Employers Association, the Swedish Employers' Association, and individual plant sources in the other countries.

a. French data refer to hourly, rather than weekly, earnings.

Table 3.3
Wage differentials in steel plants in some western countries in 1960

	U.S.	Germany	Holland	Italy	U.K.
Production					
1st helper, open hearth	179	144	155	142	282
Keeper, blast furnace	141	133	130	120	250
Charging machine operator	148	127	126	122	220
1st pourer, open hearth	148	127	115	125	179
Operator, 125-ton crane	138	117	120	122	219
Operator, 10-ton crane	114	113	119	110	187
Stoker, open hearth	107	105	115	108	179
Repair and maintenance					
Stopper maker	110	109	115	110	na
Maintenance fitter 1st class, open hearth	141	127	124	122	172
Maintenance electrician 1st class	141	124	130	122	189
Electric welder	141	113	124	122	na
Greaser, open hearth	114	109	103	110	na
Bricklayer helper	103	107	112	108	155

Source: M. Gardner Clark, "Comparative Wage Structure in the Steel Industry of the Soviet Union and Western Countries," *Proceedings of the Industrial Relations Research Association*, 1960, table 7.

Clark does not clearly indicate the size of his samples in the various countries, but his text suggests that some data were drawn from a single plant. Clark's original table also included Soviet data.

Note: Lowest-paid blast furnace and open-hearth job in each plant = 100. All figures refer to hourly base rates except for Britain, where they refer to average weekly earnings.

United States the wage structure institutionalized by CWS in 1947 had jobs with relatively high and low incentive yields, a situation that subsequently led to bargaining difficulties and reflected an industry inheritance of incentive administration problems of earlier decades.

Modern Day Incentives Administration

On issues of incentive payment, unlike that of standard base pay, the Steelworkers union and steel management failed to come to any overall agreement. In the 1940s and 1950s bargaining activity over incentives was centered at U.S. Steel Corporation and was "one of the most bitter episodes in the relations between the parties." During the incentives controversy the differences that were resolved by agreement, and more commonly by arbitration, fell into two general areas: the earnings stan dards governing establishment of incentives and the extent of incentive coverage.

The issue of incentive earnings standards concerned the adjustment or replacement of incentives upon alteration of basic conditions of work, as well as the introduction of incentives on new jobs, jobs previously not covered by incentives, or jobs previously covered either by high yielding incentives or by "submerged" incentives with earnings less than or equal to CWS base rates.

In brief, the outcome was the following. The Arbitration Board found the company was entitled to adjust post-1947 incentives when minor changes in conditions occurred. When changes of sufficient magnitude occurred, incentives had to be replaced. Whenever adjusted or replaced, incentives had to maintain prevailing hourly earnings on a job rather than a personal basis as long as previous performance was maintained. This contrasted with the handling of nonincentive jobs, where high worker earnings, deemed out of line with CWS base rates, were protected only on a personal bases, by "red circling."

Newly adjusted or replaced incentives had to offer "equitable incentive compensation," the meaning of which was disputed by the parties and adjudicated case by case by the Arbitration Board until 1969, when the Board offered its own explicit definition. The Board defined equitable incentive compensation as premium earnings opportunities of 35, 22, and 12 percent, respectively, for jobs where performance was deemed to have a direct, indirect, and secondary indirect effect upon production.

New incentives were applied where there were entirely new production processes or processes added to existing facilities, unless "some reasonable flow of connection" existed between the old and new operation. New incentives had to yield "equitable incentive compensation" but were exempt from a maintenance of earnings guarantee.

No agreement was ever reached on the revision of high yielding and submerged incentives. By the terms of the 1947 agreement management could replace submerged incentives at its discretion. After introduction of CWS, U.S. Steel pressed for explicit agreement upon standard definition of a "fair day's work" and offered to revise submerged incentives upward if high yielding incentives could simultaneously be revised downward. The union considered that the corporation was trying to recoup some of the cost of the job evaluation program by tightening standards, reducing crews, and cutting incentive earnings. Although the union initially indicated willingness to negotiate upon a fair day's work program for standardization of incentives at U.S. Steel, it has since been committed to protection of existing incentives earnings. After the 1969 Arbitration award held revision of submerged and high yielding incentives had to be settled jointly through local negotiations, no further negotiations occurred.

The issue of incentive coverage was also resolved by the 1969 Arbitration award, which provided for guidelines of 85 percent minimum incentive coverage at the company level and 65 percent at the plant level. These guidelines represented a significant extension in incentive coverage, and strict compliance with them was briefly resisted by the companies. Subsequent implementation of the 1969 award appears to have lain the incentives controversy to rest.

However, problems of incentive administration remain. For certain jobs establishment of work standards is troublesome, and the dispersion of earnings is comparatively great. For example, scarfers are responsible for burning out defects on semifinished steel, defects that may vary in extent from one lot of output to the next. In 1962 scarfers' pay in firms covered by CWS varied between $2.60 and $5.20 per hour. The coefficient of variation of scarfers' earnings was some 14.2 percent. This dispersion is considerably greater than that found for 1962 in the other occupations examined but less than that widely prevalent before introduction of CWS.

Dispersion in incentive yields is great enough to cause considerable overlap between occupational earnings distributions. For example, although scarfers were usually classified in CWS job class 7 or 8, in 1972,

15 percent had earnings greater than the base rate for job class 33 or the average earnings of all but a handful of occupations. Less extreme forms of overlap between earnings distributions were very common. To take a more typical example, soaking pit cranemen, though generally in job class 15 and recipients of the corresponding base rate, had an earnings distribution that overlapped with that of all the other hundred odd occupations covered by a 1972 wage survey, from laborers to tandem mill rollers (U.S. Department of Labor 1972).

In addition U.S. firms pay strategically positioned process workers comparatively high incentive premia. In 1972 the average incentive yield for a job like blooming mill roller frequently was as high as 58 percent, well above the 35 percent earnings opportunity figure stipulated in the 1969 arbitration award. In interviews, U.S. management officials indicated that they generally view high incentive yields as a worthwhile device for encouraging good work performance on bottleneck operations. However, in some instances high yields reflect protection of earnings on incentives that management deems out of line.

U.S. problems in incentive administration have their parallels in Britain. But in Britain there is far less centralized control over the standards for incentive compensation. The contrast between national arrangements is highlighted by U.S. arbitration awards of the 1950s, which excluded increases in output deriving from technological change as grounds for greater incentive earnings. These awards were applied to numerous specific cases and run directly counter to the informal realities and explicit agreements of British collective bargaining.

In Britain the earnings of process workers have continued to vary with opportunities for incentive wage bargaining. Under the tonnage rate schedules of the national Brown Book Agreement, in force between 1929 and 1965, the earnings of open-hearth melters were directly related to furnace output. For process workers not covered by the Brown Book, and for melters after its cancellation, earnings and output have been linked together with comparatively little constraint from central regulation. Among twenty-nine British steel plants in 1969 and 1970, the plant average for hourly earnings of manual workers varied between 50 and 80 pence, and the bulk of this variation can be explained by plant output and product type (Wilkinson 1977; n.d.).

Interviews with union and company officials indicate there is no comparable relation between earnings and output in the United States. If the Steelworkers union has successfully protected established levels of incentive earnings, U.S. management has safeguarded its prerogative to alter incentives when technological change occurs and thereby to control runaway incentives. This distinctive wage impact of modern U.S. and British steel unions is related to their different structures of bargaining, which in turn reflects an assortment of factors, including the evolution of industry labor organization and collective bargaining, historically divergent market contexts, and the character of the national industrial relations systems.

Conclusions

A Recapitulation

The available evidence suggests the most significant impetus for the establishment of internal labor markets in the nineteenth-century iron and steel industry came from underhands who demanded opportunities for advancement. These demands were raised at a time of general restiveness among less skilled workers, and a diminution of training requirements and autonomy for iron and steel production crafts caused by change in technology, industrial organization, and managerial methods. They were potent because union survival was problematic and because underhands worked in crews that had strategic responsibility for operations, equipment, and materials at bottlenecks in a large-batch production process. Although production crews were headed by a work force elite of unionized contractors, with interests in interplant mobility, over time underhands who picked up craft skills and know-how were a potential strikebreaking threat. After suffering organizational losses, the union reluctantly conceded to membership privileges for underhands and internal promotion rights.

Efficiency considerations played at most a behind the scenes and subsidiary role in the establishment of internal labor markets. Furthermore, rather than unilaterally introducing internal labor markets, as in Stone's account, U.S. steel management only subsequently maintained internal promotion practices that had already been established under the rules of nineteenth-century trade unionism. The reasons why management maintained an internal promotion policy are a matter of interpretation, which we shall come to shortly. But the record indicates that one result was the long persistence of certain distinctive features of the wage structure established during the early union era.

In the U.S. and British steel industries of the late nineteenth and early twentieth centuries, trade unions, much like discriminating monopolists, captured a share of the benefits of productivity growth, plant by plant, through mechanisms of piece-rate bargaining. Given the exclusivity of union organization, this led to wide occupational wage differentials. By insulating industry-specific jobs from competitive labor market constraints, the prevalence of internal promotion rules throughout the industry afforded broad latitude for this impact of bargaining on wage structure. Under these circumstances bargaining could have an impact on relative occuptional wages without causing shifts in employment patterns, as firms, like prospective employees, mainly concerned themselves with the expected career earnings offered and the implied average establishment wage.

Neither radical nor neoclassical theory provides an adequate framework for comprehending the resulting wage structure. Contrary to radical theory, management allowed slight pay differentiation in departments characterized by homogeneous job content and little worker bargaining leverage, but conceded wide differentials and high average pay in departments with heterogeneous job content, entrenched union organization, and dynamic productivity. The differential incidence of favorable bargaining conditions created a disparity in comparative U.S.-British wage structure which exceeded the bounds set, from a neoclassical perspective, by enterprise-human capital. In contrast to historic societal norms, for some departments British occupational pay differentials exceeded those of the United States. There also were substantial differences between the two countries in the relative position of industry departments by average pay—an indicator of expected earnings along career job ladders. Even the wages of maintenance craftsmen with interindustry mobility provided no upper constraint on wage structure, as their wages were less than those of key process workers.

In the decades after union defeat in the United States, the occupational wage structure was substantially compressed, but interplant wage dispersion remained large. With the rearrival of union organization from 1937 to 1942, wage dispersion was regarded by the parties not as worthy compensation for idiosyncratic enterprise skill requirements but as unequal pay for equal work and as grounds for inequity grievances. Interplant wage dispersion was drastically reduced in 1947 by introduction of a standard job evaluation plan that sought to preserve, as far as possible, the previous structure of average occupational wage levels.

For several reasons it is doubtful that the resulting modern industry wage structure was rational by competitive market standards. First, the job evaluation plan adopted was the subject of concerted bargaining and is very different from that first proposed by management or from plans previously employed by individual firms. Second, the previous wage structure was the result of decades of fragmented managerial administration, which was sheltered from labor market competition by exclusive reliance upon internal promotion. Incentive administration was a matter of management concern even during the nonunion era and remained problematic and controversial for years after the introduction of centralized wage regulation under CWS. In view of this record it seems unlikely that distortions in wage structure were avoided. In fact, by CWS standards, the post-World War II wage structure had high and low yielding incentives which one party or another deemed out of line.

Moreover, under modern collective bargaining in the United States and Britain, major occupational pay compression has coincided with growth in price inflation and in flat rate, cost-of-living increases. The timing and simple, formulaic mechanisms of this pay compression suggests the results of bargaining have not closely conformed to the myriad supply and demand relations for individual steel industry occupations.

Finally, comparison of the inherited U.S. wage structure with the British industry reveals the same sort of disparities in 1957 as in 1910. Adding more countries to the comparison suggests the causes of international pay disparities are not confined to either the United States or Britain.

Some Broader Implications

In brief, the iron and steel record suggests that the primary cause of internal labor markets was pressure collectively exerted by workers for employment security and advancement with consequences that included rigid internal promotion rules and a wide range of freedom from competitive constraints on wage structure. While mutually supportive, these two points are logically distinct and have their own broader implications. In at least a number of other U.S. industries, unions appear to have been responsible for introducing greater employment stability and regulation (see, e.g., Kahn 1980, 369–391; Slichter, Healy, and Livernash 1960, 178–210). But internal promotion rules can prove rigid, whatever their origins.

In general, within U.S. unionized industries, however internal promotion rules originated, their rigidity is enforced by collective bargaining agreement. No comparable source of rigidity exists for nonunion firms, which may, and at times do, depart from conventional practice to fill upper level job vacancies by external hiring. Nonetheless, rigid promotion rules apparently prevail over wider terrain and have deeper roots than can be explained by trade union impact (see Osterman, chapter 6). Judging by the steel industry's experience, four main factors appear to explain why even nonunion firms often adhere rigidly to internal promotion practices once they are established throughout an industry: the training and production requirements of modern business enterprise, implicit oligopolistic agreements, pressures from the work force, and the demands of economic growth.

In general, the mass production technology employed by large business enterprise requires reliable access to input supplies (Chandler 1977). Once established industrywide, internal labor markets assure firms of access to adequate supplies of trained workers. With interfirm mobility for industry-specific jobs generally foreclosed, external hiring which occurs in lieu of internal promotion reduces the career earnings prospects of the permanent work force and damages employee morale and the reputation of the enterprise in the labor market. There being no industry market for skilled labor, the enterprise is also not likely to base production plans on marginal additions to its permanent work force through external hiring of skilled workers, as it cannot assume the workers it wants can be recruited at a given wage.

Poaching of skilled labor is also likely to be viewed, much like price cutting, as a breach of an implicit oligopolistic agreement that redounds to the general detriment of employers. In turn, because external hiring undermines the monopoly position of enterprise workers, they are likely to view it as contrary to their collective interest. By increasing the risk of acute scarcity of skilled labor, and aggregate industry training requirements, growth can reinforce the effects of each of the factors previously mentioned.

By implication, internal promotion rules are more likely to be rigid for production workers within large firms and for workers prone to collective organization. This accords with the casual observation that, in the United States, external hiring is more commonly a live option in small firms and for managerial, technical, craft, clerical, and service personnel.

The resulting wage structure appears to be constrained, to some extent, by worker risk preferences, as evidenced by the prevalence of a common entry level wage rate in iron and steel and in other industries.

However, with bilateral monopoly prevailing between the firm and various groups in the work force, there is no good reason to expect wage structure overall to conform closely to any simple optimizing model. Aside from the entry rate, the chief operative constraints on iron and steel wage structure impinged on expected career wage earnings and the average establishment wage. These findings suggest there may generally be wide bounds for institutional influence on wage structure.

Although it redefines the constraints on wage structure, this analysis basically supports the institutional approach to internal labor markets. Pay structure departed from competitive standards in the iron and steel industry because heterogeneous job content afforded different groups in the work force varying bargaining leverage. Although very much concerned with containing work group bargaining power, management has been unable to eliminate it through union defeat, systemwide regulation, or technological change. The administrative arrangements of internal labor markets also made no very evident contribution to managerial control over work standards or worker conservatism. The preceding argument suggests job regulations were more a reflection of the underlying power relations that determined matters like work standards than an independent causal element. The conservatism of economically privileged groups in the labor force likewise appears to be more an outgrowth of their appreciation of power relations in which they possess limited but real advantages in bargaining power.

Notes

1. Fitch credits a change in union rules with driving out the contracting system from all but independent mills by 1911, and his interpretation is followed by Nelson (see Fitch 1911, 99–103; Nelson 1975, 40). In fact union restrictions only applied to the "many jobs system" in which contractors were paid for the output of more than one shift. Even these restrictions were limited. (*National Labor Tribune*, 28 June 1890, p. 4). But in any case it is misleading to identify the "many jobs system" with contracting. When holding one job for one turn, skilled workers could still contract for that shift's output, manage production, hire underhands, and pay underhands on time rates—the essence of inside contracting.
   A more accurate assessment than Fitch's was made by the British Iron Trade Association in 1900, which noted that the contract system was "very general in the rolling mills of the U.S." and was "founded on a scale, or set of ton-prices for finished rolling mill products, agreed upon between the owners of the mills and the Amalgamated Society [sic] of Iron and Steel Workers" (p. 58).

These British observers also concluded the contracting system was waning, due to the hostility of management.

2. Explicit information on hiring rules in Britain before 1886 is lacking. However, there is documentation of considerable interregional job mobility by puddlers (see Birch 1967, 246).

3. The motivation for sliding-scale agreements arose from cyclical price fluctuations. Before unionism was established, competitive wage cutting invariably occurred during downturns as firms tried to reduce costs quickly. Unions arose in part from workers' resistance to such wage cuts and their more successful attempts at recouping wage reductions during booms. Since industry technology placed a premium on continuous operations, the resulting periodic strikes were costly to either party. Sliding-scale agreements provided an automatic formula that allowed wage reductions in slumps and compensating wage increases in booms without need for renegotiation and conflict (see Elbaum and Wilkinson 1979).

4. By comparing production norms in a single New Jersey mill in 1867 with the union rules that prevailed in 1902, David Montgomery (1979, 12) suggests "dramatic improvements in puddling furnaces" occurred in the intervening years, which resulted in a 104 percent improvement in productivity. The improvements in question involve the number of puddling heats per turn and the size of the charge. According to mill owner Abram Hewitt, in 1867 puddlers in his employ worked eleven turns per week, made three heats per turn, and put 450 pounds of iron in each charge. But as Montgomery notes 1902 union rules specified eleven turns per week with five heats per turn and 550 pounds per charge.

What Montgomery overlooks is that these union rules were established in 1878 with the weight of a charge fixed at 500 pounds, and revised in 1884 to set the charge at 550 pounds. Union rules limiting a day's work to five heats per turn date from 1867 (Robinson 1920, 115–116). In light of these union measures, Montgomery's 1867 evidence cannot be accepted as indicative of industry production norms. On the contrary, the record of union work standards supports the generally accepted conclusion that productivity in puddling was virtually stagnant. This conclusion is further supported by comparison of tonnage rates and earnings of puddlers for 1890 to 1903 and 1910 (U.S. Commissioner of Labor 1904, 118; U.S. Bureau of Labor 1911–13, v. 1, 120, v. 3, 153–154; Doeringer 1968, 263–267).

5. Returns furnished to the author by courtesy of Geoffrey Martin and the University of Pittsburgh Special Collections Department, Darlington Library. I am indebted to David Montgomery for referring me to this source.

6. Adams gathered occupational wage figures for open-hearth steelmaking from inspection of a sample of seventeen returns from the 1906 *Enquiry* of Great Britain's Board of Trade.

References

Robert McDonald Adams. "A Comparative Study of the Occupational Wage Structures of the Iron and Steel Industries of Great Britain and the U.S. in the last 70 Years." Ph.D. dissertation. London School of Economics, 1958, p. 72.

John William Bennett. "Iron Workers in Woods Run and Johnstown: The Union Era 1865–1895." Ph.D. dissertation. University of Pittsburgh, 1977.

Alan Birch. *The Economic History of the British Iron and Steel Industry*. London: Frank Cass and Co., 1967.

British Iron and Steel Federation. Minutes of 5th Meeting of the Working Party on the Industry's Wage Structure, 3 April 63.

British Iron Trade Association. *American Industrial Conditions and Competition*. London: 1902.

Sam Bowles and Herb Gintis. *Schooling in Capitalist America*. New York: Basic Books, 1975.

David Brody. *Steelworkers in America*. New York: Harper and Row, 1960.

William Brown. *Piecework Bargaining*. London: Heinemann Educational Books, 1973.

Carnegie Corporation Bureau of Labor, *Wage Survey, 1891–1893*. Conducted by William Martin. The University of Pittsburgh Special Collections Department, Darlington Library.

Alfred D. Chandler, Jr. *The Visible Hand*. Cambridge: Harvard University Press, Belknap Press, 1977.

Carroll R. Daugherty, M. G. de Chazeau, and S. S. Stratton. *Economics of the Iron and Steel Industry*, vol. 2. New York: McGraw-Hill, 1937.

Peter Doeringer. "Piece-Rate Wage Structures in the Pittsburgh Iron and Steel Industry—1880–1900." *Labor History* 9 (Spring 1968):262–274.

Peter Doeringer and Michael Piore. *Internal Labor Markets and Manpower Analysis*. Lexington, Mass.: D. C. Heath, 1971, pp. 13–40.

John T. Dunlop. "Allocation of the Labor Force." *Proceedings of the Conference on Industry-Wide Collective Bargaining, May 14, 1948*. Philadelphia: University of Pennsylvania Press, 1949.

Bernard Elbaum. "Industrial Relations and Uneven Development: Wage Structure and Industrial Organization in the British and U.S. Iron and Steel Industries." Ph.D. dissertation. Harvard University, 1982.

Bernard Elbaum and Frank Wilkinson. "Industrial Relations and Uneven Development: A Comparative Study of the American and British Steel Industries." *Cambridge Journal of Economics* 3 (September 1979):275–303.

John Fitch. *The Steelworkers*. Ed. by Paul Underwood Kellogg. The Pittsburgh Survey. New York: Russell-Sage Foundation, 1911.

David Gordon, Richard Edwards, and Michael Reich. *Segmented Work, Divided Workers*. Cambridge: Cambridge University Press, 1982.

Great Britain Board of Trade. *Report of an Enquiry into Earnings and Hours of Labour in the U.K. in 1906*, vol. 6, 1911, cd. 5814. London: HMSO, 1911.

James Holt. "Trade Unionism in the British and U.S. Steel Industries 1880–1914: A Comparative Study." *Labor History* **18** (Winter 1977).

Lawrence Kahn. "Unions and Internal Labor Markets: The Case of the San Francisco Longshoremen." *Labor History* (Summer 1980):369–391.

Gabriel Kolko. *Main Currents in Modern American History*. New York: Harper and Row, 1976.

K. G. J. C. Knowles and D. J. Robertson. "Differences between the Wages of Skilled and Unskilled Workers, 1850–1950." *Bulletin of the Oxford University Institute of Economics and Statistics* **13** (1951):109–127.

David Montgomery. *Workers' Control in America*. Cambridge: Cambridge University Press, 1979.

Daniel Nelson. *Managers and Workers*. Madison: University of Wisconsin Press, 1975.

Paul Osterman. "White Collar Internal Labor Markets." In Paul Osterman, ed., *Employment Practices Within Large Firms*. Cambridge: The MIT Press, 1983.

Donald Parsons. "Specific Human Capital: An Application to Quit Rates and Layoff Rates." *Journal of Political Economy* **30** (December 1972): 1120–1143.

E. H. Phelps Brown, with Margaret H. Browne. *A Century of Pay*. London: Macmillan, 1968.

Michael Piore. "Fragments of a Sociological Theory of Wages." Papers and Proceedings, *American Economic Review* **62** (May 1973):377–384.

Sidney Pollard. *The Genesis of Modern Management*. London: 1965.

Arthur Pugh. *Men of Steel*. London: Iron and Steel Trades Confederation, 1951.

Robert L. Raimon. "The Indeterminateness of Wages of Semi-Skilled Workers." *Industrial and Labor Relations Review* (January 1953):180–194.

Jesse S. Robinson. *The Amalgamated Association of Iron, Steel and Tin Workers*. Baltimore: Johns Hopkins University Press, 1920.

Sumner Slichter, James Healy, and E. Robert Livernash. *The Impact of Collective Bargaining on Management*. Washington, D.C.: Brookings Institution, 1960, pp. 142–210.

Sons of Vulcan. *Record*, v. 1, no. 1 (1868), no. 8 (1871), no. 12 (August 1873).

Jack Stieber. *The Steel Industry Wage Structure*. Cambridge: Harvard University Press, 1959.

Katherine Stone. "The Origins of Job Structures in the Steel Industry." *Review of Radical Political Economics* **6** (Summer 1974):61–97.

Peter Temin. *Iron and Steel in Nineteenth Century America*. Cambridge: The MIT Press, 1964.

U.S. Bureau of Labor. *Report on Conditions of Employment in the U.S. Iron and Steel Industry*, vols. 1–4. Charles P. Neill, Commissioner, Senate Document No. 110, 62nd Congress, 1st session. Washington, D.C.: 1911–1913.

U.S. Bureau of Labor. "Wages and Hours in the Iron and Steel Industry." Bulletin Nos. 151 and 218 (1914 and 1917).

U.S. Commissioner of Labor. "Wages and Hours of Labor." Nineteenth Annual Report, 1904. U.S. Department of Commerce and Labor Document, no. 41. Bureau of Labor. Washington, D.C.: 1905.

U.S. Department of Labor. Bureau of Labor Statistics. "Wage Chronology—U.S. Steel Corporation and U.S.W.A., March 1937–April 1974." Bulletin 1814 (1974).

U.S. Department of Labor. Bureau of Labor Statistics. "Industry Wage Survey, Basic Iron and Steel." Bulletins 1839 and 2064 (1975 and 1980).

Frank Wilkinson. "Collective Bargaining in the Steel Industry in the 1920's." *Essays in Labour History*. Ed. by A. Briggs and J. Saville. London: Croom Helm, 1977.

Frank Wilkinson. "Earnings and Size of Plant in the Iron and Steel Industry.' Draft, n.d.

Oliver Williamson, Michael Wachter, and Jeffrey Harris. "Understanding the Employment Relation: The Analysis of Idiosyncratic Exchange." *Bell Journal* **6** (Spring 1975):250–277.

4 Variations in Managerial Career Structures in High-Technology Firms: The Impact of Organizational Characteristics on Internal Labor Market Patterns

Rosabeth Moss Kanter

There has not been much description by scholars and analysts of the actual structure of internal labor markets for managers and the career patterns that follow from these; nonetheless, there is an implicit image in the literature of the typical managerial career. This image, based on traditional, matured corporate bureaucracies, may be called the "classic functional-line ladder career" (see Kanter 1977, Rosenbaum 1979a, b). The career pattern largely characterizing those managers involved with the "core technology" of the business involves

1. functionally based careers, with movement up a long ladder in a single function,

2. a close connection between the reporting chain reflected on a formal organization chart and the usual sequence of job moves,

3. career movement that is largely linear and vertical, with moves implying promotions to a higher hierarchical level,

4. a career arena identified with a large chunk of the organization, due to high organizational centralization—moves that take place under the same general manager and within the same defined unit,

5. reluctance of units (e.g., divisions) to exchange managerial personnel,

6. a long process of development from entry-level management jobs to making key business decisions, with a large number of moves in-between,

7. achievement of a general manager post (or top management position as part of a chief executive's staff) relatively late in the career.

These patterns have been associated, of course, with tall hierarchies, vertical communication orientations, a functional bias in organizing activities, relative centralization, and slowly changing technology. In older corporate bureaucracies with these features, managers whose careers departed from the classic pattern had either extraordinary qualities or were staff managers who tended to be fewer in number, more peripheral, and isolated from internal labor markets, that is, to have fewer career opportunities in general. But for most managers in traditional firms, the classic functional-line ladder career represented the normal, legitimate achievement structure.

In newer high-technology manufacturing firms in the United States and high-tech divisions of conglomerates, however, the single career concept for managers appears to have broken down. A large number of variations on the classic pattern emerge from the particular organizational arrangements and pressures characterizing these firms. The propositions presented here should be seen as speculative, summarizing patterns that may not even be fully recognized yet by the people or the companies involved. But the career variations described can be identified often enough to warrant being labeled as new patterns.

Despite the large proportion of technical jobs in American high-tech manufacturing firms, it is relatively common in those companies to find managerial careers characterized by

1. many more options for career growth and for nontraditional moves,

2. a limited functional identification,

3. a weak connection between the reporting chain on an organization chart and the actual sequence of job moves,

4. career movement that is often nonlinear or lateral,

5. a career arena that encompasses many units of the organization rather than just one,

6. frequent exchange of managerial personnel across units,

7. a rapid process of development from entry-level management jobs to positions making key business decisions, in relatively few moves,

8. attainment of a general manager-type position (or position on a chief executive's staff) relatively early in the career.

My propositions are based on career histories of middle managers and top managers, observations of reorganizations and attendant job changes, and discussions of career development needs and concerns in five major high-technology firms whose products range from computers and word processors to large medical diagnostic devices and aerospace equipment. My observations occurred in the course of a study on the factors accounting for the degree of innovativeness of American corporations and were incidental rather than a central part of that study (the main study included field observations and/or interviewing of over 300 managers in the five high-tech firms as well as in five other nonhigh-tech manufacturing and service companies; see Kanter 1982a, b, 1983).

While all of the high-technology firms included in my research were growing, they were all old enough (more than thirty years old) and large enough (well over $500 million in sales) to have developed internal labor market patterns.

Structural Characteristics of High-Tech Firms Affecting Internal Labor Markets

Both the relative youth and the continual expansion of high-tech firms, still in an entrepreneurial phase of development, play a role in their departure from the classic functional-line ladder career that is independent of any other forces.

First, rapid growth means an expansion of managerial job opportunities, a frequent opening up of new positions, and consequently greater mobility opportunities for everyone. The hunger for people, the constant demand, associated with rapid growth means less concern for "orderly" sequences of careers or demonstrated experience and more willingness to promote for potential, to grab plausible candidates from anywhere, to move managers frequently so that they are constantly stretching to do tasks never before encountered—and indeed certain jobs may be new to an organization that is still developing its basic array of positions (Kanter, Kellner-Rogers, and Bowersox 1982).

Second, high growth and relative newness mean a greater need for obtaining high-ranked managerial personnel from external labor markets. The two younger firms in my study were much more likely than the three older ones to fill positions beyond entry level from outside; the older three had strong "promote from within" policies for line managers but would often bring in nonentry-level staff managers from outside. (Note that growth per se is not the issue, but rather, *rapid* growth. Stable and predictable growth theoretically allows hiring at the lowest entry level and promoting from within, then replenishing the supply at entry level. But unpredictable or too rapid growth does not permit advance planning or waiting for the slow internal development process to occur.)

A third consequence of growth, and rapid technological change, is less overall stability in job and organizational structures: frequent reorganizations; continual invention of new positions; and continual job creation by incumbents who, as first occupants, can define the nature of the job. Under such circumstances "vacancy chain" models of mobility, such as White's (1970), have little meaning. (Indeed for a proportion of early managers in high-tech firms, including the founding group, the very notion of "career" as a sequence of moves has little meaning; instead, managers may occupy the same nominal position with respect to the top but find that the *bottom*, the layers under them, expand as their department or function—or the whole firm—grows beneath them. Responsibility and authority increase without formal job changes; "career growth" does not only mean moving up but can occur "in place" if the territory below increases.)

As I have indicated, these three features are shared by all younger, rapidly growing organizations (Kanter and Stein 1979). But there are also four special characteristics of the organization structure of high-technology firms that give rise to a number of striking variations on the classic functional-line ladder career for managers. In other words, the nature of internal labor markets for managerial personnel is shaped by the structure of the organization, which in turn responds to its environment (especially markets but also the social-regulatory environment) and tasks (technology and technological change).

Four Characteristics of High-Tech Firms: Industry and Organization

The first organizational feature of high-tech firms is *decentralization*. Both because of complex differences between products and philosophic preferences, these firms tend to divide themselves into a large number of relatively autonomous divisions, each complete with its own general manager, and for each major function, staff heads who report to the division's general manager. In short, coordination across functions is pushed downward. Two of the firms, for example, are among the companies that find a wide variety of virtues in small-scale divisions, creating new ones when existing ones get too large. At one, which manufactures computers and other electronic equipment, corporate philosophy holds that more than 2,000 people and/or $100 million in sales reach the limit of manageability without becoming impersonal and procedure bound. Both features are seen as limiting personal growth and innovation but are values for the company. As a division reaches this limit, an elaborate "cloning" process takes place. A division will split along some subdivision of product lines (sometimes into two, sometimes into three divisions), moving employees into new plants, each self-contained and more in line with company guidelines for size (Kanter, Kellner-Rogers, and Bowersox 1982). Each subdivision will have all functions represented, thereby creating many more general manager positions and heads of staff jobs, unlike more centralized companies where the directorships are largely confined to the corporate level.

Similarly, at another firm in the aerospace business, a desire to organize around distinctive product lines or business areas, particularly as separate businesses grow, leads to a continuing process of decentralization. One of the largest divisions in the high-technology areas recently split into three operations, each with a general manager and separately managed technical and production organizations. The divisionwide staff organizations, which are decentralized from both group and corporate levels, are gradually defining responsible directors to report to the general manager of each operation and to spin off a separate staff from that remaining at division headquarters. If business development continues as planned, the division will become a group; each operation will be defined as a division with even more independence, and within each former operation still other separate business lines with their own business directors will be identified. Again, a much larger number of general management and heads-of-staff positions will be created as the decentralizing process proceeds.

The second characteristic of high-tech companies is some form of *matrix organization*. The matrix concept refers to a situation where a manager or professional has reporting relationships in two directions, or, in effect, along two dimensions of a matrix (Knight 1976, Davis and Lawrence 1977). This is an attempt to decentralize decision making even further while still maintaining coherent central direction. For example, an engineering manager might report both to a director of engineering and a program manager for a current program or activity assignment. A personnel manager might report both to the director of personnel and to the general manager. In a formal matrix these reporting relationships are considered equally important, or "solid line" in terms of what would be shown on an organization chart; such full-blown matrices are rare. But in reality the tie to someone other than the functional boss shown on the organization chart is loose, a "dotted-line" responsibility.

The idea of a matrix organization grew out of the particular needs of the aerospace industry after World War II, where a number of very large programs were carried out by teams from a number of functions assembled for the purpose of one activity. The Department of Defense wanted to make sure that there was a responsible person for each contract who could coordinate this complex team. The job of program manager was created in response to this need and is now used widely in high-technology firms. The program or product manager is a kind of general manager for that small piece of a business area, often oriented primarily toward the customer or market and sharing formal authority over those contributing to the design, production, and so on, for the program or product with the appropriate functional managers.

The significance of this kind of structural arrangement for managerial careers is twofold. First, for those operating under some kind of matrix arrangement, which is usually just a small slice of the middle managers in a company, questions of reporting and appraisal are much more complex, as at least two, and in some cases five or six, relationships are involved in helping shape a person's career. The skills needed to function in a matrix situation are also different from those required by classical forms of organization; interpersonal and personal characteristics count for more in situations where the demands for communication, conflict-resolution, and persuasion on technical matters of those from other fields are essential (see Farbstein 1982, Summers 1983). In addition matrix forms of organization open up a number of new career options. The program or product manager position, as a kind of junior general manager, represents an advancement opportunity often attainable much earlier in the career than a business manager position might be in a traditional manufacturing firm. This earlier opportunity for decision making is useful to firms relying on rapidly changing technical expertise because of the superiority of recent education. Furthermore the interchange that takes place across fields may help people learn the technical content of other areas in a way not possible in a more functionally oriented organization.

Related to both of these features is a third: looser authority structures and heavy reliance on *teams* and other *participative vehicles* (Kanter 1982b, 1983). For a number of reasons connected with the age of high-technology firms, the age of their work forces, the complexity of their operations, the speed of change within them, and the propensities of entrepreneurial founders who are often still present as forces, high-technology firms often use a large number of interdisciplinary task forces or special project teams to develop new procedures or to solve problems. It is common for innovative high-technology companies to make assignments that have critical implications across areas rather than to individuals: for instance, a team of functional managers from a number of fields may assemble to create a five-year production and marketing plan for a new product. At one computer company, the establishment of formal interdepartmental of cross-functional committees was the usual way managers sought to improve the performance of their own unit. (This is consistent with the common finding that greater uncertainty or nonroutineness in tasks and technology is associated with a greater reliance on vertical, horizontal communication as a coordination mechanism and greater discretion at lower levels— that is, more teams, more participation (see Van de Ven et al. 1976, Perrow 1970).

At the largest division of one of the firms, for example, the use of task forces is frequent, and a number of task forces on divisionwide policy issues report formally to a steering committee composed of top management and representatives of middle management. These task forces draw people from across the hierarchy, both from those with technical knowledge to contribute to the project and those who could benefit from a developmental opportunity or accurately represent a particular, relevant constituency. In most cases the task forces have a life of six months to a year and take only a portion of the manager's or professional's time. But occasionally, when the recommendations are critical to the organization, the task force might meet full-time for an intense period; a task force on the development of new business information systems, for example, might work together in a conference room for ten weeks, while subordinates temporarily act as managers of the relevant functions.

The team method has a number of implications for managerial careers. Teams not only create relationships across functional boundaries but may serve as training grounds for people who otherwise would have no opportunity to learn about particular issues or to demonstrate their skills with respect to them. Furthermore for many older top managers these task forces or teams often serve as an opportunity for challenge and recognition that is no longer possible in their jobs. Thus the existence of large numbers of participative mechanisms are useful for both those in early as well as later stages of their careers. For young managers who may feel frustrated in their ambitions by a boss unwilling to recognize their talents, a special assignment to a task force or team may be a way to short-circuit the boss and make relationships that will speed career progress; indeed, it is not uncommon for young people in high-technology firms to shoot ahead because of a special assignment rather than their regular job. At the same time for those near the end, when opportunity appears blocked and growth is slow or nonexistent, teams serve as a welcome alternative.

A fourth issue facing high-technology firms in particular is a desperate *need to motivate and retain technical talent*. This has led such companies to search for ways to reward outstanding technical performers who wish to remain "individual contributors" because they are more enthusiastic about technical than managerial work or lack the skills to become managers but have a great deal of technical expertise to contribute. In the classic functional-line ladder career it was often impossible for such people to contribute to policy decisions affecting their work or to feel that they were advancing or being recognized without moving on to management jobs. (In 1970 the most negative responses came from MIT graduates in engineering who after 11 to 19 years out of school remained staff engineers. The most satisfied were the few who had become general managers, but their satisfaction seemed to derive from the autonomy of higher positions rather than the management of people; see Bailyn 1982.) A related pressure is to overcome technical obsolescence, a clear problem for firms in industries with rapidly changing technology. Technical obsolescence is related to organizational variables such as job design and career structures as well as to individual variables such as age and distance from formal education. Innovation declines when engineers and scientists remain on project teams too long (5 years or more; see Katz 1982). Technical obsolescence often results from lack of participation in job-related decisions (Shearer and Steger 1975), but those with challenging assignments have been found to regain technical knowledge on their own (Thompson and Dalton 1971).

One result of these pressures is the attempt to build in a new set of career options that extend management status and compensation for "individual contributors" without having to actually put them in charge of people.

Other General Environmental Pressures

In addition to the four special organizational characteristics of high-technology firms, there are two broad aspects of the environment affecting all manufacturing firms—indeed, to some extent all U.S. corporations—that combine with the unique features of high technology to produce career variations. These involve the proliferation of issue-oriented staff functions and the attendant managerial opportunities this creates. First, competitive pressures as America reels from the effects of foreign competition have created for most companies a greater awareness of the need to plan and conduct periodic market assessments using new analytic tools and data-processing equipment. Second, regulatory pressures and other nonmarket forces of the 1960s and 1970s brought with them the growth of staffs designed to interface with regulatory and public agencies and to ensure that the company maintained its procedures in accordance with societal demands. "Strategic planners" are the beneficiaries of the first kind of pressure, along with market researchers, human resource planners, and some aspects of financial management. Personnel and related departments have been the chief beneficiaries of the second, as they have incorporated affirmative action, sometimes safety and health and community relations activities.

There is a noticeable pattern in the movement of these kinds of issue-oriented activities from the periphery to the corporate mainstream. Initially, companies often handled these new demands by using outside consultants, outside law firms, public relations agencies, academics, or government employees. But gradually, as internal competence grew, a more permanent staff from within the company would develop. No longer the temporary problemsolvers at the periphery, such people now became part of a relatively specialized professional and managerial hierarchy, and specialized career pathways soon would follow. Sometimes the internalization of the function and development of career paths would result in a loss of status for the activity. For example, it is quite common to have the analyst or issue manager for a pressing current external demand report in to the top of the organization because of the urgency of solving the problem immediately. But as the tools for dealing with it become routinized, it is possible to send the staff back in to the appropriate department to be managed by those that are professionals within the staff area. Under the circumstances an environmental affairs expert with direct reporting links to the office of the chief executive when the problem first surfaces may gradually disappear into an environmental affairs office within an engineering or product design department, or a vice-president for affirmative action may disappear into a junior coordinator position within a personnel or human resources function.

Whatever the currently pressing issue, then, we can expect to see the analysts who advise with respect to it enjoying the privileges of high status, managerial titles, and reporting to high levels; this is indeed the case at the moment with respect to "strategic planning" or "productivity improvement" in many companies.

Five Variations in Managerial Careers

It is impossible to discuss the management group in high-tech firms without including a variety of technical and staff professionals. The very term "manager" is misleading in many high-technology firms, for it is possible, given the proliferation of staffs and people in high status analyst roles, to have large numbers of people with "manager" in their titles and equivalent reporting level who in fact work without staff. The title of manager has come to connote a high-level status, a set of privileges, and a closeness to the top, rather removed from its original meaning as the supervisor of the work of others. The manager/nonmanager distinction is more often used to signify the difference between high-level salaried and hourly employees than it is to clearly differentiate managers from professionals who have no people management responsibilities.

The organizational characteristics and environmental pressures impacting on high-tech firms lead to five variations on the classic functional-line ladder career for managers. I argue that these variations are already identifiable in high-technology firms and may perhaps someday be acknowledged as career tracks.

The first variation is the *lateral-cross unit advance*. This career structure begins by resembling the classic functional-line ladder. For perhaps five to ten years a manager moves up within a particular function in an orderly and apparently linear fashion—for instance, to director of engineering or director of personnel for a decentralized unit. From then on the career consists of retaining the same title but moving to even larger units and ultimately to ever higher groupings of units—for instance, from director of engineering in a small facility, to director of engineering for an operation, to director of engineering for a division, to director of engineering for a group of divisions. In short, after a rather early point in the career, a single locality or a single unit under the same general manager no longer provides opportunities for career movement; decentralization, however, provides many more opportunities to attain a high-level position in the top management team rather early in the career. Advancement then involves jumping across to another subsidiary or division in what looks on paper to be a lateral move with respect to height in a hierarchy but in fact constitutes a more responsible position. While there are clear status gradations in terms of size or importance of the unit, there is nothing else linking the jobs— no formal ladder, no reporting relationships. The chain is an implicit one.

For some staff managers this pattern involves, in effect, "moving up a dotted line." For example, let's visualize a personnel director of the small Boston components division of a computer manufacturer who reports directly to the general manager of that operation who controls her salary, performance appraisal, budget, and day-to-day activities, and only indirectly, on a "dotted line," to a group director of personnel. But the personnel link is the more important one for career progress, so the manager next moves on to be personnel director of a larger San Francisco operation, now reporting directly (on a solid line) to the new general manager and still on a dotted line to the group director of personnel. This, then, is the equivalent of a dotted-line career path. Whereas in the classic functional-line ladder career, a solid line on the organization chart which reflects reporting relationships was also highly likely to be correlated with career sequences (in part because of the height of most traditional hierarchies), in the new style world of high-technology firms there is a clearer split between the immediate authority embodied in the reporting relationship and the longer-term career embodied in the indirect, sideways, or dotted-line professional relationship.

A second variation on the classic career is closely related to the first: the growth of *"generalist tracks."* Decentralization, matrix structures, and the attendant need for large numbers of program or product managers as well as general managers of operating units means that high-technology firms have a great need for generalists who can serve as integrators, managing across functions while having profit and loss responsibility for a particular product or activity. Once on a generalist track, which may occur relatively early in the managerial career because generalist positions now penetrate much lower in the organization, advancement means moving in size of product, program or unit.

Entry into these tracks is often surprisingly nontraditional. Despite a heavily technical emphasis in the five firms, those who are excellent technical managers of engineering or production often become too specialized or never have the opportunity to show their skills as generalists. Instead general managers and program managers may come out of the less central but more integrative functions where knowledge and experience are gained in terms of market or business management issues. Even in a highly technical company with large numbers of engineers, it is not unusual to see a manager or professional from marketing, or occasionally personnel, become a product manager; then having demonstrated skills in this small arena, he or she could get a series of business manager assignments leading to a general manager's job in a small operation. In one case a lawyer with an MBA moved from his entry position, a legal staff job, to a general managership (accompanied by a vice-presidency) in five years, between the ages of 33 and 38; he had worked in only one other company previously, for two years, and before getting his MBA had worked for a law firm. His "sponsor," who gave him his first chance to move from the legal specialty to a more general problem-solving assignment (selling off a failing business line), was himself the youngest general manager in the company, who had spent only a year as an engineer ("and not a very good one," he says) with the firm before moving into marketing and from there accumulating generalist experience and getting increasingly larger chunks and combinations of businesses to manage.

The generalist track is clearly one of the most important routes to the top in high-technology organizations—even more important than moving up the engineering or production hierarchy, despite the length (and thus apparent opportunity) in those more technical ladders. In part, as I have already indicated, generalist positions begin quite low in the organization because of decentralization and matrix or partial matrix structures. But also, since technical knowledge can become obsolete quickly in such firms, the generalist track represents a way to move off a functional-line into a position where the manager does not have to claim technical mastery. Furthermore the constant change such companies face, in technology and products as well as in internal systems, creates many opportunities for "project managers" or "development managers" rather than those who merely administer the routine.

Movement along the generalist track is sometimes quite speedy, especially for those who develop reputations as "troubleshooters" who can be sent in as the product manager or general manager over a failing activity and turn it around. The need for troubleshooters is a function of business conditions in high-tech firms. Because of rapid technological changes, the cost structures of industries with heavy R&D components, and the high uncertainty quotient in new product performance, high-technology firms may be plagued with trouble spots that do not reflect incompetence so much as realities of the industry. Furthermore for those companies in aerospace that work for single, large customers and must bid or contracts years before the work is completed, inflation and other external economic factors can create problems with potential cost overruns, requiring troubleshooters who can increase efficiency or convert possible losers into winners. Thus troubleshooters are a kind of generalist specializing in turnarounds, smoothing the inevitable internal bumps in externally successful high-tech firms. Troubleshooters may be sent on a rapid sequence of assignments for several years, with increasing dollar value reflected in each program or product. These assignments are typically short: a year to eighteen months. Having proved their value in rescue operations, and having become known to top management because of the publicity value of such assignments, these managers then enter the general manager sequence with responsibility for a more stable ongoing operation, now spending more time at each—perhaps three to five years—before moving on. At one firm in particular, several individuals were identified to me as "rescue artists" or "miracle workers" whose careers grew because of the turnarounds they effected.

In both of the two variations I have thus far identified, I recognize that I am making the career structures sound more orderly than they appear to the people involved in them. While I have encountered some conscious attempts in high-technology firms to identify both of these patterns with a particular sequence of moves that will eventually develop the kinds of high-level talent the company needs, many of the actual moves are ad hoc responses to current needs rather than part of an explicit program for development, in part because of the constant pace of change in high-technology firms.

A third career variation is idiosyncratic but important in the lives of many people in high-techology companies: the *extra-hierarchical leap*. As should be clear by now from my description of the key organizational features of many high-technology companies, the formal hierarchy as reflected on an organizational chart is quite misleading in terms of actual working relationships and opportunities for contribution and career growth. Even though high-technology firms can produce organization charts that represent the same neat array of boxes linked by hierarchical chains of command that can be produced in more traditional manufacturing firms, such charts reflect only one layer of organizational reality. The vast array of acknowledged dotted-line relationships, which are often not shown on the charts, add a second dimension, and the heavy use of team mechanisms and participative vehicles add still another. At one of the computer companies I studied, the "real" or operative organization chart was described as resembling a "plate of spaghetti," and the firm as resembling a "family," a "guild," and "tribe on a Pacific island," or an "assemblage of 20,000 entrepeneurs" (see Farbstein 1982, Kanter 1983).

The fact that people on special assignments, task forces, or program teams may be in close working contact for periods of time vastly multiplies the opportunities to make relationships, learn skills, demonstrate skills, and make unusual career moves that could never be predicted by considering either a job chain or an organization chart. For example, in one of the more engineering-intensive companies, a young female personnel manager with no technical background was assigned to be a member of an information systems planning task force chaired by the production manager of a different facility. Since one of the task force's first jobs was to familiarize themselves with the systems in use in other major companies, the woman had an unusual opportunity to learn this field, and her skills and intelligence impressed the production manager with her potential to move into his area. In several other cases unusual job offers have resulted from the contacts made on task forces involving leaps across functions, locations, and levels.

Such random moves are considered extra-hierarchical because they are idiosyncratic, apparently fortuitous rather than planned, and occur outside of job chains or anything that the formal, hierarchical structure could predict. Nonhierarchical aspects of the organizational structure make it likely that people will encounter opportunities for such moves. (Obviously, such moves occur occasionally in *all* companies; I propose that they are much more common under the structural features of high-tech companies.) In some high-technology firms there is so little explicit attention to formal career paths that to many employees these kinds of leaps represent the only way they feel one can get another job until reaching rather high-level positions. In short, preexisting personal relationships or the chance to impress a hiring manager in another area with one's skills and abilities constitute one of the primary ways that jobs are secured in high-technology firms today, despite the current efforts on the part of many of those firms to put more explicit career development programs in place. (Career development programs are most often addressed to nonmanagerial personnel and do not substitute for the personalized or fortuitous nature of many managerial career moves.) At the same time it should be noted that the very legitimacy of leaps or jumps across fields independent of the hierarchy means that there are more opportunities for people to put themselves eventually in positions of generalists.

A fourth variation on the classic managerial career pattern has already been mentioned: the *dual ladder* or *professional ladder*. This involves the design of explicit career ladders for professionals or technical employees in which advancement along the technical track supposedly parallels advancement along a managerial track. Thus professionals with demonstrated skill and appropriate length of service can be paid and treated as though they were managers, with the attendant privileges, recognition, admission to managerial functions, and signs of status. In some firms special technical achievement may be recognized in the form of appointment as a "corporate engineering fellow" or the award of a prize for outstanding work. Or research budgets may be given for proposals that are particularly significant. Other incentives for this pattern include the sharing of patent rights, sabbaticals, or company-supported continuing education. The analogies to university statuses are not accidental, as companies try to create for their scientists and engineers a feeling that they are receiving status and recognition equivalent to that of their university or research institute counterparts. Some companies, in traditional as well as high-tech areas, have dual ladders for sales personnel (a professional sales track) and personnel experts as well. But it is not clear that these ladders work well or are seen as other than second best.

The fifth variation characterizes the careers of a few: the *high-level analyst pattern*. This pattern refers to the tendency of the firms to bring in a few analysts close to the top of the organization to solve particular problems or advise on major aspects of strategy. There are a number of anomalies in this pattern. Such analysts are often young, fresh from school or from a company that may not be in the same industry, unfamiliar with the products, and largely inexperienced in the technology characterizing the firm's core technology; yet their reporting level is high, they attend key meetings, and they may advise on important questions of strategy or philosophy that involve the exercise of their analytic skills or special knowledge base. Such would be the case, for example, for a business school graduate hired as a special assistant to the CEO of a manufacturing firm and then made vice-president of strategic planning a year and a half later. There is, literally, almost no place for such analysts to go after they have completed their assignments (see AMBA Executive 1979). To go back down into operations appears to be a loss of status and sometimes requires a skill they do not possess. Yet without this experience, they are blocked in terms of further moves around the top echelons of the organization. It appears that their career path is likely to involve intercompany moves rather than mobility within a single organization. Or they may remain in the functions but move from analyst serving as staff to the top to department head building a set of functionaries below. Both are stabilizing moves from what is otherwise an unusual and anomalous position.

Issues and Tensions

In high-technology manufacturing firms, and others that come to resemble them, there are a number of variations on the classic functional-line ladder managerial career structures that have become legitimate options—and in the case of the first two, even preferred routes to the top. The classic functional-line career has not disappeared in high-tech firms, but it has been augmented by another set of possibilities.

The existence of these variations match the directions recommended by those studying the changing career desires of individuals. Schein (1978) identified a variety of "career anchors" representing different core values individuals might hold with respect to ideal job sequences, with the implication that organizations should provide for all of them. Hall (1976) proposed the need for "protean careers" managed by the person, not the organization, to meet the needs of "mobiocentric people" who value freedom, growth, flexibility, and change. But while the potential fit between high-tech internal labor markets and individual preferences may be good, it is important to note that the development of the career variations was driven by structural characteristics of the organization, in turn a function of environmental factors, and labor supply variables seemed to play only a small role. This is consistent with the argument made by many labor market analysts that the scarcity of labor is not the determining factor in job design (Kalleberg and Sorenson 1979); people are expected to, and often do, bend to structure and change preferences accordingly (Kanter 1977).

The existence of a more varied and less rigid internal labor market in a high-tech environment does not solve all career problems for individuals, however. The lack of orderliness in careers, the constant addition and modification of positions, the fall out of favor of some skills and tasks as others rise into prominence, the same reliance on personal networks and interpersonal skills found in other settings (Kanter 1977) but at even lower levels—all can make it difficult for anyone to plan a career in a high-tech firm. Furthermore some people still get blocked from further career progress. I have argued, in effect, that the opportunity structure is looser or more open for managers in high-tech firms because of the number of career routes unavailable in more traditional industries. But the variations may exist for only a fraction of the managerial work force. And there are also new sources of blocked mobility introduced by these same structures while old ones are not entirely eliminated. In the traditional manufacturing firm, as represented by "Industrial Supply Corporation" in *Men and Women of the Corporation*, I identified three major structural sources of blocked mobility (Kanter 1977, 1979) in addition to external changes (e.g., slowed overall organizational growth) or idiosyncratic individual problems:

1. Dead-end jobs with short ladders, low ceilings for mobility, and limited exit from the job category (primarily characterizing clerical jobs and many lower-level factory jobs).

2. Nontraditional career histories, or a wrong route *in* to a high-mobility job (inappropriate background for next moves and no way to fill holes in experience).

3. The "pyramid squeeze" (because of pyramidal shapes and restriction to hierarchical movement, more eligible candidates than openings at the levels above, especially in later years of managerial careers).

The career variations in high-tech firms are not altogether free of these problems, and they add other sources of career blockage as well:

1. Functional over-specialization/high-level dead end (rising high in a particular function because of successful performance and knowledge of its technical content but reaching a dead end because too old and too senior to gain other experience to move on to the more promising generalist/general manager track).

2. For analysts and some professional staff, incongruence between reporting level and eligibility for other jobs—the appearance of high status relatively early in the career but no place to move after that within the company.

And wherever large skill discontinuities exist between otherwise linked positions (obvious career moves) because of rapid change in markets or technology, blockage will also occur.

Several of the managerial career structures outlined are quite different from one another and require incompatible skills and experience. In some cases we can predict tensions arising from this. There is already a gap and a conflict between the internal labor market for managerial jobs requiring hands-on technical experience and/or product knowledge and that for analyst positions. In the first case it implies a longer, slower process of development for both the remaining classic functional careers and some generalists; in the second, it is possible to start up high and fast while young, using educational credentials instead of company experience, but the entire career structure is much flatter. Older functional managers and some who have waited a long time for general manager or product/program manager jobs appear to resent the "young hotshot MBAs" reporting directly to top corporate officers or the younger professionals moving directly into high staff jobs at the top of their division. At the same time, because of the flatter opportunity structure for analysts and their more generalizable skills, compared to those that must have solid product/market/business area knowledge and credibility with the technicians below, they will show less company loyalty, enhancing their careers by company hopping to "trade up." The hands-on managers, in contrast, will probably change companies less often, if at all. The increases in company hopping noted by executive recruiters in the late 1970s and early 1980s were probably accounted for largely by analysts, professionals, and troubleshooters, adding to the base number of managers who had reached apparent dead ends and were looking for moves. Those on classic functional paths or generalist tracks are more likely to find their careers centered in one company.

The importance of lateral-cross unit advance and related patterns suggests that geographic mobility will continue to be a necessity for managers, since moving across units often implies geographic relocation. Two of the companies I examined were unusual among high-tech firms in having a major geographic cluster of many facilities in and around a single city; in one case a helicopter network had once linked the more distant locations within a region. Most high-tech operations are spread across the country—and the world—so as to not exhaust the technical talent in any one area.

Implications for Other Sectors

The elaboration of internal labor markets in the large modern day corporation and the formal or informal career paths associated with them, has been viewed in strikingly different ways. To some analysts who assume that there is a fundamental and irreconcilable conflict between the interests of capital and labor, internal labor markets function as a control device that ensures a more docile and stable work force motivated to conform because of the promise or hope of attaining the next levels in job progressions (Edwards 1979). Evidence does show that the "moving," high in opportunity, identify more with the organization and suppress more of their grievances than those "stuck," with low opportunity for advancement (Kanter 1977). To others who assume that there is a posible harmony of interests between organizations and individuals, internal labor markets integrate the organization's needs for succession planning and an available pool of trained talent with the individual's need for growth and progress (Schein 1978).

However, there are also a number of specific conditions that allow internal labor markets to develop, conditions that differentiate industries and firms as well as sectors within the same firm. These conditions, clearly present in the high-technology firms I studied, do not exist to the same extent in other industries. They are indigenous in technical and general management areas within high-tech firms rather than other management fields. For example, internal labor markets are likely to be developed and utilized when there are losses, noneconomic or economic, associated with filling management jobs from outside and gains, interpersonal, organizational, or technical, to filling jobs internally. In effect, internal labor markets are likely to be more elaborate where

1. tasks require a high degree of firm-specific knowledge;

2. tasks are high in uncertainty but put a premium on ease of communication and trust (Kanter 1977, ch. 3) and therefore favor long-established relationships;

3. there are large numbers of openings and cost savings to internal recruitment;

4. internal candidates may be groomed or prepared for the job because of its close relationship to a previous job, so there is a minimum "down" time;

5. there is high competition for labor with specific skills, and, as a retention device, employees with those skills are offered the inside track for better job functions;

6. there is a longer learning curve to master the area and/or greater reliance on employees' discretion and judgment, so that the pay differential for seniority is worth it to the organization;

7. organizational cohesion and unity are important, and there is a "culture of pride" (Kanter 1983) stressing the abilities of employees which would be disturbed by external hiring;

8. there is low routinization, the structure may be loose or changing, and formal rules or procedures minimal (so persons rather than systems are the repositories of knowledge, and career mobility functions not only to retain those persons but also to spread their knowledge and to integrate parts of the organization as they move across units);

9. change is constant and valued, and people learn to seek and use new information so that the organization is not forced to hire from outside as its only change strategy when crises demand new responses (Kanter 1983).

Under these largely characteristic conditions of high technology firms, we could expect a more elaborate internal labor market for managers by a number of measures including: more openings filled from within, more people eligible for more positions, more variety in the kinds of moves, and more overall movement.

High technology is now the leading edge of American industry in terms of economic growth, financial success, stock market glamour, and popular excitement. Thus it is natural to wonder what will happen across industries over time. Will other industries come to resemble the patterns identified with it, through emulation or as a necessity for survival? Or, on the contrary, will the relatively young high-tech firms rigidify as they age, settling into the more hierarchical patterns of the past?

I have pointed to four classes of environmental and situational variables that shape organizational structure and, with it, internal labor markets for managers: The social and economic environment includes labor force characteristics—attitudes and values as well as skills— organizational fads and fashions, and overall economic conditions in the society. The political and regulatory environment adds tasks and roles to organizations, from labor relations to affirmative action. Industry characteristics include the rate of technological change, speed of turnover of product generations, and competitive situations. Finally, firm characteristics, especially company age, reflect the rapidity of growth, and presence of the entrepreneurial/founding generation.

The first two classes of variables clearly affect many traditional industries as well and should help move them closer to high-tech patterns. The last two, on the other hand, should move high-tech firms closer to the traditional model as they age and if or when growth slows and products mature.

So we could expect some degree of convergence: more analysts tracks, more overall career variety, more teams and participative vehicles, and more "extra-hierarchical leaps" and "dual ladders" in traditional firms; but perhaps a tightening of the internal labor market and a shift in the balance of emphasis from the variants back to the classic functional-line career in high-tech firms if matrices are unraveled and decentralization wanes.

But I would not expect convergence to be complete either. Radical decentralization, loosened authority, and a change orientation will probably never characterize traditional industries with mature products in declining markets to the same extent that these features define and dominate high tech. And the relative "permanence" of the features associated with the high-tech firms I studied, even in companies forty and more years old with slower growth than counterparts, indicates that their internal labor markets may constitute a new organizational form, appropriate to their founding era (Stinchcombe 1965) and always maintaining many of their unique features.

This chapter has suggested several of the ways that managerial—and related professional—careers appear to vary in high-technology firms. Many of these firms are too young and keep too few records to yet permit detailed analyses of career histories. But from the experiences of the older and larger firms, it is possible to extrapolate the emerging patterns shaping the internal labor market for managers.

References

The AMBA Executive. 1979. "One Step Below Top Management: A Critical Point in My Career." In M. Jelinek (ed.), Career Management. Chicago: St. Clair Press, pp. 186–192.

Bailyn, Lotte. 1982. "Trained as Engineers: Issues for the Management of Technical Personnel in Midcareer." In R. Katz (ed.), Career Issues in Human Resource Management. Englewood Cliffs, N.J.: Prentice-Hall, pp. 35–49.

Davis, Stanley, and Paul R. Lawrence. 1977. Matrix. Reading, Mass.: Addison-Wesley.

Doeringer, Peter B., and Michael Piore. 1971. Internal Labor Markets and Manpower Analysis. Lexington, Mass.: D.C. Heath.

Dunlop, John. 1966. "Job Vacancy Measures and Economic Analysis." In The Measurement and Interpretation of Job Vacancies. New York: Columbia University Press, pp. 27–47.

Edwards, Richard. 1979. *Contested Terrain*. New York: Basic Books.

Farbstein, Ken. 1982. "Achieving at CHIPCO: Enterprise and Innovation as a Collaborative Bargaining Process in a Successful High Tech Firm." In *Stimulating Innovation in Middle Management*. Cambridge, Mass.: Goodmeasure, Inc., pp. 111–128.

Hall, Douglas T. 1976. *Careers in Organizations*. Santa Monica, Cal.: Goodyear.

Kalleberg, Arne L., and Aage B. Sorenson. 1979. "The Sociology of Labor Markets." *Annual Review of Sociology* 5:351–379.

Kanter, Rosabeth Moss. 1977. *Men and Women of the Corporation*. New York: Basic Books.

Kanter, Rosabeth Moss. 1979. "Differential Access to Opportunity and Power." In R. Alvarez and K. Lutterman (eds.), *Discrimination in Organizations*. San Francisco: Jossey-Bass, pp. 52–68.

Kanter, Rosabeth Moss. 1982a. "The Middle Manager as Innovator." *Harvard Business Review* **59** (July–August):95–105.

Kanter, Rosabeth Moss. 1982b. "Power and Entrepreneurship in Action: Corporate Middle Managers." in P. L. Stewart and M. G. Cantor (eds.), *Varieties of Work*. Beverly Hills, Cal.: Sage, pp. 153–172.

Kanter, Rosabeth Moss. 1983. *The Change Masters: How People and Companies Succeed through Innovation in the New Corporate Era*. New York: Simon and Schuster.

Kanter, Rosabeth Moss, Myron Kellner-Rogers, and Janis Bowersox. 1982. "Organizational and Management Dilemmas in Successful, Growing High Technology Firms." In *Managing Growth*. Cambridge, Mass.: Goodmeasure, Inc., pp. 71–114.

Kanter, Rosabeth Moss, and Barry A. Stein. 1979. "Growing Pains." In *Life in Organizations*. New York: Basic Books, pp. 255–273.

Katz, Ralph. 1982. "Managing Careers: The Influence of Job and Group Longevities." In *Career Issues in Human Resource Management*. Englewood Cliffs, N.J.: Prentice-Hall, pp. 154–181.

Kerr, Clark. 1954. "The Balkanization of Labor Markets." In E. W. Bakke et al. (eds.), *Labor Mobility and Economic Opportunity*. New York: Wiley, pp. 92–110.

Knight, Kenneth. 1976. "Matrix Organization: A Review." *Journal of Management Studies* 13:111–130.

Perrow, Charles B. 1970. *Organizational Analysis*. Belmont, Cal.: Wadsworth.

Rosenbaum, James E. 1979a. "Career Paths and Advancement Opportunities." In R. Alvarez and K. Lutterman (eds.), *Discrimination in Organizations*. San Francisco: Jossey-Bass, pp. 69–84.

Rosenbaum, James E. 1979b. "Tournament Mobility: Career Patterns in a Corporation." *Administrative Science Quarterly* 12:220–242.

Schein, Edgar H. 1978. *Career Dynamics*. Reading, Mass.: Addison-Wesley.

Shearer, R. L., and J. A. Steger. 1975. "Manpower Obsolescence: A New Definition and Empirical Investigation of Personal Variables." *Academy of Management Journal* **18**:263–275.

Stinchcombe, Arthur. 1965. "Social Structure and Organizations." In J. G. March (ed.), *Handbook of Organizations*. Chicago: Rand McNally, pp. 142–193.

Summers, David. 1982. "Achieving at MEDCO: Conditions Supporting Innovation by Managers in a Well-Run Company." In *Stimulating Innovation in Middle Management*. Cambridge, Mass.: Goodmeasure, Inc. pp. 129–148.

Thompson, Paul H., and Gene W. Dalton. 1976. "Are R&D Organizations Obsolete?" *Harvard Business Review* **56** (November–December):105–116.

Van de Ven, A. H., A. L. Delbecq, and R. Koenig. 1976. "Determinants of Coordination Modes Within Organizations." *American Sociological Review* **41**:322–338.

White, Harrison C. 1970. *Chains of Opportunity: System Models of Mobility in Organizations*. Cambridge, Mass.: Harvard University Press.

5

The Transformation of the Industrial Relations and Personnel Function

Thomas A. Kochan and
Peter Cappelli

Social scientists are becoming increasingly aware of the influence an organization's structure exerts on its decisions and strategy. The link between administrative structure and strategy and decision making, for example, is of longstanding interest to organizational theorists (Chandler 1962, Simon 1957, 1964, Thompson 1967, Lawrence and Lorsch 1967). Microeconomists have also addressed the question of how internal structural variations influence the management of discretion and the response to external pressures (Leibenstein 1978, Slichter, Healy, and Livernash 1960, Slichter 1941, Freeman and Medoff 1979). Industrial relations researchers in both Britain (Gospel 1973, Thomson 1981) and North America (Freedman 1979, Kochan 1980, Godard and Kochan 1981) have shown renewed interest in the role and structure of industrial relations and personnel departments. This work is being driven by a view that management is now the dominant force for change in employment practices and that employee, union, and government behavior are largely reactions to management-initiated events. Indeed, we will argue that this proposition is more true now in large U.S. corporations than at any time since the 1930s.

Thus, to understand employment relations in modern firms, we first need to understand the role and structure of the organizational units responsible for formulating and administering labor policies. This chapter will review changes in the role of personnel-industrial relations units over time and will use an historical overview to explain variations in the structure and influence of these units as well as to predict changes

Partial support for this research was provided by the Alfred P. Sloan Foundation. The views expressed in this chapter are those of the authors and do not represent those of the Sloan Foundation. Helpful comments on an earlier draft were received from Robert B. McKersie, Sara Rynes, Deborah Kolb, Audrey Freedman, Charles A. Myers, and Paul Grehl.

in the future. Our focus will be on the broad patterns in the evolution of personnel and industrial relations units. A more thorough discussion of the internal structure and functions of modern personnel departments can be found in Pigors and Myers (1981, pp. 52–67).

Perspectives on Organizations and Managerial Behavior

The role of management is to allocate rationally resources in a manner that promotes the long-run economic interests of the firm. Whether those interests are operationally defined in classical terms as profit maximization, growth, or some multiple sets of objectives (Cyert and March 1963), the labor force serves as one key set of resources that must be managed efficiently. Since labor costs are an important component of total costs, one task of management is to minimize the costs of its human resources.

In addition to cost minimization, managers must deal with unpredictability in employment relations. The work force is analogous to other sources of environmental uncertainty or unpredictability that firms seek to minimize (Thompson 1967). Thus another key objective of management in dealing with its human resources is to develop and maintain predictable and stable relations. While at times concern for costs and for stability will lead to the same strategies, at other times trade-offs may exist between these objectives. It is important therefore to examine the interplay between these two objectives over time.

Finally, since the goals of employees and employers partially conflict, the relationship between the firm and its employees takes on the characteristics of an implicit or explicit bargaining relationship. The relationship is most explicit when employees are organized and formally represented in collective bargaining. An explicit exchange or bargaining relationship is also present in situations where individuals hold sufficient individual bargaining power based on their labor market alternatives to require the firm to negotiate. In situations where sufficient individual power is not present and employees are not formally represented by a union, the bargaining relationship is more implicit as the firm adjusts its employment policies and compensation system in response to labor market questions, employee expectations and motivational requirements, governmental regulations, threats of unionization, and so on. Thus another objective of the firm in managing its human resources is to insure that the firm is an effective bargaining agent—that it has sufficient power, control, and discretion to achieve a bargain that protects its economic interests, organizational autonomy, and flexibility in its deployment of human resources (Fox 1971). Indeed, concern for maintaining flexibility is an increasingly important benchmark against which managers assess their human resource management systems (Foulkes 1980).

Three key sources of external pressure have influenced employment policies for managing the work force and the organizational structures used to implement them: (1) market pressures, (2) the threat or presence of a union, and (3) government regulations. Pressures from product markets, for example, lead management to attempt to maximize output in times of growth and to economize on the use and cost of labor in times of market decline or excess capacity. Scarcity in key labor markets, on the other hand, forces firms to maintain adequate compensation and working conditions and to attend to recruitment and development strategies to avoid manpower shortages. The threat or actual presence of a union is expected to not only increase costs but also to increase the pressures on management to develop policies to reduce the uncertainty and threats to stability that can come from bilateral negotiations. The presence of a union therefore requires management to make trade-offs between stability and cost minimization objectives. Government regulations pose additional costs and, depending on the enforcement strategies, can threaten the stability of production. Analysis of the intensity and relative importance of these three sets of external pressures will help explain the evolution and current status of employment policies within firms and the organizational structures used to carry them out.

The effects of the external market, unions, and government pressures cannot explain the entire range of variation in employer policies and practices in managing its work force. Organizational theorists are increasingly documenting the effects of top managerial values, philosophies, and the "organizational culture" that evolves out of efforts to shape the organizational behavior of members in a way that is consistent with the perspectives of top executives (Van Maanen and Schein 1979, Ouchi 1981). The study of organizational cultures is gaining momentum within the field of organizational behavior, largely in response to the interest in Japanese management and the policies of U.S. firms that use similar strategies to create all-inclusive cultures to socialize employees and shape behavior. Part of this strategy includes the development of comprehensive human resource management policies. The ultimate objective is to develop ways of integrating the needs of employees with the objectives of the firm (McGregor 1961, Argyris 1964). Firms that have adopted this approach have clearly strengthened the role that personnel and human resource management plays in implementing, if not in shaping, the overall business strategy of the firm.

The typical way a complex organization manages environmental pressures and discretion is through a structural division of labor. Specialized units, referred to in the organizational literature as boundary spanning units, are assigned responsibility for managing the firm's relations with particular aspects of its environment (Thompson 1967, Lawrence and Lorsch 1967, Aldrich and Herker 1977). This leads to a differentiation of management into separate decision-making centers or functional units, each of which tends to develop its own set of specialized goals and priorities (Kochan, Cummings, and Huber 1976). Thus internal managerial decision making also takes on a political character, as specialized units compete for power and influence in the management structure. The power of a boundary unit and its influence within management in turn depends on (1) the importance of the environmental pressure that it is responsible for, that is, the extent to which the attainment of cost, stability, or organizational autonomy and flexibility objectives can be influenced by that aspect of the environment within the boundary unit's responsibility, and (2) the effectiveness of the unit in achieving a favorable bargain in its dealings with this aspect of the environment.

In the case of industrial relations, a symbiotic relationship can develop between the management professionals in an industrial relations-personnel group and the employees, union, or government agencies with which they negotiate (Goldner 1970). The greater the potential threat or cost to the organization posed by the work force, union, or government agency, the more power the personnel-industrial relations group will be allocated by the organization. Kochan (1975), for example, found that the power of labor relations representatives in city management (relative to other city management officials) was largely a function of the power of the unions with which the city dealt. The growth of industrial relations specialists in private firms has been found to be related to similar pressures (Kochan 1980, p. 194, Beaumont and Deaton 1980). On the other hand, to *maintain* power over time, the personnel-industrial relations unit must manage these threats effectively and continue to perform well in achieving the firm's objectives. The symbiotic relationship also remains important to the maintenance of the boundary unit's power. If the external threat posed by the labor market, union movement, or government declines, the industrial relations unit's power is likely to decline.

How well the boundary unit is doing and the acceptability of the strategies used to manage relations with employees, unions, and the government are judgments ultimately made by executives outside of the personnel-industrial relations function. This adds another political dimension to the personnel-industrial relations role. It must adapt to or influence the perceptions, values, strategies, and judgments of top management and other competing organizational groups in order to preserve its power.

In summary, changes in the intensity of three sources of external pressure, both over time and across organizations, have had important effects on the power and functions of personnel-industrial relations units: (1) market pressures, (2) unions, and (3) government regulations. Each has posed threats to the labor cost, stability and predictability, and organizational control and autonomy objectives of employers. These threats have varied in degree over time. Understanding variations in the intensity of these pressures over time, along with the dynamics of internal management culture, politics, and strategy, will help explain the power that the overall personnel-relations unit has in the firm. Understanding changes in the relative importance of the three sets of pressures and in top management strategy will also help explain shifts in the relative power of subunits within the broad personnel-industrial relations function.

We will now use this broad conceptual framework to interpret the historical evolution and changing role and power of industrial-personnel units within large American firms. To do so, four historical periods are noted: (1) 1900 to 1935 when the personnel-industrial relations unit first began to emerge as a professional staff function within major firms, (2) 1935 to 1960 when the industrial relations (or more particularly the labor relations subgroup) rose to the dominant power position within personnel-industrial relations departments, (3) 1960 to 1980 when the industrial relations unit generally maintained its power or experienced a gradual but generally unnoticed decline in power, whereas the personnel-human resource management specialists regained power and influence, and (4) the early 1980s, which indicate that the roles of personnel and industrial relations are undergoing fundamental re-structuring and change.

Origins of the Personnel Function

The personnel-industrial relations function was in many ways a creation of the pressures brought by World War I and the availability of human engineering and other management techniques emerging out of scientific management. Before that, decisions concerning hiring and employment were made entirely by line management, with each supervisor or foreman hiring and managing his own work force. (A description of this "drive" system is provided by Jacoby, chapter 2.)

The war brought with it an entirely new set of environmental pressures. The increased demand for wartime production was accompanied by labor shortages produced by conscription and a drop in immigration. This pressure from markets—shortages in the labor market and growing costs of production losses in the product market—increased the importance of relations with the labor force to the firm. Management therefore began to respond by creating specialized employment departments to administer relations with the labor force. They were aided in this endeavor by the diffusion of ideas and techniques coming out of the scientific management movement (Locke 1982). This response was also encouraged by pressures from wartime government agencies.

To meet market and government pressures, the new employment departments made several changes in existing management practices. First, as estimates of staffing needs became centralized, hiring decisions were taken away from independent foremen and supervisors. Second, selection and placement decisions became based on tests similar to those used by the government to place conscripts into various skill and trade groups. The tests were used to reduce the inefficiences associated with misplaced workers. These placement decisions and promotion policies were also centralized so that the reduced pool of skilled labor could be allocated in a manner that would serve the most pressing needs of the firm as a whole.

Within personnel departments, power was clearly concentrated in the sections concerned with raising production, such as human engineering. What one would by contemporary standards consider the labor relations function—dealing with problems associated with unions— was a relatively unimportant concern in the personnel department since unions did not represent many workers (less than 5 percent of the labor force), and the range of issues over which they had influence was limited. This would change with the new circumstances of the depression, as would the relative position of these units within the personnel department.

The Rise of Industrial Relations, 1935–1960

The tremendous economic decline associated with the Great Depression removed many of the pressures that had brought the personnel function to its position of influence. With the drop in demand, there was little pressure to increase production through productivity gains; with the increased unemployment it was no longer as difficult to meet manpower needs. Pressure to cut labor costs could be met by simply cutting wages. Meanwhile, the firm faced more pressing problems from other aspects of the environment brought about by the collapse of product demand and prices. Interest in the personnel function therefore declined.

That decline was short-lived, however, and ended in 1933 with the rising challenge from the trade unions. The challenge came for several reasons. First, the system of welfare capitalism could no longer protect workers in these new economic circumstances, and they looked for an independent influence on the employment relationship. Second, the birth of the Congress of Industrial Organizations (CIO) provided a new and more appropriate vehicle for organizing workers in the mass production industries that had become the backbone of the economy. Third, and most important, the New Deal encouraged the growth of unions by both the tone of the Roosevelt Administration and the legal requirements contained in the National Labor Relations Act (NLRA).

Millis and Montgomery (1945) found that trade union membership rose from less than 3 million in 1933 to 4.4 million in 1935, and then on to 13 million by 1944. The concern to management, however, was not simply the increased probability of becoming organized. The new labor movement associated with the CIO was also of a more militant type. They sought to extend union influence into a number of areas traditionally associated with management prerogatives, and they were much more inclined—and able—to engage in effective industrial disputes (Taft 1939).

The unions brought a new kind of environmental pressure to management. The payroll costs associated with union demands were an obvious pressure, but far more important was the potential instability that the labor movement brought to the operation of the firm. From the viewpoint of management the problem was that disputes were unpredictable and could occur over practically any issue. With union influence exerted on virtually every aspect of the employment relationship, it was impossible for management to predict which issues might lead to disputes and how the terms and conditions of employment might be affected.

The personnel departments moved to combat the growing pressure from union organizing at first by pursuing aggressive antiunion tactics, including organized violence and industrial espionage. When the NLRA was upheld as constitutional in 1937, and as unions continued to win recognition, these efforts decreased.

Management then responded to the growing labor unrest in both organized and unorganized shops by adopting new policies and creating new departments to handle them. Dunlop (1955) pointed out that the unions' ability to turn grievances into organizing issues forced management to make all personnel policies explicit and to centralize policy-making to prevent unions from exploiting differences in treatment. With collective bargaining came the need for management specialists to interpret and administer the technical aspects of contracts and the growing number of rules concerning work (Slichter, Healy, and Livernash 1960). The National Industrial Conference Board's (NICB) 1940 survey found that over 80 percent of firms surveyed had a union function and that half these firms had separate divisions just to handle union problems. Union relations, they found, was already one of the most important personnel functions. Dietz (1940) argued that it was assuming a very important position with top management. By 1946 the NICB's new survey found that seven out of eight personnel directors in major manufacturing firms reported directly to the company president. These departments were growing for another reason as well: to keep track of new legislative requirements associated with unionization. The additional wartime regulations further increased the responsibility of these departments.

These new departments sought to address the problem of labor unrest and to bring stability to labor relations. They did so by substantially altering management's approach to labor policies. Perhaps the most revealing insight into the management changes comes from the Golden and Parker (1955) study, *Causes of Industrial Peace under Collective Bargaining*. Their list of these changes in strategy included the following:

1. The full acceptance by management of collective bargaining and unions.

2. The view that a strong union is an asset to management, so the workers' allegiance to their union must not be alienated by a company.

3. Widespread union-management consultation and information sharing.

These changes by management were based on the recognition that the problems of labor unrest stem from worker demands and that the union could be a stabilizing influence on these demands. Strong unions and union leaders can control their membership and bring the firm stability in industrial relations, albeit for a price. Given that the existence of unions was seen as inevitable, management worked for stability in labor relations by cooperating with and stabilizing the position of union leadership in hopes that stable labor relations would result. By taking this position of course the industrial relations specialists in management were also working to secure their own position within the management hierarchy. Stabilizing the unions meant that they were more likely to survive and to continue bringing the pressures on management that led to the rise of the labor relations staff in the first place (obviously, if the unions disappeared, so would the need for labor specialists in management). Further, by stabilizing the unions' functions and the position of their leaders, labor relations managers ensured that they would continue to be able to deal with union pressures in their own expert way, a manner that provided stability for the firm and enhanced the unit's position within management. Thus the symbiotic knot was tightened.

In practice this new relationship involved the creation of new institutions for handling conflict and new rules for governing employment policy. Slichter, Healy, and Livernash (1960) provide the most thorough guide to these arrangements. They emphasized the importance of grievance procedures and arbitration for resolving conflicts while maintaining stability and of collectively determined rules, such as seniority provisions, that help reduce the sources of conflict. Many of these arrangements help to consolidate the union's control over its members. The dues check-off and other forms of union security are perhaps the most notable examples, but union control over training programs and promotion through seniority arrangements gave the union power over its members, helping the leadership guarantee stability. In contract negotiations new developments such as pattern bargaining protected the political interests of both the union leaders and the management negotiators by providing a settlement criterion that avoided strikes and a settlement level that allowed both sides to appear as though they had done a good job. The development of long-term contracts, cost-of-living escalators, and other wage-adjustment formulas were additional innovations that increased stability. Later the development of productivity bargaining served much the same role, allowing management negotiators to win contract changes that the firm demanded while giving the unions something in return to take back to their members.

Management achieved the stability it sought in labor relations but did so at the cost of narrowing its prerogatives (Slichter, Healy, and Livernash 1960). Within the personnel function, for example, there usually existed separate menagement divisions assigned to propose and implement policy on manpower, safety and medical issues, training, wages and benefits, and so on. Following the rise of collective bargaining, these issues were no longer set by management but were determined jointly with the union. One consequence of this development was that it tremendously increased the power of the labor relations subunit within the personnel function, for it now had an additional role in developing policies that in the past had been set unilaterally by other personnel subunits.

The narrowing of management prerogatives had an adverse impact on firms' operating costs. Adapting to changes now became a more time-consuming and costly affair, as the union had to be consulted when new equipment ws brought in or when jobs were changed, and so on, and issues frequently went to arbitration. Union influence on work rules generally led to practices that reduced flexibility and productivity. Taking a harder line may have led to fewer restrictive rules, but it also would have increased the risk of industrial disputes. (Northwest Airlines, for example, has historically pursued such a policy and has experienced both a lower level of restrictive practices and a higher level of industrial disputes.) By contemporary standards the years from 1940 through the 1960s have represented a period of comparative economic expansion, especially for the manufacturing sector. Industrial disputes in periods of expansion were very costly actions because the loss of production translated into lost sales opportunities (Hazard 1957) (note the similarity with wartime periods). Slichter, Healy, and Livernash (1960, 946) concluded from their case studies that the costs of industrial disputes in that period led management to yield on many of these issues: "The pressure for concessions (from management) was increased by the war and by large profits of the post-war boom, which made managements extremely reluctant to lose production."

They went on to argue that the goal of maintaining production and achieving stability in labor relations had in some ways supplanted the goal of winning contracts favorable to management: "Company operating executives or industrial relations executives did not want their records marred and their chances for advancement jeopardized by labor trouble. A stoppage of production would look bad on their record. . . ."

Another cost associated with unionization is the higher wage and benefit costs represented by the union differential. There is evidence indicating that the union wage differential increased through the period of union growth, from the 1930s through the 1950s (Douglas 1930, Lewis 1963). (See Rees 1974 and Freeman and Medoff 1981 for later estimates of union wage differentials.) But the impact of the union differential on the firm's competitive position depended on how much of the associated costs could be passed on to consumers, and that in turn depended on whether competitors are also paying the union rate.

Commons (1919) noted the benefits that unions gained by being able to organize an entire product market, thereby taking wages out of competition. In the mass production industries—even where the product markets were extremely competitive—unions were able to organize virtually the entire industry and to enforce a common wage rate through pattern bargaining (Seltzer 1951, Maher 1961, Eckstein and Wilson 1963, Levinson 1964). Wages became a common cost for firms, and an increase in the union rates in the industry therefore did not increase the relative production costs in any given firm and threaten employment prospects. In the regulated transport industries this process was formalized, and the Interstate Commerce Commission and Civil Aeronautics Board adjusted prices to cover the higher labor costs associated with union settlements.

Even where the industry was not completely unionized, a number of factors kept the union differential from imposing a severe burden on organized firms. First, the U.S. economy had a much more regional character than it does today; industries tended to be concentrated geographically (in the northeast and industrial midwest), making them easier to organize. The rise of the nonunion, industrial sun belt was yet to come, and most important, regional manufacturers tended to serve their own markets and not to compete with the larger, unionized firms. There were always nonunion, organized packers in the meat industry, for example, but until recently they served small, regional markets. The economy was also relatively closed to lower-priced non-union competition in the form of foreign imports, a situation that would change with the development of exporting industries in Asia and with the various currency reform programs.

Finally, firms are thought to be more able to pass costs on when the demand for products is increasing. This was generally the case from the 1940s through the 1960s, and the belief that the inflation during this period was driven by demand contributes to this view (Samuelson and Solow 1960).

As unions increased their influence, the power and position of management professionals dealing with unions also increased. A 1944 survey found that most firms were planning to strengthen their employee relations function after the war (Connecticut Life 1944). By 1952 a Bureau of National Affairs (BNA) survey found that, in about 70 percent of the large firms surveyed, the personnel-industrial relations function was thought to be as important to the firm as production, marketing, or finance (BNA 1952). In over 80 percent of the firms contract negotiations were viewed as one of the most important personnel functions—if not the most important. (In contrast, the 1929 NICB survey found that only 5 percent of the firms surveyed even had labor contracts.) A follow-up survey in 1959 found that the position of these departments had increased: "it is difficult to avoid the conclusion that in prestige, acceptance, and authority, the Personnel/Industrial Relations department stands at a higher level today than it did at the beginning of the decade" (BNA 1959, 13).

Within the general field, the units handling union negotiations continued to rise in power and position. The annual surveys conducted by Yoder and Nelson (1950 to 1959) found that even the titles were changing; from personnel director to industrial relations director, reflecting the new influence of union relations. Just as the rise of manpower issues during World War I brought forth personnel journals and training programs, the rise of union issues between the 1930s and 1950s led to the founding of schools or centers of industrial relations in the major industrial states and to journals of industrial relations (*Industrial and Labor Relations Review* in 1946 and *Industrial Relations* in 1961).

Union growth in the private sector slowed and then stopped in the late 1950s, but the industrial relations groups had by then stabilized their relationship with the unions and strengthened their position within the firm. The movement toward greater predictability of relations and the maintenance of stability apparently continued as indicated by a survey of labor relations executives conducted by the Conference Board in 1978 (Freedman 1979, Kochan 1980). That survey found that the labor relations function had become highly centralized. Ninety-two percent of all firms placed primary responsibility for developing overall policies at the corporate level—in the hands of either the top labor relation executives (60 percent) or the chief executive officer (32 percent). Indeed, most corporations had clearly established procedures and well-defined areas of responsibility for preparing for negotiations, establishing targets for agreements, coordinating strike plans, and so on. These arrangements again helped reduce the uncertainty and unpredictability of collective bargaining.

Further evidence of management's concern with stability in industrial relations can be seen from another aspect of the survey that asked these executives to assess the effectiveness of various aspects of the industrial relations function in their firm. The respondents gave the highest effectiveness ratings to the aspects of their work that reduced conflict; the ability to avoid "unnecessary" strikes, the avoidance of legal maneuvering, the ability to coordinate labor policies within management, and to cooperate with the union. They assigned lower effectiveness ratings to specific bargaining outcomes, such as the ability to achieve management goals, or to their ability to introduce changes. The lowest level of effectiveness was reported for aspects of the employment relationship that concern individual workers, such as attitudes and productivity issues. (Not suprisingly, few efforts were reported underway to address problems associated with attitudes and productivity.)

Responses to questions about bargaining goals reinforced the view that management's primary concern in negotiations was to maintain the status quo, to secure the stability of their relationship with unions, and to seek necessary changes in an incremental fashion. The wage criteria given the greatest weight in the survey were comparisons, either with industry patterns or other competitors. The predominant nonwage goal was to maintain their present relations with unions. This was given a higher priority than achieving substantive changes benefiting management. The only exception was in the area of employee job assignment where management sought to tighten their control over existing procedures.

Through the late 1970s management continued to pursue stability in its relations with unions. It made further adaptations to unionization and collective bargaining by formalizing its internal procedures and decision-making structures and by pursuing bargaining goals that minimized the chance of conflict. These arrangements contributed to the stability of the unions, their leaders, and to management's relationship with them. At least in the highly unionized firms the labor relations function continued to enjoy considerable autonomy and influence. There were a number of important changes occurring in the firms' environment, however, that set the stage for a transformation in the personnel-industrial relations function and in the relative position of the labor relations group within it.

The Resurgence of Personnel, 1960–1980

While the industrial relations professionals were pursuing stability in collective bargaining, a gradual expansion and increase in the power and importance of the personnel functions outside of industrial relations occurred across most large corporations. The growth of personnel during this period is largely attributed to the increase in government regulations, the growth in demand for workers who were outside the traditional scope of collective bargaining (managers, professionals, and technical employees), and the emergence of nonunion options for new plants and firms. The latter development was both caused by and spurred on by the use of advanced personnel-behavorial science techniques to structure personnel systems in nonunion plants. These developments will be reviewed in turn later.

Perhaps the most important force for change in the personnel-industrial relations function in the period since 1960 has been the rise of government regulations in the workplace. This view is confirmed by a 1977 Conference Board survey of personnel executives. Two-thirds of the 673 respondents cited government regulations as "a major or primary influence for change in their company's personnel management over the past ten years" (Janger 1977, 2). Dunlop (1976) estimated that between 1960 and 1975, the number of regulations administered by the U.S. Department of Labor tripled—from 43 to 134. The most important of these regulations were those dealing with employment discrimination. Although Title VII of the Civil Rights Act of 1964 was the basis of the employment discrimination legislation, the pressures on firms continued to increase through the 1960s and 1970s as the Equal Employment Opportunity Commission, the Office of Federal Contract Compliance (responsible for enforcing Executive Order 11246 governing affirmative action requirements of government contractors), and their state-level equivalents developed regulatory and enforcement procedures. Throughout this period consent decrees concerning discrimination and the litigation that came with them increased both in number and complexity.

Virtually all employers were affected by some aspect of these laws and regulations. Failure to comply raised the possibility of costly litigation, potential penalties, and the loss of government contracts. Employers responded to these pressures by changing their organizations, in particular by establishing a unit or group with responsibility for monitoring compliance with these government regulations. Typically, this unit fell within the personnel function. The 1977 Conference Board survey found that 97 percent of the firms surveyed had an EEO unit and that 95 percent of these firms assigned that unit to the personnel function (Janger 1977, 38).

Meeting the government requirements and establishing programs of affirmative action required new levels of analytic sophistication. Employers had to survey the requirements of their jobs, identify the relevant characteristics of their labor force and of the outside labor pool, and establish a plan for meeting both the affirmative action plans and their own manpower needs. Research by the firm focused on rates of turnover and promotion, on recruitment procedures and success, and on forecasts of future manpower needs—information that would later be useful for manpower planning. Furthermore these programs had to be coordinated with general business plans (e.g., projectd growth rates), a process that laid the foundation for the advanced forms of human resource planning currently used in many large corporations (Walker 1980).

Legislation also appeared in other areas, especially occupational safety and health and pension reform. Again these regulations raised the possibility of penalties and litigation for noncompliance. They also increased the need for substantial data collection. Once more these responsibilities were allocated to the personnel function. Ninety percent of the firms in the 1977 Conference Board survey reported that pension management fell within the responsibility of the personnel department, while 72 percent indicated that health and safety programs were housed within the personnel function (Janger 1977, 38).

The pressures on management from government regulations led first to the establishment of specialized boundary units to administer relations with the government and later to increased importance for these units as the regulations grew. The results from the Conference Board survey are supported by responses to another survey conducted by O'Reilly and Anderson (1981). They found that between 1973 and 1978 clerical staff increased by 114 percent and professional staff by 83 percent in the personnel departments of Fortune 500 firms, the additional employees coming largely to handle increased government regulations.

Studies by Foulkes (1975) and Burack and Miller (1976) also found that the management units responsible for handling government regulations had increased in importance. Our own current research on changing practices in industrial relations reinforces the view that these units were becoming more important than those concerned with labor relations. The director of industrial relations for a major defense contractor put it as follows:

> It used to be that labor relations was the elite part of industrial relations. This was because it was the only aspect of the business that could shut down the operation. This is no longer so. With the growth of ERISA, EEO, and other government regulations, the rest of industrial relations has grown in importance so that now there is little innovation coming from labor relations.

The power and influence of personnel units grew during this period for another reason; they had the skills to meet a new set of manpower problems that developed first in the 1960s. The structure of the U.S. economy began to shift away from the established manufacturing sector and toward more technical fields, such as those associated with the space race, advanced communications, and defense systems, and toward service industries. With this change came an increase in demand for technical, managerial, and professional workers relative to the demand for unskilled workers. As skills became more differentiated, workers became less interchangeable, and shortages in particular areas became more common. Furthermore many of these jobs required firms to make substantial investments in individual workers who then became very costly to replace. In short, technical and professional manpower became a real problem for firms, and the skills needed to solve these problems were exactly those that personnel departments had developed to deal with government regulations, manpower planning, training and development.

Because performance in these new jobs was more dependent on the individual worker, the previous systems of personnel administration based on a collective approach became less appropriate. Positions became more difficult to supervise and performance standards more difficult to establish as individual employee ability and motivation became more crucial to performance. A more useful approach to personnel was one oriented toward the interests and concerns of workers as individuals. Personnel executives with backgrounds in psychology and the behavioral sciences were more suited to these new approaches than were those with backgrounds in labor relations. Janger (1977, 13) notes that the problems of manpower and the individual orientation toward work increased the importance of the personnel units in the general employee management function:

A possibly equally significant change [in addition to the effects of EEO legislation] in the corporate work force has been generated by the growth, disposition, and the more sophisticated technological requirements of the company. The resultant mix of levels, skills, and localities produces a heterogeneous mix of groups and individuals. . . . Managing diversity—especially diversity in people—makes the personnel job significantly more complex and more critical.

While the other aspects of personnel-industrial relations were finding new responsibilities and influence, the labor relations function was undergoing a secular decline. The main reason for this change was that the pressure from unions had declined. By the late 1970s union membership had fallen from a peak of 33 percent of the nonfarm labor force in the mid-1950s to approximately 24 percent. This occurred despite the rise of public sector unionism. Thus the decline in private sector unionism is steeper than the aggregate union membership data suggest. On average therefore firms were less likely to have to deal with unions. More important, the industrial distribution of the organized sector was changing: the newest industries, the newest firms in existing markets, and the newest plants in existing firms all tended to be nonunion. In other words, it was no longer the case that unions were an inevitable fact of life, and the call for management to accept their existence, as exemplified by *The Causes of Industrial Peace* in 1955, no longer seemed necessary. Firms were successfully pursuing nonunion options. Indeed, one-third of the partially unionized firms in the Conference Board survey of labor relations (mostly those with less than a majority of current employees unionized) indicated that preventing additional organizing ranked as a higher priority than achieving favorable results in collective bargaining (Freedman 1979). As will be noted later, the incremental growth of the nonunion sector throughout the 1960 to 1980 period laid the foundation for the fundamental transformations in the personnel-industrial relations units that appear to be occurring in the early 1980s.

The Current Transformations

The possibility of maintaining nonunion operations combined with the rise of psychology-based, individual-oriented personnel policies gave management a new method for avoiding unions, an alternative to the labor relations approach. Since the 1960s there has been an increase in the application of psychology-based organizational development (OD) programs (Beckhard 1969, Schein 1969), work organizational innovations (Walton 1979, 1980), and comprehensive personnel policies (Foulkes 1980). The adoption of these innovations has helped firms establish and/or maintain nonunion operations. In contrast to the labor relations approach of supporting the position of the union and stabilizing its relations with management, these new approaches seek to bypass or substitute for the union and establish direct communications between management and workers. In addition to matching the benefits secured by unions through collective bargaining, they are also concerned with the organization of work, the leadership style of supervisors, the involvement of individual employees or small groups in decision making, and other worker concerns. These techniques have grown to the point where they constitute a competing system of industrial relations (*Business Week* 1981).

Given the fit between these new behavioral science strategies, the pressures from labor markets and government regulations and the union avoidance side "benefits" that they helped produce, it is not surprising that these new approaches gained increasing acceptance and approval among top executives. Indeed, these efforts began to develop an internal momentum of their own, as top executives recognized their potential for developing an organizational climate or culture that both attracted the high-level managerial and professional talent needed to prosper and embedded a strong humanistic dimension in the firm's personnel policies. In short, top executives were given the technical tools needed to create an organizational culture that was congruent with the ideas being promoted by the leading management theorists of the time (McGregor 1961, Argyris 1964, Likert 1967). By the end of the 1970s the commitment of some of these firms had escalated to the point where some management researchers have argued that they are now permanently embedded within the culture of these firms (Foulkes 1980, Ouchi 1981). To the extent that this is true, the policies of these "strong culture firms" may be less responsive to short-run changes in external environmental pressures than those firms where top management has not fully internalized these values and diffused them throughout the organization. While no systematic data exist on the extent to which these innovations have diffused across firms and industries, there is sufficient case study (Foulkes 1980) and causal data available to suggest that they are primarily concentrated in the same type of "cutting edge" firms that Millis and Montgomery (1945) noted were the heaviest users of the union substitution policies of the 1920s, namely the largest, fastest growing, and most profitable firms and industries.

The spread of these programs has generally contributed to the decline in power of the traditional industrial relation unit, since typically this unit lacked the expertise to develop and the inclination to adopt these innovations within established bargaining units. Indeed, industrial relations managers were often cited as major opponents of work innovation programs in the 1970s because these efforts threatened to disrupt stable relationships that had been developed over the years between the industrial relations managers and the union representatives. Perhaps the best example of this internal conflict between industrial relations and personnel that occurred during the 1970s is found in the experience of General Motors in its efforts to develop a quality of working life program:

GM's traditional-minded chief labor negotiator, George B. Morris, Vice-President for Labor Relations, saw QWL as a surrender of management powers. . . . As a concession to both Bluestone [the union vice-president who supported the program] and Stephen Fuller [the vice-president of personnel], Morris agreed to a letter of understanding with the UAW. In it, he recognized the "desirability of mutual effort to improve the quality of work life," and agreed to a joint Committee to Improve the Quality of Work Life with responsibility for reviewing and evaluating all QWL programs. The Committee . . . met only occasionally in the first years of its existence. The failure of the Committee to pursue actively any QWL programs was due to the suspicion with which Morris viewed the notion of QWL. (Spector 1981, 7)

By the early 1980s this particular conflict had played itself out at General Motors. The vice-president of labor relations retired and was replaced by the former director of the quality of working life program for the corporation, not by an individual whose career had been concentrated within the industrial relations function. In turn the quality of working life program was then made part of the director of labor relations' responsibility in recognition of the close interdependence between union management relations and the quality of working life improvement efforts.

The pressure to develop new innovations such as QWL helped bring other aspects of the personnel function into areas traditionally the prerogative of the labor relations group. Continuing changes in the environment, however, were at the same time threatening the long-term prospects of the stable system of union relations that had become associated with the labor relations function.

First, as noted earlier, the fundamental assumption of the system of stability—that unionization should be accepted as inevitable—was no longer valid. Even in the most organized industries, many multiplant firms were maintaining or developing some nonunion operations. The ability to develop and maintain unorganized plants had a great deal to do with the aggressive industrial development programs in the right-to-work states.

Second, this nonunion presence contributed to a reduction in the cost that industrial disputes presented to firms. By maintaining some nonunion capacity, firms could maintain at least some production during strikes, a development that was accentuated in some cases by new technology that can be kept in operation by supervisory staff. Thus firms may be able to maintain more capacity during industrial disputes than in the past. Because product markets have been considerably weaker in the recession-filled 1970s and 1980s, firms have not been under as much pressure to keep production up. Lost sales opportunities are not as great when production is halted because of industrial disputes, and therefore the losses and uncertainty associated with potential disputes are less of a burden to the firms. The benefits provided by the system of stability associated with the labor relations unit, however, are not as great as in the past.

More important, the costs of the stable labor relations system have been increased by the more competitive economic environment of the 1980s. Firms now are less able to pass on to consumers the higher costs associated with this labor relations system. One reason is that product markets generally have been weaker, and with excess supply/capacity, price competition tends to increase. Thus labor costs are no longer "taken out of competition" because the unions have no longer "organized the entire product market." Part of the reason is, as noted earlier, that even unionized firms have successfully maintained nonunion plants. Yet even where domestic industries remain substantially organized, such as rubber and autos, the product market may not be fully organized because low-wage foreign competition is taking an increasing share of the domestic product market. It is no longer possible, for example, for U.S. auto makers to pass on common labor costs to consumers when consumers can purchase lower-priced foreign cars. And in the transport industry, deregulation efforts have produced a similar effect because prices no longer necessarily rise to cover higher labor costs. One result of this increased pressure on labor costs has been that operating management has focused its attention more directly on labor relations and human resource management issues.

In short, the environment associated with labor has changed. The pressure associated with unions and industrial disputes has declined, and with it, the benefits associated with the system of stability. Changes in outside environmental factors, meanwhile, have vastly increased the costs associated with that system. In many cases these costs led to pressure from top management to get out from under this system.

One option open to firms was to press for nonunion status through decertification or reorganization of facilities. Clearly these were areas where the labor relations unit has no expertise nor, one might think, any inclination to participate. The human resource groups, on the other hand, have exactly the skills necessary to develop programs that keep unions out. The other option was to pursue changes through the collective bargaining system. Management needed to secure fundamental changes in existing relations. These changes are typified by concession bargaining (Cappelli 1982) that departs from the system of incremental adjustment associated with the labor relations approach of the 1960s and 1970s. They cut across the primary goal of the labor relations staff because they are likely to cause instability.

The labor relations units were already suspect by top management for having helped produce the system perceived to be the cause of current problems. Further their approach to labor relations was based on support of the union leaders and an incremental approach to changes. Information from the Sloan case studies indicates that in some firms the labor relations staff tended to argue initially that it was not possible to secure the changes that top management wanted. As a result a number of firms have formed new management teams or task forces involving operating managers, financial and strategic planning experts, human resource staff, and in some cases top corporate executives to plan and oversee concession negotiations with the labor relations staff. These groups are, for example, more willing to communicate directly with workers, seeking to change the union's position from the membership up. In some cases they are willing to confront relatively weak unions with sets of "no win" options (e.g., concessions or massive unemployment). In other cases, where unions represent a higher proportion of current workers, management has offered, in return for contract concessions, a broader agenda for union and individual worker participation (*Business Week* 1982).

Not surprisingly, the labor relations function is currently under a great deal of stress. In the airline industry, for example, where deregulation has forced these changes to occur rapidly, the top labor relations executives in 6 of the 26 major carriers were replaced in 1982. The situation varies according to the circumstances in each industry of course, and in some industries the labor relations unit has been able to secure at least some of the changes that top management desired. In virtually every case, however, some aspects of the human resource management approach were introduced—most often, direct communications with workers.

It may be too early to tell, but it would appear that these changes have fundamentally altered the position of the labor relations unit within the firm. Top management no longer shares the unit's concern with stability, and the costs associated with the unit's traditional approach no longer seem worth the benefits. The human resources management professionals and their individual-based planning and small-group participation methods seem more in line with the preferences of top management and can be more easily integrated with the firm's growing interest in strategic planning. One visible sign of this transformation is that the top executive in the firm responsible for personnel-industrial relations now tends to be given the title vice-president of human resources. Shaeffer (1982) reports that approximately 46 percent of a sample of large industrial and financial firms consider this executive to be part of "senior" management, a percentage expected to increase to 53 percent in the next five years. O'Reilly and Anderson's 1981 survey of Fortune 500 firms also found, for example, that between 1969 and 1979, 45 percent of responding firms elevated their top personnel position to the vice-presidential level.

In short, human resource management is growing in importance within most firms, the skills and methods of human resource management professionals are increasingly being carried over to the management of unionized employees, and top executives and operating managers are becoming more involved in decisions involving employment policies. While it may be too early to say which of these management groups will emerge as the dominant force in personnel-industrial relations in the future, it is clear that the distinction between labor relations, human resource management, and operating management will become increasingly blurred as firms attempt simultaneously to control production costs, increase employee communications and involvement, maintain stable union-management relations where unions exist, and avoid new opportunities for union organizing.

While these are all signs that the personnel function is gaining power and status, its position relative to other functions should not be over-stated. Despite these trends, in many organizations personnel still carries an image of lesser status, power, and importance than competing functional groups such as finance, marketing, operations, and strategic planning.

Summary

Throughout the historical periods reviewed in this chapter, firms have faced a variety of environmental pressures and have responded by creating special boundary units to manage those pressures. The position and influence of these units within the firm have varied directly with the importance of the corresponding pressures and with the unit's success in handling them. Specifically, firms have faced pressures from three areas: markets, unions, and government regulations. They responded by creating the personnel-industrial relations function and special units within it, such as labor relations and human resources management. The position of these functions within the management hierarchy has varied over time with the nature of the environmental pressures associated with them. Pressures from shortages in labor markets and the need to increase production led to the rise of a personnel function in World War I; the failure of the personnel response (welfare capitalism) in the new economic environment of the depression and the rise of labor unrest led to the creation and growing influence of the labor relations unit. Other aspects of the personnel function developed and grew in importance with the tighter labor markets for technical and professional employees and the growing government regulations of the 1960s and 1970s. At the same time the environment facing the labor relations unit began to change, and the gradual decline in pressure from the labor movement led to a gradual decline in the influence of the labor relations unit. In the most recent period a major transformation of power is under way within these units as firms cope with a confluence of environmental pressures. Growing competition and the inability of unions to organize product markets has greatly increased the costs of the system of stable labor management developed by the labor relations unit. Firms are turning to the human resources unit, to line executives, or to new labor relations professionals to develop a new set of relations with unions and individual employees. In addition the new interest of firms in strategic planning has benefited human resources groups since they have the skills necessary to participate in the planning process.

Given the many changes in the relative position of these units over time, it would be difficult to imagine that the current balance of power within management will remain stable in the future. In order to understand the changes that are likely to occur within management, one must consider the changes in environmental pressures that the firms are likely to face as well as their current internally generated policies or "cultures" that may have a certain force of their own. In general, one might expect that in industries where the labor movement is growing weaker, the labor relations unit will continue to lose power. If government regulations continue to decline in importance (or government relations are stabilized and enter a maintenance stage similar to the labor relations of the 1970s), the corresponding management unit will also lose power. Where labor markets grow more slack and firms face more immediate pressures for survival from declining product markets, one may expect the personnel-industrial relations function in general to lose influence to operating, finance, and other functional units.

More specifically, one might wonder what influence the change in management's approach to unions may have in the long run. At least some firms have abandoned the approach associated with labor relations units that stressed stability. Another potential problem area is where firms are continuing to pursue policies consistent with their long-run organizational culture but inconsistent with current environmental pressures. Will firms that have traditionally been able to maintain employment and pursue innovative human resource management strategies be forced by tougher market circumstances to abandon that approach? Again the answers depend on the nature and intensity of the future environmental pressures that firms will face and the ability of their organizational culture to withstand or adapt to these pressures.

In the next decade the durability of the human resource management systems and cultures associated with nonunion growth firms in the 1960 to 1980 period is likely to be challenged by environmental pressures, while the unionized firms attempt to merge some of the innovations developed in these systems into their existing collective bargaining relations. Meanwhile, the labor movement will undergo a reappraisal of its traditional organizing and bargaining strategies in response to the management successes of the past two decades. The interaction of these employer and union strategies and the trends in the three sets of environmental pressures reviewed in this chapter will shape the role of the personnel-industrial relations profession in the years ahead.

References

Aldrich, Howard E., and Diane Herker. "Boundary Spanning Roles and Organization Structure." *Academy of Management Review* 2 (April 1977): 277–230.

Alexander, Maguus W. "Hiring and Firing." *American Industries* (1915).

Argyris, Chris. *Integrating the Individual and the Organization.* New York: Wiley, 1964.

Balderston, C. Canby. *Executive Guidance of Industrial Relations.* Philadelphia: University of Pennsylvania Press, 1935.

Beaumont, P. B., and D. R. Deaton. "Personnel Management in the Management Hierarchy." *Management Discussion* (Winter 1980).

Beckhard, Richard. *Organizational Development: Strategies and Models.* Reading, Mass.: Addison-Wesley, 1969.

Bingham, W. V. "Management's Concern with Research in Industrial Psychology." *Harvard Business Review* 20 (1931):40.

Burack, E. H., and E. L. Miller "The Personnel Function in Transition," *California Management Review* 18 (1976):32–38.

Cappelli, Peter. "Concession Bargaining and the National Economy." In *Proceedings IRRA*, Madison, 1982.

Chandler, Alfred Dupont. *Strategy and Structure: Chapters in the History of the Industrial Enterprise.* Cambridge: The MIT Press, 1962.

Cyert, Richard Michael, and James G. March. *A Behavioral Theory of the Firm.* Englewood Cliffs, N.J.: Prentice-Hall, 1963.

Dietz, J. Walter. "New Trends in Personnel Policies." *Personnel* 16 (1940): 97.

Donald, W. J., and E. K. Donald. "Trends in Personnel Administration." *Harvard Business Review* 18 (1928):143.

Douglas, Paul H. "Plant Administration of Labor." *Journal of Political Economy* 27 (1919):544.

Douglas, Paul H. *Real Wages in the United States, 1890–1926.* Boston: Houghton Mifflin, 1930.

Douglas, Paul H. "Wartime Courses in Employment Management." *School and Society* 4 (1919):692.

Dunlop, John T. "The Growth of the Relationship." In Clinton S. Golden and Virginia D. Parker (eds.), *Causes of Industrial Peace under Collective Bargaining.* New York: Harper, 1955.

Dunlop, John T. "The Limits of Legal Compulsion." *Labor Law Journal* **27** (February 1976): 67–74.

Eckstein, Otto, and T. A. Wilson. "The Determination of Money Wages in American Industry." *Quarterly Journal of Economics* **56** (1962):379.

Foulkes, Fred. "The Expanding Role of the Personnel Function." *Harvard Business Review* **53** (1975):71–74.

Foulkes, Fred. *Personnel Policies in Large Non-Union Companies*. Englewood Cliffs, N.J.: Prentice-Hall, 1980.

Fox, Alan. *A Sociology of Work in Industry*. London: Collier-Macmillan, 1971.

Freedman, Audrey. *Managing Labor Relations*. New York: The Conference Board, 1978.

Freeman, Richard B., and James L. Medoff. "The Impact of Collective Bargaining: Illusion or Reality?" In *U.S. Industrial Relations 1950–1980: A Critical Assessment*. Madison: IRRA, 1981.

Godard, John H., and Thomas A. Kochan. "Canadian Management Policies, Structures, and Practice under Collective Bargaining." In Morley Gunderson and John C. Anderson (eds.), *Union Management Relations in Canada*. Reading, Mass.: Addison-Wesley, 1982.

Golden, Clinton S., and Virginia D. Parker. *Causes of Industrial Peace under Collective Bargaining*. New York: Harper, 1955.

Goldner, Fred. "Division of Labor: Process and Power." In Mayer Zald (ed.), *Power in Organizations*. Nashville, Tenn.: Vanderbilt University Press, pp. 97–143.

Gospel, Howard F. "An Approach to a Theory of the Firm." *British Journal of Industrial Relations* **11** (July 1973):211.

Hazard, Leland. "Wage Theory: A Management View." In George W. Taylor and Frank C. Pierson (eds.), *New Concepts in Wage Determination*. New York: McGraw-Hill, 1957, pp. 32–50.

"Industrial Relations Programs in Small Plants." New York: National Industrial Conference Board, 1929.

Janger, Alan. *The Personnel Function: Changing Objectives and Organization*. New York: The Conference Board, 1977.

Kahler, Gerald E., and Alton C. Johnson. *The Development of Personnel Administration, 1927–1945*. Monograph 3. Bureau of Business Research and Service, University of Wisconsin, 1971.

Kochan, Thomas A. "Determinants of the Power of Boundary Units in Interorganizational Bargaining Relations." *Administrative Science Quarterly* **20** (September 1975):434–52.

Kochan, Thomas A., L. L. Cummings, and George P. Huber. "Operationalizing the Concept of Goals and Goal Incompatabilities in Organizational Research." *Human Relations* **29** (1976):527–54.

Lawrence, Paul R., and Jay W. Lorsch. *Organizations and Environments.* Cambridge: Harvard University Press, 1962.

Leibenstein, Harvey. *General X-efficiency Theory and Economic Development.* New York: Oxford University Press, 1978.

Levinson, Harold M. "Pattern Bargaining: A Case Study of the Automobile Workers." *Quarterly Journal of Economics* **74** (1960):296.

Levinson, Harold M. *Postwar Movements of Prices and Wages in Manufacturing Industries.* Washington, D.C. Study Paper No. 21. Joint Economic Committee, 86th Cong. 2nd Sess., 1960.

Levinson, Harold M. "Unionism, Wage Trends, and Income Distribution, 1914–1947." *Michigan Business Studies* **10** (1951).

Lewis, H. Gregg. *Unionism and Relative Wages in the United States.* Chicago: University of Chicago Press, 1963.

Likert, Rensis. *The Human Organization.* New York: McGraw-Hill, 1967.

Locke, Edwin A. "The Ideas of Frederick W. Taylor: An Evaluation." *Academy of Management Review* **7** (1982):14–24.

Lovett, Robert F. "Present Tendencies in Personnel Management." *Industrial Management* **65** (1923):331.

Maher, John E. "The Wage Pattern in the United States." *Industrial and Labor Relations Review* **15** (1961):1.

McGregor, Douglas. *The Human Side of the Enterprise.* New York: McGraw-Hill, 1961.

Millis, Harry A., and Royal E. Montgomery. *Organized Labor.* New York: McGraw-Hill, 1945.

"The New Industrial Relations." *Business Week,* May 11, 1981, pp. 85–98.

Organization of Personnel Administration. New York: National Industrial Conference Board, 1946.

O'Reilly, Charles A., III, and John C. Anderson. "Personnel/Human Resource Management in the United States: Some Evidence of Change." Unpublished manuscript, 1982.

Ouchi, William G. *Theory Z.* Reading, Mass.: Addison-Wesley, 1981.

Personnel Activities in American Business. New York: National Industrial Conference Board, 1940.

The Personnel Executive: His Title, Functions, Staff, Salary, and Status. Washington, D.C.: Bureau of National Affairs, 1952.

The Personnel-Industrial Relations Function. Washington, D.C.: Bureau of National Affairs, 1959.

Pigors, Paul, and Charles A. Myers. *Personnel Administration.* 9th ed. New York: McGraw-Hill, 1981.

Rees, Albert. "Strikes and the Business Cycle." *Journal of Political Economy* **60** (1952):37–82.

Rees, Albert. *The Economics of Trade Unions.* Chicago: University of Chicago Press, 1974.

Robbins, E. C. "Development of Personnel Records." *Harvard Business Review* **15** (1937):362.

"Salaries and Allocation of Duties in 150 Personnel Departments." The Connecticut General Life Insurance Company, Hartford, Conn., 1944.

Samuelson, Paul A., and R. M. Solow. "Analytical Aspects of Anti-Inflation Policy." *American Economic Review* **50** (1960):117.

Schein, Edgar H. *Process Consultation: Its Role in Organizational Development.* Reading, Mass.: Addison-Wesley, 1969.

Seltzer, George. "Pattern Bargaining and the United Steelworkers." *The Journal of Political Economy* **59** (1951):322.

Shaeffer, Ruth. *Who Is in Top Management?* New York: The Conference Board, 1982.

Simon, Herbert A. "On the Concept of Organizational Goals." *Administrative Science Quarterly* **9** (1964):1–22.

Simon, Herbert A. *Administrative Behavior.* New York: The Free Press, 1957.

Slichter, Sumner H. "The Current Labor Policies of American Industries." *Quarterly Journal of Economics* **43** (1929):393.

Slichter, Sumner H., James J. Healy, and E. Robert Livernash. *The Impact of Collective Bargaining on Management.* Washington, D.C.: The Brookings Institution, 1960.

Slichter, Sumner H. "The Management of Labor." *Journal of Political Economy* **27** (1919):813.

Slichter, Sumner H. *Union Policies and Industrial Management.* Washington, D.C.: The Brookings Institution, 1941.

Sobotka, Stephen. "Union Influence on Wages: The Construction Industry." *Journal of Political Economy* **61** (1953):127.

Spector, Bert. "General Motors and the United Automobile Workers." Harvard Business School Case 9-481-142. Boston: Harvard Business School Case Services, 1981.

Taft, Philip. "Some Problems of the New Unionism in the United States." *American Economic Review* **29** (1939):313.

Thompson, James G. *Organizations in Action.* New York: McGraw-Hill, 1967.

Thomson, Andrew W. J. "The Changing System of Industrial Relations in Great Britain: Book Review." *Industrial and Labor Relations Review* **35** (October 1981):128–129.

Van Maanen, John, and Edgar H. Schein. "Toward a Theory of Organizational Socialization." In Barry M. Staw (ed.), *Research in Organizational Behavior*, vol. 1. Greenwich, Conn.: JAI Press, 1979, pp. 209–264.

Walker, James W. *Human Resource Planning*. New York: McGraw-Hill, 1980.

Walton, Richard E. "Work Innovations in the United States," *Harvard Business Review* **57** (July–August 1979):88–98.

Walton, Richard E. "Establishing and Maintaining High Commitment Work Systems." In John R. Kimberly and Robert H. Miles (eds.), *The Organization Life Cycles*. San Francisco: Jossey-Bass, 1980, pp. 208–290.

Yoder, Dale, and Roberta J. Nelson. "Industrial Relations Budgets—1950–1959." *Personnel* **27–56** (1950–59).

6 White-Collar Internal
       Labor Markets

Paul Osterman

The American labor force increasingly wears a white collar. In 1960 the Census classified 43 percent of the work force as white collar; in 1980 the proportion stood at 52 percent. In 1900 the proportion stood at 12 percent, and as late as 1940 it was 24 percent (Kocka 1980, 19). This trend has not, of course, gone unremarked. Developments as diverse as the decline of unionization and the unemployment rates of inner city youth have been popularly attributed to the growing dominance of white-collar employment. Yet when we inquire more deeply, it emerges that very little is known about the nature, evolution, or even the definition of white-collar work.

The first difficulty is simply defining the term. Although in a colloquial sense we may understand the phrase "white collar," a little probing reveals complications. We might at first think that it denotes working with one's mind and not with machines, but this would exclude typists and computer programmers who are clearly tied to machines. We might focus upon location and distinguish between office and factory work, yet we all know that offices are staffed by employees—service workers, messengers, repairmen—whom we would not consider white collar. Some scholars shift the discussion to attitudes and distinguish white-collar workers by their identification with the goals and well-being of the firm. However, the widespread alienation of many clerical workers and the constant turnover of computer professionals cast doubt upon this strategy. We might also argue that white-collar workers are "overhead" rather than "production" employees, but bank tellers and typists for temporary help firms are production workers.

Definitional confusion has not prevented a substantial literature on the subject. Some of this research has been undertaken by labor economists, for example Freeman's work on high-level professionals (Freeman 1971), Schultz on clerical labor markets (Schultz 1962), and scattered studies of white-collar unions. However, the economics literature is not very plentiful, and most of it emphasizes the external, rather than internal, labor market. In fact there appears to be no available study of white-collar internal labor markets.

Most material on conditions of white-collar employment is found in the sociology literature. These studies, both ethnographic and quantitative, are rich sources of insight. The classics, the works of Mills (1951), Lockwood (1958), Crozier (1971), and Whyte (1956), have shaped modern images of white-collar work. However, these efforts and the sociology literature in general tends to focus on alienation, work groups, job satisfaction, and power. They provide only light treatment of topics such as unemployment, job security, wage determination, and internal labor markets. To put the problem differently, this strand of work accepts the organizational structure and career lines as given and inquires about individual adaptation. We wish to understand the nature and determinants of the structure.

This concern is given some topicality by evidence that the structure of white-collar work may be changing. For many years the wage differential between white- and blue-collar workers has steadily narrowed, but more recently the white-collar workers have shared the burden of the recession. Hence the traditional advantage in employment security enjoyed by white-collar workers may be eroding. Partially related to this development, but also growing out of other considerations, is the increasing use of temporary and part-time workers in white-collar occupations. This is occurring for relatively unskilled clerical jobs as well as for more technical occupations. Finally, the spread of microelectronics signals a wave of technological change pointing to the office of the future. Although no one is in a position to describe accurately that transformation, it already seems apparent that the nature of many white-collar occupations will be affected.

A workable grasp of white-collar internal labor markets would be helpful for understanding these developments. For example, the rules that define internal labor markets were established to allocate employment security and insecurity. Although the rising white-collar unemployment rate is partially attributable to the supply characteristics of white-collar workers, to the extent that demand considerations do play a role, then it is to the rules of the internal labor market that we must turn.

Internal labor markets constrain employers' flexibility in allocating labor. With the rules well established and enforced by custom or unionization, one strategy for increasing flexibility is to subcontract work to firms that operate under a different employment system. Hence the rise in the use of temporary help services can be interpreted as a particular response to the nature of white-collar internal labor markets.

Finally, since the path of technological change depends in significant ways on the context in which it is introduced, the nature of job security arrangements influences worker response. Formal and informal rules concerning job definition and reassignments shape the configuration of a technical innovation and also the consequences for the labor force. Hence the form that the office of the future will take depends upon the characteristics of the internal labor markets in which it is introduced.

This chapter seeks to describe and analyze white-collar internal labor markets by reporting the results of intensive interviews with Boston area employers. The difficulty in defining white-collar work, and the enormous variety of white-collar occupations, leads us to finesse the definitional question and narrow the scope of the research by examining four occupations: clerical employees, low-level managers, sales workers, and programmers. These occupations were chosen because they seem to represent fairly the range of skills, wages, and working conditions found in white-collar work.

Beyond the definitional issue another difficulty is ambiguity about career lines and progressions. Most accounts of white-collar work (and the research reported here supports this) stress the fluidity and flexibility of job ladders. The managers interviewed by Rosabeth Kanter (1978, 132) seem typical: "People in the same position disagreed among themselves about its place in the organizational career map. Twenty distribution managers identified seven routes to their jobs . . . and they imagined that there were three likely and seven rare moves from their job."

We thus find ourselves in an uncomfortable position. First, we cannot agree on a workable definition of the subject matter. We have resolved this for the moment by simply choosing to examine four typical occupations. However, even among these occupations it is apparent that there is enormous variation in employment structures and outcomes. And, to make matters worse, one characteristic that these occupations probably share is somewhat poorly laid out career paths. All of this suggests that, if we are to make sense of any empirical findings on the nature of white-collar internal labor markets, we need a framework in which to organize our thinking. Hence, before we turn to the research itself, we will first lay out such a framework.

A Theoretical Framework

Students of internal labor markets generally take the entire firm as their unit of analysis. The implicit assumption is that firms are unitary in their central employment characteristics, and hence it is appropriate to speak of *the* internal labor market of a given enterprise. The briefest reflection shows that this assumption is unfounded. In high turnover "secondary" firms there are some workers who repair machines and are treated differently than the typical worker, and in the most privileged "primary" firm marginal employees inhabit the fringes. Yet the problem of heterogeneity within the firm goes well beyond this. Most enterprises contain several different internal labor markets operating with different rules and procedures.

Once stated, the point about different job ladders within the same firm is self-evident at the level of pure description. Clerical workers, managers, and production workers may work under the same roof, but their job circumstances are quite different. The difference is not simply a matter of pay levels or job security, though these are important. Rather the industrial relations rules under which they operate differ. In some respects these employees might as well be in different firms. The issue, however, is more complicated than that since some personnel rules extend across job ladders within the same firm.

The existence of different job ladders within firms would be of only mild interest if the distribution of occupations across ladders were predetermined by technological considerations or other factors exogenous to the firm. However, to a perhaps surprising extent, firms can exercise some discretion in their employment practices. Consider the various alternatives firms can take in organizing their typing tasks. Typing can be treated as a responsibility of secretaries. In this case typing is accomplished under reasonably stable working conditions and as part of a job that has some, albeit truncated, career possibilities. An alternative is to organize large typing pools. Then the employment is likely to be high turnover, low wage, and with few advancement chances. Another alternative is to subcontract the task out to a temporary help service so that the companywide policies (such as affirmative action or job posting), which even those in the typing pool enjoy, would not apply. This range of choice thus raises the twin issues of characterizing the kinds of choices firms make and understanding the determinants of more choices.

Employment Subsystems within Firms

How might one usefully begin to think about the existence of different
internal labor markets within firms? Elsewhere I have developed a
theory of industrial relations subsystems, and I will summarize those
ideas here (Osterman 1983). The basic argument is that subsystems,
or internal labor markets, within firms can be classified as one of three
types: *industrial, craft,* and *secondary* subsystems.

In industrial subsystems employees have a limited number of ports
of entry and progress along clearly marked job ladders. Well-defined
procedures and company norms govern job security rules. Training is
provided by the firm and can be on the job or take the form of brief
courses. Limited ports of entry make interfirm mobility difficult. It is
important to realize that these arrangements extend well beyond blue-
collar work: managers work under industrial rules as do many technicians and professionals.

Craft subsystems are characterized by greater mobility and more
loyalty to the skill or profession than to the firm. The skills are not
very firm specific, and hence workers have more market power than
under industrial arrangements. Mobility, which is often penalized under
industrial arrangements, is more commonly rewarded here. Examples
of white-collar occupations that operate under craft subsystems are
computer programmers and some high-level salesmen.

Secondary subsystems contain jobs with few advancement opportunities. They lack career prospects, either within or between firms.
These jobs tend to be low skilled and poorly paid, though this is not
always the case. Most important, they lack clear linkages to future jobs.
In white-collar employment examples include many clerical occupations
and jobs such as mailroom staff and messengers.

The usage of the terms "craft," "industrial," and "secondary" differs
in important ways from conventional meanings. For example, craft
workers in our sense may not have the historical feeling of solidarity
and self-awareness about their trade which is commonly thought to
be an important attribute of craft occupations. Instead we are empha-
sizing portability of skills and flexible ports of entry. Similarly, conventional use of the term "secondary employment" often implies harsh
and arbitrary discipline and lack of industrial jurisprudence. However,
secondary subsystems in large firms are different: there are generally
personnel rules that extend across all subsystems and are oriented
toward procedures and due process.

Perhaps the most significant difference among the three subsystems lies in the nature of the training arrangements. Industrial subsystems are characterized by training conducted within the firm. The training need not be extensive, but it is under the firm's control. Hence companies have some significant degree of influence over the supply of trained workers. By contrast, craft skills are generally learned outside the firm. Firms may occasionally train workers whose jobs are organized along craft lines, but this is uncommon. The consequence is that shortages and bottlenecks for skilled labor can develop. Occupations organized along secondary lines generally lack extensive training investments by firms since these occupations entail high turnover.

In general, firms can, and often do, seek to alter their internal mix of subsystems. They may, for example, wish to transform the internal labor market of an occupation from one subsystem to another. Or, when adding new tasks to the production process, they may be able to choose into which kind of subsystem to place them. Of course, firms do not enjoy complete discretion, there are technological and market constraints that limit their freedom. There is, however, enough scope for choice that the question of how and why firms attempt to alter their mix of subsystems is an important topic. This involves understanding what attracts and repels firms to the different subsystems and what techniques are available for exercising choice.

Secondary subsystems are attractive for employers because workers can be used more flexibly than under the other two arrangements. Secondary workers are relatively powerless to resist management decisions. For example, large firms frequently employ secondary workers in jobs slated to be abolished due to technological change (Hacker 1979). Usually firms have much more flexibility with respect to staffing plans and hours of work when the jobs are secondary. Craft workers have the power to change employers, while industrial workers have union protection or a tradition of unwritten work rules. It is important to realize, however, that the firm does not necessarily desire high turnover; even in secondary positions this can be costly. What the firm seeks is a lack of career commitment and a moderate turnover level, both of which permit maximum flexibility in the design of work tasks and the deployment of the work force.

For secondary subsystems to be a feasible choice, two conditions must be met: jobs that can be learned rapidly, and an elastic supply of secondary workers available to fill them. Rapid learning is important because the expected tenure of secondary workers is low. If the job takes too long to learn, the worker may well be gone before producing useful output. However, it is important to realize that rapid learning is not always equivalent to low skill. A relatively complex job can be learned rapidly if workers coming to the firm already possess certain skills. Thus there is no reason why, in principle, work requiring a college degree cannot be organized along secondary lines. From the viewpoint of an observer standing outside the firm, certain jobs may seem highly skilled even though from the firm's perspective they may be taught in a short time and hence are appropriate for secondary rules. (Many part-time or adjunct professors are employed in universities under secondary conditions despite their possession of a Ph.D.)

Although secondary subsystems can be staffed with a work force whose personal characteristics are different than what one might expect, this arrangement is not likely to be stable. The classic secondary worker is a target earner who is not fully committed to the work force. Sporadic participation and high quit rates characterize this group. If employees in secondary jobs have different expectations, then over time unrest and either unionization or the threat of unionization will develop. Furthermore the relative stability of the firm's labor force will lead to the emergence of informal work rules and expectations that will draw the firm into the industrial system.

If secondary subsystems are often appealing, craft subsystems are generally disliked because they are prone to skill shortages and to sharp wage movements. These difficulties arise because firms have limited control over training, and hence cannot regulate the availability of skilled labor, and because the considerable mobility between firms leads to market wage setting which implies unpredictable wage patterns. But the periodic shortages and unpredictable wage movements make it difficult for firms to engage in long-range planning.

The implication of the preceding arguments is that industrial subsystems emerge for two quite different reasons: one relating to the firm's attack on craft systems and the other to workers' attack on secondary arrangements. The existence of these two very different origins of industrial subsystems helps explain some of the confusion in the literature over what welfare interpretation to attach to internal labor markets. Some industrial subsystems result from efforts of firms to transform craft arrangements into industrial ones because the latter offer the firm considerably more control and predictability. What distinguishes this kind of transformation is that the firm is gaining control at the expense of its labor force. The other case, which is quite different, is where secondary subsystems are transformed into industrial ones. In these instances the industrial subsystems represent clear improvement in the conditions of the labor force.

Firms have a variety of techniques available for altering their mix of subsystems and moving tasks from one subsystem to another. Temporary help services and subcontracting, job redesign, the creation of new job ladders and training programs, opening or closing ports of entry into job ladders, or spatial relocation are examples of available devices. The empirical section of this chapter will take up some of these in more detail. The important point for now is that such techniques are commonly used.

In summary, we have argued that it is inappropriate to regard firms as largely unitary in their employment characteristics. Rather they are composed of industrial relations subsystems that vary considerably in their rules, procedures, and employment outcomes. What lends this analysis special interest is that firms have some freedom of choice concerning in which subsystem different tasks are performed. This permits us to contemporaneously observe the emergence and transformation of internal labor markets, and hence understanding the origins of these institutions need not be purely a historical exercise.

Beyond this theoretical interest the analysis of subsystems also has practical importance. If over time the fraction of occupations organized along secondary lines increases, then we may expect to see higher turnover and more unemployment. Hence the so-called natural rate of unemployment depends, in part, upon the organization of occupations within firms. Another point is that any shift in the direction of craft organization may lead eventually to shortages of skilled workers and production blockages, a pattern already observed in several craftlike occupations. Hence decisions by firms on their subsystem structures have important implications for a range of labor market outcomes.

The Interviews

We conducted a series of interviews with managers of twelve largely white-collar firms in the Boston area. The choice of firms was dictated by considerations of access, but the industries were diversified and reasonably representative of downtown office employment.[1] However, from a national perspective financial and insurance institutions are over-represented and manufacturing firms under-represented.

For each firm we administered a lengthy questionnaire on four occupations: salespeople, low-level managers, computer programmers,
and clerical workers. These occupations were chosen because they seem
representative of the range of white-collar work. The questionnaire
mapped the job ladders for each occupation and asked a series of
detailed questions about skills, training, working conditions, wage setting, and hiring criteria. In addition we conducted open-ended interviews
to develop information on job design and the evolution of personnel
policy.

In the next section we employ the questionnaire results to determine
what the internal labor markets of the four occupations have in common
and in what ways they differ. These data will provide some of the first
quantitative information available on white-collar internal labor markets.
We will then use the open-ended interviews to study instances where
firms sought to change the internal labor market for some of the occupations. This will shed light on the dynamics of the subsystems.
Finally, we will take up the question of differences across companies
(as opposed to across occupations) and, in so doing, will identify some
major issues outside of the analysis of subsystems.

Differences and Similarities across the Occupations

Perhaps the first question one might ask about the subsystems or internal
labor markets is how open are the job ladders. An industrial-type internal
labor market is characteristically closed to the outside; one must enter
the ladder at the bottom and move up. In contrast, in the craft subsystems
entry occurs at all levels. Secondary subsystems are similar to the craft
model in this respect (though, of course, the rewards for mobility are
quite different).

A portion of the questionnaire mapped the structure of the job ladders
for each occupation. We asked the respondents to identify the top,
middle, and lowest (or entry) job in each ladder. We then asked a series
of questions about each job within the ladder including, How common
is entry into this job from outside the company? How common is entry
into this job from another ladder elsewhere in the company?

The responses to these two questions are presented in table 6.1 It is
apparent that the results for entry from outside the firm conform to
what we would expect from the subsystem analysis. Managerial occupations, the occupations which we argued most closely conformed
to the industrial subsystem model, are the most closed to outside. Only

Table 6.1
Openness of job ladders

	Sales	Managerial	Computer	Clerical
Entry from outside the firm (entry from outside is common or very common)				
Top jobs in ladder	28%	10%	40%	25%
Middle jobs in ladder	16	0	50	70
Entry from other ladders in the firm (entry from elsewhere in company is common or very common)				
Top job	0	30	0	27
Middle job	0	22	0	44
Entry job	42	77	60	50

10 percent of the firms reported that entry into the top job from the outside was common or very common, and none of the firms reported such for the middle jobs in the ladder. In contrast, computer-programming jobs, which we argued are organized along craft lines, are very open to the outside. Forty percent of the firms reported common or very common entry into the top job, and 50 percent into the middle job of the ladder. Clearly this internal labor market is far from the conventional picture. Clerical occupations, which are largely secondary in nature, are embedded in relatively open job ladders, with the ladder being just slightly less open at the top than the programming jobs and more open in the middle position. Finally, sales positions are at the managerial end of the continuum but are somewhat more open. As we shall see, sales occupations are in a transitional period, and over time we may expect to observe them moving in the direction of craft arrangements.

The basic conclusion is that there is considerable variety in the openness of white-collar occupations. Occupations within the same firm differ quite sharply in the extent to which outsiders have access to the preferred positions. From this perspective it makes no sense to speak of a uniform white-collar internal labor market; the notion of subsystems accurately describes the system.

When we turn to ease of entry from other ladders within the same firm, a different picture emerges. In analyzing the data on entry from elsewhere in the company it seems most helpful to distinguish between the entry position at the bottom of the ladder and the two higher positions. For all four occupations access from elsewhere in the company to the bottom of each ladder is quite easy. Several examples may help give a sense of how this works. Many firms have established internal training programs for computer programmers and hence recruit employees from elsewhere into the entry position of that ladder. Similar efforts are underway for sales workers. Managers are naturally recruited from within, and many low-level managers have moved up from clerical supervisory positions. Although one might not expect much movement into secondary clerical jobs, in fact it seems to happen commonly. These flows largely include people who transfer from other secondary subsystems, for example, messengers, mailroom workers, and bank tellers.

If all the ladders are open at the entry position to internal movement, they vary considerably in the ease of entry at higher levels. Programming positions easily accessible from outside the firm are essentially closed at the higher levels to inside movement. This is presumably due to technical barriers; one cannot enter as a senior systems analyst unless one knows how to do the job, and no one in the firm not part of the job ladder is likely to have the skills. Sales positions are similar in their technical requirements at higher levels and hence are also closed. Managerial and clerical positions, both of which have lower technical entry barriers, are moderately open to inside movement but not strikingly so.

In summary, the job ladders present a complex picture. Entry from the outside is common in the craft and secondary subsystems, that is, for programmers and clerical workers. Outside entry is virtually impossible for the industrial subsystem, managers, and quite difficult for salespeople. These findings cleave very closely to our expectations. When we turn to inside movement, however, complications arise. All of the occupations are very open to inside movement at the entry position. It is important here to note that the question which elicited this information asked how common actual entry was, not whether in principle it was possible. Hence there does appear to be considerable intrafirm movement in all four occupations across job ladders. The open-ended interviews confirmed this impression. Hence these white-collar occupations seem to have a common characteristic that may distinguish them from manual work, considerable intrafirm movement at the bottom of job ladders. This supports the impression of somewhat vague career patterns noted by other observers of white-collar occupations. Finally, movement at upper levels within the firm is very difficult for technical occupations regardless of which subsystem they represent, and in this case the managerial and clerical occupations (which are nontechnical) have more in common than is true along most other dimensions.

Having described the structure of the different job ladders, the next step is to examine several additional characteristics of the occupations in order to discern wherein they differ, how they are similar, and what light these characteristics shed on the nature of the subsystems. Table 6.2 contains data on each of the occupations. The notes accompanying the table explain the construction of those variables which are likely to be unfamiliar.

The first three lines of table 6.2, which contain data on compensation, turnover rates, and expected duration of employment, confirm our expectations concerning the characteristics of the different subsystems. For the entry and the top jobs in the ladder the salaries of sales, manager, and programming occupations are well above those of clerical employees. However, the annual turnover rates of programmers and clerical workers are similar and are much higher than those of the other two occupations. A similar pattern holds for expected tenure with the firm.[2] This supports the notion that turnover is high for both craft and secondary subsystems but is rewarded in the case of craft workers.

A central determinant of job structure is often thought to be the characteristics of the skills required. This argument has two parts. First, and most simply, the level of skills is expected to be higher for the better-paid occupations. This is simply due to the fact that greater rewards are required to induce the longer training period that high skills require. The argument developed earlier concerning subsystems is silent on this issue, and there is no reason to doubt the logic.

A more controversial point concerns the specificity of skills. A skill is said to be specific if it cannot be easily transferred from one firm to another. For example, a particular configuration of machines or an idiosyncratic work procedure may mean that persons trained in one firm cannot easily perform seemingly comparable tasks elsewhere. The specificity of skills is a central consideration of human capital, and by extension neoclassical, labor theory and would generally be used to explain the structure of job ladders and subsystems. For example, if skills are highly specific, then firms will be unwilling to hire from the outside into the top of job ladders since individuals so hired are unlikely to be productive. Hence, in our case, we would expect that managerial skills are more specific than computer skills since more outside hiring

Table 6.2
Characteristics of different occupations

	Sales	Managerial	Computer	Clerical
Annual compensation for entry job	$21,000	$17,895	$18,674	$9,370
Annual turnover rate	0.15	0.11	0.21	0.29
Expected number of years new hire will remain	8.5	11.7	8.7	3.9
Minimum educational level required for training[a]	4.2	3.6	3.4	1.5
Months required for average entry proficiency	22.2	14.4	8.8	5.1
Skill specificity[b]	2.7	2.2	2.8	2.9
Importance of personality[c]	2.0	2.2	2.3	2.2
Control[d]	2.0	2.0	2.2	2.6
Importance of merit in promotion[e]	0.95	0.83	0.88	0.72
Importance of merit in wage setting[e]	0.75	0.72	0.63	0.45

a. A score of 1 indicates less than a high school diploma, 2 a high school degree, 3 a community college education, 4 some four-year college, and 5 a college degree.
b. Firms were asked fourteen multiple-choice questions to which they could respond in one of four ways: always true, usually true, usually false, always false. Two questions were: If you can do the job at one company, then you can quickly perform as well at another. Although skills may seem similar, each company's procedures are so different that movement among them involves substantial retooling. The replies were coded in such a fashion that a score of 1 indicated high firm specificity and 4 no specificity.
c. This scale also results from some of the type of questions described in note b. The questions were: Personality and manner are as important as skills in this job. If a person gets along well with his fellow workers, then he is well on the road to being successful at this job.
d. This scale also results from some of the questions described in note b. The questions were: Employees can control their pace of work. Employees are often left to their own judgment as to how to handle problems. People set their own goals for each day's work.
e. In these questions the respondents were asked to estimate what percentage of wage increases were due to merit and what percentage to seniority or across the board and also the relative weights (as measured in percentages) of these considerations in affecting promotion decisions.

occurs in the latter occupation. Also, if skills are specific, then employees will be less likely to quit since they will have difficulty finding another job that fully utilizes their skills. By this logic clerical employees, with the highest turnover rates, should have the least specific skills. In contrast to this analysis, the arguments developed concerning the determinants of subsystem structure place less emphasis on technological considerations (skill specificity) and more on considerations of control and flexible deployment.

Lines three through seven of table 6.2 present data on the skills involved in each of the occupations. It is apparent that the argument concerning skill level is generally correct. Both in terms of the minimum level of education required to train successfully an entry worker and the length of time it takes to perform at an average level of proficiency on the entry job, it is apparent that clerical occupations rank distinctly lower than the other three. Hence at least this secondary occupation is lower skilled than others. The highest skilled occupation—sales—also receives the highest compensation, whereas managers and programmers, whose skill levels seem comparable, do not differ very much in salary.

However, if we turn from the level of skills and look at their nature, then it seems apparent that the skill-based explanation of the subsystem structure is weakened. The questionnaire asked a series of questions designed to measure specificity, and these were used to construct the index reported on line six. Two facts stand out. All of the occupations score on the nonspecific side of the index's midpoint. Evidently, these four occupations have fairly general skills in that they can be transferred between firms without difficulty. As we might expect, the managerial occupation is the most specific (it would involve the most idiosyncratic knowledge of the given firm); however, the differences in scores across the occupations seem minimal. Although there is no standard against which to judge these differences, it does not seem likely that skill specificity can explain differences in subsystem structure. This does not prove in any sense the alternative argument, but it tends to strengthen our confidence in it and undermine rather severely the human capital explanation.

The questionnaire probed other aspects of skill, and the four occupations also display very little variation along these other dimensions. Proficiency is more important than personality for all four occupations. However, the margin is surprisingly small. Clearly the small work groups and frequent interactions involved in white-collar employment make the ability to get along with others an important dimension of job success. The control variable is intended to measure how much initiative individuals have in carrying out their duties. The pattern of the variable follows our expectations, with clerical occupations having the least control, programming ranking just above clerical, and managerial and sales occupations displaying the most control. However, the spread among the occupations is not great.

It would appear from this analysis that, while the level of skills clearly varies across white-collar occupations, the nature of those skills shows less variation. These four, and perhaps other, white-collar occupations seem to share similar kinds of skills which are not strongly firm specific, tasks in which personality is an important attribute of skill, and roughly similar amounts of individual control over the flow of work. It does not appear that the nature of the skills involved is helpful in explaining the differences in job structure across the four occupations or three subsystems.

The final two lines of the table provide information on wage and promotion rules. Two findings stand out quite clearly. First, for all of the occupations merit is a more important consideration in promotion than it is in wage determination. Evidently, firms are more concerned with insuring that the highest quality individuals move to positions of responsibility than they are with merit considerations in pay. Second, it is evident that there are differences across the occupations with respect to the importance of merit. Merit is consistently least important in clerical work and consistently most important in sales. Merit plays a roughly comparable role in promotion for managerial and computer occupations but is clearly less important with respect to wage determination for programmers. These findings are consistent with the view that merit is most important for those occupations which are most central to the firm's success (sales) and is least important for the more peripheral occupations (clerical). The greater importance of merit in promotion than wage setting is also consistent with this interpretation.

In summary, it appears that the characteristics of the four occupations differ in ways that support the arguments developed earlier concerning industrial relations subsystems. In addition some of the similarities are also consistent with the subsystem perspective. The patterns of compensation and turnover clearly conform to our expectations. With respect to rules, the differing degrees of openness of the ladders and the role of merit considerations are consistent with our expectations. Finally, the differences across subsystems do not seem to be related to technical considerations such as the degree of skill specificity although they are related to the level of the skills involved.

To develop deeper insights into the determinants of the subsystem structure and the nature of white-collar internal labor markets, we will now turn to the question of why and how firms alter the conditions under which a given task is performed or seek to change their mix of subsystems.

The Dynamics of Change

One advantage of the concept of industrial relations subsystems is that it provides a framework for interpreting many changes in personnel policy. Most previous research on internal labor markets views current arrangements as static and more or less permanent and turns to historical analysis to uncover the sources of change. However, if one looks inside seemingly monolithic firms and distinguishes among the subsystems, the opportunity for observing change is substantially increased. Most firms are at any given time altering their mix of subsystems at the margin, and observation of this process should yield insights.

The Sources of Change

Personnel officials do not regularly evaluate their employment systems or ask fundamental questions about staffing arrangements. The day-to-day business of hiring, wage setting, dealing with the government, and handling miscellaneous problems occupies most of their time. Nonetheless, on occasion it becomes necessary to reexamine long-standing arrangements or to consider how to structure new tasks. Often the motivation for such a reconsideration lies in some of the issues—the desire for flexible deployment, unpredictable changes, technological change—which were discussed earlier.

A recurrent debate among labor economists has been whether disturbances in product markets rebound into the labor market. A clear example of such an effect occurred in the fields of financial sales and services. Traditionally, commercial lenders at banks—the people responsible for lending out bank funds to business customers—have worked in a stable and secure environment. They spent their entire working life at the same institution and managed a stable portfolio of loans. Because banks and other financial institutions operated within spheres of influence, the lenders did not require extremely high skills or aggressiveness. All of this led to organization along industrial lines.

This pattern has been shaken in recent years by the intensification of competition among financial institutions. Deregulation of financial markets and a generally heightened competitive atmosphere has led to aggressive incursion by banks into each other's territories and the entry of nonbanking institutions into markets traditionally limited to banks. The consequence is that the labor market for commercial lenders changed sharply. Skill requirements increased as lenders were forced to seek out aggressively prospects and as a consequence be both better judges of risk and better salesmen. Banks now pirate lenders from each other. This is due to a shortage of the more skilled lenders as well as to the somewhat lengthy training period (nearly two years) required to produce a competent lender. It is no longer the expectation that lenders spend their careers at one bank, and job hopping is now fairly common. In short, the market for lenders is shifting from an industrial to a craft subsystem.

What is notable about this development is that the trigger was in the product, not the labor, market. Furthermore many of the labor market arrangements have remained unchanged: despite the increasingly craft nature of the work firms continue to conduct their own training. This of course may change as the new system becomes institutionalized, and the training arrangements may come to resemble those of programmers with training conducted outside the firm.

Another striking aspect of this change is that it involves a transformation of an industrial subsystem. Implicit in most writings on internal labor markets, and indeed in much of the literature on industrial relations, is the view that the industrial pattern represents the final, or "highest and best" stage in the evolution of work patterns (Kerr et al. 1960). Yet in this case we observe the breakdown of the industrial arrangement. Furthermore there is no reason to believe that this represents in any sense a worsening in the welfare of the labor force.

A second motivation for management to shift tasks from one subsystem to another lies in shifting labor market conditions. A good example is computer programmers. Historically, programming was organized along craft lines. Programmers learned their skills in college, in proprietary schools, in programs run by manufacturers, or on their own. Little basic training was conducted by firms. Programmers moved easily from one company to another. This arrangement always posed some difficulties; for example, in earlier years programmers were casual about documentation and often insisted on working with their own idiosyncratic programs rather than developing standardized routines (Kraft 1977, Greenbaum 1979). This problem was solved by enforcing industrywide standards. However, another problem developed. Craft organization means that decisions concerning how many people should be trained lie outside the control of firms, and in recent years shortages emerged, leading to sharp wage increases. This became extremely troublesome, not simply because labor costs were rising seemingly out of control but also because turnover and shortages disrupted production.

These problems became especially difficult for firms that do not offer state-of-the-art opportunities for their programmers. These companies—particularly financial institutions—require a great deal of routine programming; yet they found themselves bidding in an open market for people who preferred more challenging positions. Thus these firms found themselves with an overqualified, high-turnover, expensive staff and also prone to shortages.

For these reasons craft organization became increasingly undesirable for many firms. The obvious solution was for firms to train their own programmers. Arguing against this was the fear that any programmer trained at the company's expense would soon leave and enter the auction. Nonetheless, as pressures built and the craft subsystem became very burdensome, firms sought to shift programming from craft to industrial organization and to do so in a way that avoided losing their trainees.

Firms proceeded to recruit internal candidates into training programs and to fill many of their programming positions from these programs. However, several steps were taken to avoid the turnover problem. Only employees who had been with the firm for several years were eligible, on the asumption that these people had demonstrated some commitment to the firm and also had developed some ties. In addition, the training and skills were truncated. Rather than teaching the full range of programming skills, the training was limited to a level necessary to meet company-specific needs for routine "maintenance" programming. These limitations reduced the attractiveness of the trainees on the outside market. Hence a combination of social selection—drawing from a different pool of people than college-trained programmers with a commitment to the profession—and truncated trained helped transform the nature of the work. Of course even in the firms that were the most successful with this strategy the higher level, or systems, programming jobs continued under the former craft system. However, the extent of that system was successfully limited.

Technological change is a third impetus for altering the subsystem patterns within firms. A good example of this is the impact of word-processing and other computer-based office systems on secretarial work. In most firms secretaries perform a variety of tasks, including typing, filing, and administrative and organizational tasks. The latter responsibilities make secretarial jobs higher skilled than other clerical work and provide firms with incentives to maintain a fairly stable secretarial work force. As a result in many firms secretarial work is organized along industrial lines, albeit with truncated ladders.

New office technologies have provided firms with the opportunity to rearrange these work patterns. In particular, word-processing and intraoffice communication capabilities enable firms to split off the lesser skilled aspects of secretarial work from the higher skilled tasks and create two categories of jobs where before there was one. The first category is a word-processing or typing pool which acts as a centralized resource for the firm, while the second group is a reduced number of administrative secretaries. This new arrangement in turn permits firms to recruit different kinds of employees for the two new jobs, with the word-processing pool taking on the characteristics of a higher turnover secondary subsystem and the secretarial group retaining its previous character. This pattern is not widespread. However, a number of firms are experimenting with it, and it seems likely to grow in importance.

In summary, we have identified several different reasons why firms might choose to alter the organization of particular tasks. Disturbances in product markets may change the kind of skills required for a job, and this may in turn transform the organization of the labor market for an occupation. In the case of commercial lenders at banks, a job previously organized along industrial lines shifted in the direction of craft work. The opposite movement is occurring in computer programming; labor market developments, in particular the emergence of shortages and rapid increases in wages, have led firms to transform craft into industrial arrangements. Finally, the nature of new office technologies has been such that firms can increase the proportion of their work force organized along secondary lines.

Thus far the discussion has detailed several techniques firms use to alter subsystems. Additional approaches are available, and a brief discussion of them will shed further light on the dynamics of change in white-collar occupations.

One very common technique is to increase the use of temporary workers. This is accomplished either through temporary help firms or by establishing a temporary help pool within the firm itself. In virtually all firms whose managers we interviewed, the volume of work asssigned to temporary workers was increasing. The use of "temps" has the advantage of avoiding any explicit or implicit commitment to the worker and is hence a clear example of a secondary subsystem. Most of these firms have recently made such extensive use of temporary workers that they are establishing their own internal temporary pool to eliminate the middlemen. In fact the circumstances where this is not being done sheds light on the motivation of the development. The few firms that have not established or are not considering their own in-house temporary services are those where a large fraction of the work force is unionized or is (in the view of management) in danger of unionization. In these cases management is reluctant to establish an internal secondary subsystem for fear that unionization will ensue. Outside agencies are seen as a safer, albeit more expensive, choice.

The use of temporary workers to shift work in a secondary direction suggests, in Braverman's (1974) terms, the desire of firms to "degrade" the occupation. This is not, however, an inevitable tendency. The interviews also turned up examples of job redesign intended to transform work away from a secondary structure. These occurred in instances where firms came to feel that the high turnover rates inherent in secondary subsystems imposed unacceptable costs. Such a perception was more common in firms with a greater than average commitment to internal promotion and training and which therefore sought to maintain a more stable than average labor force. An interesting example, and one that shows that technical innovation can result in upgrading jobs, occurred in a firm that processes insurance claims. For many years when a claim arrived, the processing was divided among several people: one person only opened mail and sorted the contents, another person would gather and assemble all of the records in the files on the claimant, and a third would use the assembled records to calculate the correct claim. When the files were computerized, the ease of information retrieval led to all of these tasks being assigned to one person. Rather than technological innovation, subdividing jobs in this instance, jobs were recombined; as a consequence turnover was reduced, and a pool of people more generally familiar with the firm's operations and procedures came to be available for promotion.

Variation across Firms

We have focused on differences among occupations and have ignored variation across firms. Such a perspective is inherent in any attempt to gain a "first-round" understanding of the topic, and indeed the subsystem perspective seems to describe successfully the central tendency among firms. Nonetheless, the interviews did develop evidence of interfirm variation.

We found examples of variation in each of the subsystems—industrial, craft, and secondary. For instance, in most firms clerical work is unstable and provides little future. Yet in a few companies the jobs are permanent and have virtually no turnover. Likewise, several companies hired high-level college-trained programmers and yet managed to avoid the extreme craft-related instability. There are also firms that have an effective internal bidding system, and hence mobility out of secondary subsystems is more likely than would otherwise be the case.

In order to understand what causes this variation across firms, it is necessary to consider a set of conditioning variables. These are characteristics of the firm's internal and external environment that modify the attempt to achieve flexible deployment, low wages, minimal supervision, and the other similar goals discussed earlier. Three such conditioning variables seem to be important: company culture, fear of unionization, and government regulation.

Perhaps the most significant of these conditioning variables is company culture. Firms seem to vary in their attitudes and philosophy concerning "human resources development," and these differences have real effects, independent of the external environment, upon employment patterns. It is important to understand that all firms have a culture. This is not a concept limited to the most innovative group of firms. For our purposes the key dimensions or attributes of the culture concern a commitment to inside promotion, resources devoted to training, and an attitude toward merit versus seniority.

A few of our firms stood out from the others in having a strong, almost overriding, commitment to inside promotion and internal training. The firms that fell into this group were extremely averse to outside hiring at any but entry jobs, and they made this work by expending considerable resources on internal training. There was also a strong sense among these firms that they offered lifetime jobs. Within this group two subgroups can be distinguished according to their attitude toward merit pay and promotion. In one, the firm is likely to be unionized or regulated, and thus operates on a strong seniority system. In the other, often high technology, the workers are nonunion, and pay and promotion are heavily influenced by merit considerations. In both, turnover is low and job ladders are available for all subsystems, but the kinds of people each firm attracts and the atmospheres of the firms do differ. To the extent that both subgroups provide lifetime jobs, they adhere to what the popular press has termed the Japanese model (although this is a misnomer since Japanese firms employ large numbers of women in secondary positions with no chance of advancement, and they also make extensive use of temporary help services; see Rehlin 1978).

It is beyond the scope of this chapter to enter into a detailed discussion of why culture differs across companies, but it is evident that no single factor provides an adequate explanation. Age of the firm, ideology of top management, industry, profitability, and the character of the union, if any, all seem important. It is not clear whether, with time, the practices of the more innovative firms will converge to the norm or whether instead the new patterns will diffuse more widely. In any case it does appear that for a few outlying firms culture influences practices concerning subsystems.

The second conditioning variable is unionization or fear of unionization. In two of the firms we interviewed clerical workers were union members, and in one other a sufficiently large fraction of the work force was unionized so as to raise the fear that clerical unionization was a possibility. These firms all made very heavy use of temporary help services in order to take advantage of secondary subsystems, but the clerical workers within the firms received better than average wages, had effective bidding opportunities for jobs elsewhere in the company, and had very low turnover rates. It is not possible to go into a discussion why these particular firms were unionized, but it is worth noting that each was in a regulated sector.

The final conditioning variable is government regulation, particularly affirmative action programs. These programs, which have been more effective than generally believed (Osterman 1982), influence the structure of subsystems largely through constraints they place on promotion paths. One common goal in government enforcement is to achieve the "appropriate" proportions of target groups within each occupation. In our context the difficulty firms often face is a shortage of women in higher-level occupations. In order to provide a defense for these shortages and, in some cases, in genuine efforts to overcome them, firms which feel themselves under pressure have introduced job posting and bidding schemes. Under these programs all jobs up to a certain level are posted, and all employees are able to apply. In principle then the job ladder for even the lowliest secondary subsystems job extends to the top of the bidding range.

Although job posting appears to change the nature of the job ladders dramatically, in practice the effect is considerably less sweeping. In a variety of ways the potential impact is mitigated. Some firms require managers to interview inside candidates but permit them to hire anyone. Other firms limit the number of jobs that must be posted. In still other firms more mundane considerations block the effectiveness of the posting system. For example, the time lag between posting and closing of jobs is so short that only through informal word-of-mouth channels are most jobs effectively available. Finally, educational and experience requirements for many jobs simply place them out of reach for low-level employees. The consequence of all of this is that job posting, which on its face is a revolutionary change in white-collar industrial relations, is most commonly a way for clerical workers to move from one clerical job to another across departments. It is a mechanism for lateral, not vertical, mobility. Having said all of this, however, there are a few firms that can demonstrate that posting has led to increased clerical upward mobility, and it is clear that in all firms affirmative action pressure has raised a set of issues and expectations and created a nascent institutional structure which may over time be of consequence.

Conclusion

We began by noting that little analysis is available concerning the internal labor market for white-collar workers. This is not simply due to absence of work but also to the enormous heterogeneity of white-collar employment, a heterogeneity which makes even definition of the subject matter difficult. Therefore we proposed a scheme for classifying the numerous occupational categories into one of three types of internal labor market or industrial relations subsystems. The interviews which were then reported had a twofold purpose. First, they provided a description of the character of the internal labor market for four occupations, a description that has hitherto been unavailable. Second, we sought to learn if the similarities and differences among the occupations' job ladders, skill structure, rewards, and other industrial relations variables corresponded to the analysis of the subsystem approach. In general, the patterns we observed were consistent with the subsystem view. Furthermore, when we examined cases where firms have sought to alter the subsystems for certain tasks, the motivation and strategy also were consistent with the broader arguments we developed. However, we did identify three considerations—company culture, unionization, and government regulation—that seem to have independent influences on the nature of white-collar internal labor markets

In some respects this analysis of white-collar internal labor markets is incomplete. There remain several issues that we cannot resolve here, but it is important to note them. The first concerns the treatment of women in white-collar employment. It should be obvious to any student of office work that women play a unique and problematical role. They are the dominant labor supply to a major category of white-collar employment—clerical work—and indeed much of the growth in total white-collar employment in the twentieth century is due to the entry of women into this area. However, women are clearly under-represented in other white-collar occupations, and there is persuasive evidence that sex discrimination plays a major role. Furthermore women are also employed in those occupations slated for significant technological change, and they are often denied the implicit employment guarantees that men receive.

Sex discrimination in fact is a significant part of white-collar employment, and the sexual division of labor in the office may serve as a useful way of distinguishing white- from blue-collar work. Having noted this, however, we cannot proceed much further. A variety of unresolved questions remain. How is the discriminatory pattern maintained in the face of labor market competition among firms? Do the discriminatory practices reflect profit maximization by firms or instead the weight of social convention and norms? Can the influx of women into the labor force be partially explained by the efforts of employers to recruit a secondary labor force for the rapidly expanding clerical occupations? To what extent is the organization of clerical work predicated upon the availability of a flexible female labor force? Do gender considerations play a role in the organization of other office occupations? How can we take into account legitimate sex-based differences in employment patterns that arise from the preferences of some women for part-time or occasional work?

It is apparent that satisfactory answers to these questions require an extensive research effort beyond the scope of white-collar internal labor

markets. Nonetheless, recognition of the industrial relations characteristics of different clusters of occupations within the firm will provide
a useful framework for examining the role of sex in allocating labor
and in shaping the organization of work. This should rightly shift the
analytical focus away from the employment preferences of individual
workers and toward the view that the organization of work is a strategic
decision made by the firm.

The second major unresolved issue concerns wage determination.
We spoke of this in passing in the discussion of merit versus seniority
in pay and promotion, but there is clearly a great deal more ground
to cover. There is an extensive literature on blue-collar wage determination which emphasizes the importance of a rigid internal wage
structure, of wage contours, and of union politics or the threat of unionization. It is apparent that in some respects the white-collar situation
is different. Unionization plays less of a role, and personal merit is
evidently more important. The frequently expressed ethic of white-
collar wage determination is that of a flexible structure, individual wage
setting, and no automatic or seniority-based increases. At the same
time, there are clear hints of other processes at work. For example,
firms participate in local community wage surveys and also make heavy
use of valuation or "point" systems, such as the Hay System, in arriving
at their internal wage structure. The fear of unionization is evident in
many cases, and this may influence wages. Considerations of bureaucratic politics may also influence wage determination and the internal
wage structure. All of this suggests that it may be fruitful to devote
more effort to white-collar wage determination.

Finally, we must confront the issue we introduced early in this chapter,
the definition of white-collar work. The point here is not to satisfy
some arid desire for definitional neatness but to see if in fact some
occupations share enough in common to merit study as a group. It
does seem clear that certain occupations are linked together in a common
personnel system. For example, job posting and the frequency of entry
at the bottom of job ladders from elsewhere in the firm leads to linkages
among the occupations. At a more general level these occupations seem
to have two characteristics in common: they are concerned with the
manipulation of people and information (as opposed to the transformation of physical material which is characteristic of what is termed
blue-collar work), and they are located in a bureaucracy. The extent
that it is possible to identify these common elements among occupations
leads us to a definition of white-collar work.

What appears to be helpful about this definition is that it points to what might be termed the "technology" of white-collar work. In blue-collar occupations the technology is the engineering process or blueprints which indicate how the physical product is to be produced. This technology plays a major role in every analysis, from neoclassical to institutional to Marxist, of blue-collar work. No such readily identified technology is apparent for white-collar work. What we suggest here is that there are two aspects to white-collar technology. One is the physical technology of information processing. As already noted, that technology is in a period of transformation. The second, and more often overlooked, strand of white-collar technology is the sociology of bureaucracy. Organizations and bureaucracies can be usefully viewed as social systems with their own requirements and rules. The definition and structure of white-collar jobs, and clusters of occupations, must be consistent with these rules of bureaucracy. Hence the nature of bureaucracy must shape white-collar work in much the same way that the nature of an assembly line shapes the jobs of auto workers. If we are willing to view bureaucratic sociology as a key aspect of white-collar technology and then move to understand its interaction with the technology of information processing, we may find that this is a helpful new way of understanding and interpreting the current shape and the future direction of white-collar work.

Notes

This research was made possible by the cooperation of the Tri-Lateral Council on Quality Education and its member firms. Portions of the research were supported by a grant from the U.S. Department of Labor. Helpful suggestions were made by Margaret Lobel, and I am grateful for the comments of seminar participants at Boston University and MIT.

1. The industries in our sample were insurance, banking, utilities, computers, and consumer products manufacturing.

2. The data on expected tenure refer to people hired from outside the firm into the ladder. In many cases some of the incumbents on a job also came from elsewhere in the firm, and their expected tenure differs from the outside hires (it is usually longer).

References

Braverman, Harry. *Labor and Monopoly Capital*. New York: Monthly Review Press, 1974.

Crozier, Michel. *The World of the Office Worker*. Chicago: University of Chicago Press, 1971.

Freeman, Richard B. *The Market for College Trained Manpower*. Cambridge: Harvard University Press, 1971.

Greenbaum, Joan. *In the Name of Efficiency*. Philadelphia: Temple University Press, 1979.

Hacker, Sally. "Sex Stratification, Technology, and Organizational Change; A Longitudinal Case Study of A.T. & T." *Social Problems* 26 (June 1979):539–557.

Kanter, Rosabeth. *Men and Women of the Corporation*. New York: Basic Books, 1978.

Kerr, Clark, John Dunlop, Frederick Harbison, and Charles Myers. *Industrialism and Industrial Man*. Cambridge: Harvard University Press, 1960.

Kocka, Jurgen. *White Collar Workers in America, 1890–1940*. Beverly Hills: Sage, 1980.

Kraft, Phillip. *Programmers and Managers*. New York: Springer-Verlag, 1977.

Lockwood, David. *The Blackcoated Worker*. London: Allen and Unwin, 1958.

Mills, C. Wright. *White Collar*. New York: Oxford University Press, 1951.

Osterman, Paul. "Affirmative Action & Opportunity; The Impact of the Contract Compliance Program on Female Turnover." *Review of Economics and Statistics* 54 (November 1982):604–612.

Osterman, Paul. "Employment Structures Within Firms." *British Journal of Industrial Relations* (November 1983).

Rohlen, Thomas. *For Harmony and Strength: Japanese White Collar Organizations in Anthropological Perspective*. Chicago: University of Chicago Press, 1974.

Shultz, George. "A Nonunion Market for White Collar Labor." In *Aspects of Labor Economics*. Princeton: Princeton University Press, 1962, pp. 107–146.

Whyte, William F. *The Organization Man*. New York: Simon and Schuster, 1956.

7

Job Training, Employment Practices, and the Large Enterprise: The Case of Costly Transferable Skills

Paul Ryan

Introduction

The internal labor markets of large U.S. manufacturing firms have been described as eminently suited to the development and utilization of job skills. The detailed subdivision of labor limits the amount to be learned on a job, frequently to minimal levels. The system of job ladders and internal promotion permits the development of skills through the informal, economical method of on-the-job training, while the rules that price and allocate labor within the enterprise ensure the willingness of incumbent experienced workers to train their juniors by removing the threat the latter might pose to their job security and earnings. The provision and finance of job training is then a matter of little concern, as the skills in question can generally be learned rapidly as part of the performance of job tasks without incurring significant loss of output—a process described vividly by Piore as "osmosis" (Piore 1968, Doeringer and Piore 1971).

The degree to which training is without cost has, however, been exaggerated. Training costs for mainstream production and office work do indeed commonly lie well below levels suggested by indirect estimates based on the pattern of earnings over an individual's life cycle (Mincer 1962). At the same time investments in job skills exceed significantly the negligible magnitudes inferred both from the studies referred to here and by those who hold the formation of enterprise internal labor markets to be unrelated to skill and training requirements (Stone 1973).[1] The presence of non-negligible training costs does not, however, in itself threaten the provision of skills. The very subdivision of labor creates in job skills a strongly enterprise-specific or idiosyncratic content which, along with its presumed institutional embodiment (the seniority provisions of the upgrading system), discourages the turnover of experienced workers and makes it feasible for the employer to finance at least in part the costs incurred during the period of training without placing its investment in jeopardy (Becker 1964, Doeringer and Piore 1971). The result is a system of skill development in U.S. manufacturing which is by European standards remarkably informal, rapid, and economical.

However, not all the skills used by large employers can be fitted into this description. In a significant number of cases, even where labor is fully subdivided, training for a skill remains a protracted affair, the value of output during training stays low (and training costs high) for long periods, while the resulting skills and knowledge prove highly transferable between firms. In manual work such situations arise in two contexts. First, there are the craft specialists such as maintenance and tool room workers whose advanced skills and long training provide the preconditions for the low-skill levels required of the mainstream production work force. Second, there is an important category of production work itself—jobs such as those of metal and wood machinists, sewing machine operators, and welders where the limited level of mechanization leaves a requirement for manual dexterity that can be developed fully only with extended practice and experience. It is this manual knack, common to all uses of the skill, that endows it with a high degree of transferability.

In the nonmanual area the skills of typists and office machine operators provide analogies, although the learning period is distinctly shorter than for the manual skills. The nonmanual occupations add a further dimension to the category: jobs that require a considerable degree of vocational knowledge in addition to practical work experience. The work of technicians, computer programmers, and lower professional workers requires a significant period of prior vocational schooling so that training for such jobs will also be marked by significant costs, while the role of the school suggests that the resulting knowledge and skills are likely to be highly transferable between employers. In all of these instances the picture of job training as short, informal, cheap, and employer-specific falls down in one or more respects.

The chapter will analyze the provision and finance of training for such skills, in particular for production jobs in large enterprises. A significant volume of employment is involved. Roughly one in every eight workers (12.1 percent) falls into the categories machinist, tool-maker, welder, mechanic, sewing machine operator, baker, secretary, typist, computer programmer, or technician (U.S. *Census of Population*

1970, PC(2)-7A, table 1). Moreover, when employers have complained of skill shortages, often one or more of these occupations has been involved. Little attention has been paid by economists to the problems arising when, even after management attempts to subdivide labor to the maximum consistent with the particular technology and product, the production process still requires many workers whose training is long and costly and whose skills and knowledge are highly transferable to other firms.[2] As they take a considerable length of time to master, the manual skills in question may be described as quasi craft. Indeed they constitute a significant subset of the skills and knowledge of the worker in craft forms of the internal labor market.[3]

It will be argued that the provision of training for costly transferable skills is directly affected by the wage structures of enterprise internal labor markets. In this chapter I discuss (1) the provision and finance of training in the absence of wage rigidity, (2) the origins of a wage structure whose flexibility is constrained by considerations of equitable payment and maintenance of bargaining power, (3) the implications of wage rigidity for the provision of training, with particular reference to the role of proprietary and state schools, and (4) the implications of the analysis for the quality of job training and economic performance.

The absence of comprehensive measures of the costs of training or the transferability of skills will inevitably restrict much of the discussion to the formulation of hypotheses to be checked against what limited data are available. Evidence will be drawn primarily from survey data and secondary sources, but reference will be made frequently to a case study of employer-sponsored training for a costly transferable skill, a study that generated many of the hypotheses that this chapter attempts to evaluate with more broadly based evidence. The training program in question involved the welding of heavy gauge steel plate as part of the fabrication of large tanker ships in a major U.S. shipyard during the 1970s. An outline of the economics of the training program can be found in Ryan (1980). For present purposes it is sufficient to establish, first, that the skill involved did indeed take a considerable time to master. After six to eight weeks of supervised practice in a vestibule school, at least one further year of production experience was required in order for a worker to attain experienced levels of proficiency. Second, training costs were substantial. The long duration of low net output during training imposed an average cost of training (to both firm and trainee) of more than $5,500 ($1975) per trainee, a cost at that time borne in its entirety by the employer. The welding skills produced were also highly transferable to other employers. The rate of voluntary turnover among welders who had recently joined the ranks of the experienced ran at the rate of 68 percent per year in a time of severe recession. Finally, the shipyard's welders were indeed caught up in an enterprise internal labor market, with the rules governing their pay and job movement decided in a plantwide collective bargaining agreement. The internal market was, however, of the open, not the closed, variant: welders were commonly hired from the external market at all levels of proficiency from the Beginner's hourly rate of $3.99 to the Mechanic First-Class rate of $5.26. Moreover the internal market was by no means located in the primary segment of the external labor market. The job rewards of experienced welders were widely perceived as lying toward the low end of the distribution in the market for experienced welders due to the adverse working conditions of a shipyard environment. To the extent therefore that the shipyard typifies any slice of the broader labor market, it is the lower rather than the higher end of the primary segment.

The Provision and Finance of Training in Competitive Theory

The analysis of training for costly transferable skills can best begin with the implications of orthodox theory, with its assumptions of competitive markets and wage flexibility. The injection into such a model of a wage structure dictated by institutional rather than market-clearing considerations will be seen to change drastically its implications for the provision of job skills.

Training in job skills may occur in a school (formal training) or as part of productive work (informal training, including simple learning by doing). The agent involved in providing the training may be the employer, a state school system, the military, or a technical institute or a correspondence school. Competitive theory treats the source of training as a matter of secondary interest, determined by the relative efficiency of learning in the various possible environments (notably school versus job-based training). What is of interest in competitive analysis is the issue of finance, a matter wholly distinct from that of provision and determined wholly by productivity gains due to the training. Of course, in a capitalist society the skills embodied in a person are his or her inalienable property; the employer cannot in a competitive market appropriate any of the benefits of training by paying the trained worker less than the market wage for the skill in question. The high transferability of the skill will foil all such attempts, leaving employers neither willing nor able to finance, even in part, training in transferable skills (Becker 1964). Any firm that subsidizes training in transferable skills by paying trainees more than their value products during training will find that, when it reduces the pay of trained workers to recoup its outlay, the result is an exodus of experienced labor to its competitors, the "poachers" who both are willing to pay the market rate and are able to do so because they have not made any outlays on training themselves. The trainee must therefore bear the burden of low output during the training period in the form of low earnings; the return is the achievement of high levels of pay once trained. He or she may look to the state for assistance, but certainly not to the employer.

There is therefore good reason to expect that provision and finance will be completely separate facets of training in costly transferable skills, with provision falling to the firm or to an independent school depending on relative cost-effectiveness and finance to the trainee. Should efficient training involve formal schooling, the employer will then require separate schooling as a condition of employment; where training is provided on the job, trainees are paid the value of their net product during the training period. The orthodox literature on training is dominated by a picture of job-based training provision combined with trainee-based finance in the shape of earnings foregone during training (Mincer 1962, Rosen 1972).

The analysis is depicted in figure 7.1 for the case where trainee output is measurable at low or zero cost, as it will be in principle for the handicraft skills with which this study is in part concerned.[4] The growth of trainee net output during a period of on-the-job training is depicted by a learning curve $y(t)$. The curve lies below the time-on-job axis at first, which is the period when the trainee contribution to production (if any) is more than offset by the costs of instruction and trainee interference with the production of others. Competitive theory predicts then that, for a fully transferable skill, the wage-experience curve $w(t)$ will follow $y(t)$ exactly. In contrast, the pay and productivity of trainees in "no-training" jobs would remain a constant w_0, with the trainee bearing the cost aw_0c of earnings foregone during the training. In between these two extremes is the case of a less progressive wage-experience relationship, such as $w_1(t)$. The firm now invests in trainee skills to the extent of area ade, leaving the trainee a much smaller share (area dw_0b). The steepness of the wage-experience profile determines therefore the division of training costs between the two parties. Under

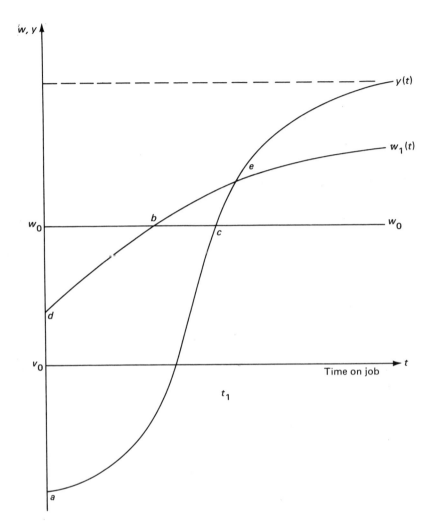

Figure 7.1
Output and wages in relation to training and experience

competitive conditions wage differentials must be as great as productivity differentials in the learning of transferable skills so that the firm's share is reduced to zero.

The Sources of Wage Rigidity

In practice, however, the wage structures of internal labor markets fail to exhibit the flexibility required if the allocation of training costs is to reflect competitive forces. The incumbent labor force has used with success the methods of legal enactment (statutory minimum wage) and collective bargaining to impose a floor to trainee wages independent of market-clearing levels. This discussion will concentrate on the role of collective bargaining. The legal minimum wage does indeed provide a potential constraint upon wage flexibility, but it is one that is superseded in enterprise internal markets by the higher minima established by collective bargaining (Osterman 1980, ch. 4).

Trade unions, in their bargaining activities, may seek to limit the degree of differentiation in the wage-experience relationship to a level well below that in productivity for two reasons: considerations of equitable payment, on the one hand, and the maintenance of bargaining power, on the other. The issue of equity is by no means unambiguous. First, a concept of fairness that looks to equal rewards for equal outputs will be satisfied by a situation where pay tracks productivity during the training period, thereby imposing no constraints on a competitively mediated distribution of training costs. Other concepts of equity are often more influential. It may be felt that personal needs or customary levels of payment should be reflected in the pay of trainees. The criterion of personal need is particularly relevant, as the training opportunities of internal markets are generally made available, not to young workers with their general lack of family responsibilities, but to workers in their twenties and older, many of whom support a family (Thurow 1969, Osterman 1980).[5] The criterion of customary payment is relevant to workers undertaking retraining or upgrade training. The reduction of their pay to value product during this training would imply a marked reduction in their standard of living, something that would strike many unionists as unfair and to be resisted in bargaining. Finally, in on-the-job training, as trainees perform production work, it may be thought unfair not to pay them at levels at least comparable to the lowest grades of production work no matter how low their net productivity is claimed to be in practice. To the extent that such concepts of equity are influential in the work force and backed up by bargaining power, the flexibility of the wage-experience profile will prove constrained in practice.

An allied, and potentially more powerful, set of influences upon the wage-experience relationship are the requirements for the maintenance of bargaining power. If a significant degree of bargaining power is necessary for a group of workers to be able to impose a concept of equity on the wage structure, similarly consideration of fair payment may serve to buttress the bargaining power of the worker association. When youth or trainee labor is available to employers at rates well below those of experienced workers, a strong incentive exists for the employer to allocate work to the former group, to the detriment of the job security, access to overtime, and promotion prospects of the incumbent work force. It is not just equitable to insist that trainees be paid a high wage; it is also the most effective way of neutralizing the threat they would otherwise pose to experienced workers.

The argument is clearest in the case of craft markets. Craft unions have historically sought to control the supply of labor to their occupations, by restricting employer utilization of apprentice labor (maximal apprentice/journeyman ratios) and by reducing the differential between apprentice and craft rates of pay. So effectively has the latter strategy been pursued that in modern times employers have shown increasing reluctance to take on sufficient apprentices to keep a trade stocked with well-trained craft workers.[6]

In the enterprise variant of internalization, the argument differs in detail but carries similar implications for wage structure. A weaker role for the requirements of bargaining power might be inferred in enterprise than in craft markets, partly because of the lower levels of unionization and partly because of the different methods by which bargaining power is established and defended in enterprise markets. In the unionized case even considerable differentiation in earnings by experience need not pose a threat to the job security and earnings of incumbent senior members. The rules of the internal market function to protect the position of established union members from erosion under the influence of potential competitors within the enterprise. Thus the jobs of senior workers are usually well defined, and the pay rates guaranteed, by systems of job evaluation. Similarly, access to the scarce jobs that offer desirable pay and conditions is regulated by promotion rules that give dominant weight to length of service (Tillery 1972). To the extent that such rules are enforced, the mere existence of a pool of relatively cheap trainee labor need not threaten the bargaining position and job rewards of experienced workers. Indeed it has been argued that it is this very removal of the positions of experienced workers from such competition which ensures their cooperation in the training of the inexperienced (Doeringer and Piore 1971, 33).

Rules of this kind cannot, however, be considered sufficient for the protection of experienced workers. Without parallel support in wage structures, such rules would prove distinctly inadequate. A pool of cheap trainee labor within the enterprise creates at the very least an incentive for employers to increase the relative magnitude of trainee to experienced job slots. While the earnings of the senior work force would not be immediately affected by such a move, its job security and access to overtime would most certainly be threatened. The experienced and senior work force has therefore a direct interest in limiting the trainee differential in pay.

The threat posed by trainees to the bargaining position of experienced workers hinges upon a separate factor: the open-ended nature of the employment contract, particularly as it relates to the activities of trainees. If trainees were inevitably characterized by a long period of low net productivity, then their very unproductiveness would mean that they posed little or no threat to senior workers. Why would the firm want to allocate work to trainees when little would be obtained in return? In practice, however, the productivity of trainees is intrinsically variable. There is usually the possibility of specializing trainees for particular job tasks in order to make them relatively productive at an early stage in their training—at the expense, of course, of their progress in learning. Cheap trainee labor presents an incentive to do just that; the control of management over production methods provides it with the opportunity to do so. The experienced work force finds then that it lacks direct means to prevent such adverse movements in the blend of learning and producing during training. Vigilance and a willingness to take collective action when it is felt that management has overstepped the bounds offer no outlet to a procedurally bound work force. The labor contract itself might be rewritten to impose restrictions on the freedom of managerial action in this area. Instances of such contractual limitations can be found, but their efficacy is highly dubious. Who is to say when a trainee has spent sufficient time on a particular phase of the job, especially when job content is subject to change? Instead of trying to write the exhaustive labor contract, the superior alternative is to remove the incentive to management to engage in the intensive use of trainee labor by limiting the trainee differential in pay.[7]

Inspection of the rules of unionized enterprise markets does indeed on occasion reveal concern on the part of unionists lest the training function be used to erode the position of experienced workers. Provisions that relate to training matters reveal two partly contradictory concerns. The first is the desire to spread training opportunities around among the existing membership to augment its skills and job prospects. At the same time explicit restrictions may be placed upon management's ability to engage in high levels of training activity against the interests of current members. Protective clauses in labor contracts take the form of stipulations that "training programs should not 'displace' or detrimentally affect employees who ordinarily performed work to which trainees were assigned" or of stipulated limits to the number of employees who can be trained within a given period (U.S. Department of Labor 1969, 20). Such restrictions are indeed rarely found in collective agreements. However, both their relative rarity and the more general willingness of unions in enterprise markets to leave the training function to managerial control are taken to reflect not so much the absence of conflict of interest as the defusing of potential conflicts through the indirect route of high trainee pay.

The wage clauses of collective bargaining agreements are consistent with these generalizations. In most cases no provision is made for the payment of an explicit trainee rate during the learning period. Thus the previously mentioned survey of training provisions of all major agreements found that of the 7.3 million workers covered in 1967, only 0.34 million had contracts that made an explicit reference to trainee pay. For 70 percent of these workers, trainees were to be paid the full rate for the job, and transfers the rate for their former assignments. In the great majority of contracts that remained silent on the issue, however, wage progression during training was limited to the (generally narrow) range of rates bargained for particular jobs. Only 24 percent of affected workers were subject to some form of explicit progress payment during training (U.S. Department of Labor 1969, table 6).

The argument is underlined by the limited size of trainee differentials in the minority of instances where they are included in collective agreements. No comprehensive data have been developed on this point, but it can be illustrated from the handful of major agreements selected by the BLS for its *Wage Chronology* series.[8] Table 7.1 presents the rules governing payment of trainees in a group of occupations where the incidence of primary employment, non-negligible training costs, and skill transferability is likely to be relatively high. In no case does the pay of trainees fall more than 18 percent below the maximum rate for the job. The Boeing/IAM agreement is particularly striking in this respect. The maximum intensity and duration of trainee differentials applies to craft trainees, who take two and a half years to eliminate the 17 percent shortfall between their rate and that of the experienced craftworker. Moving down the hierarchy of job grades, to arc welder and drill press operator, for example, the trainee differential which is strictly limited already in the case of the craft trainee shrinks still further in both extent and duration.

The training program for shipyard welders is consistent with these observations. The minimum wage provided no active constraint on the wage-experience curve. Trainees were paid twice the minimum wage, even during their initial weeks of vestibule training away from the job. The high floor to trainee wages reflected the effects of a series of negotiated flat-rate wage increases which, during the preceding eight years alone, had actually raised the trainee rate from 67 to 76 percent of the fully experienced rate, an endemic excess supply of trainee labor and excess demand for experienced welders notwithstanding.[9] The union had bargained for the compression of an already limited experience differential in pay. Management had resisted, but not with sufficient intensity to deny success to the union. The union thereby succeeded in fusing a popular concept of equity with the requirements of contract ratification in a context where the sheer scale of the firm's training effort had introduced into the ranks of the local a large minority of youthful trainees.

"The younger members have to be pleased too" stated a union negotiator, "and they're not interested in better pensions." The experience differential in pay, never closely attuned to that in output, had actually evolved under the influence of union-bargaining strategy in a direction opposite to that suggested by competitive forces.[10]

The arguments have been couched thus far in terms of the unionized enterprise market. Yet many primary sector employers remain nonunion, while the nonmanual employees of nearly all enterprise markets fall outside collective bargaining. Beyond the minimum wage what is there to prevent the accommodation of pay differentials to productivity differentials during training? For manual workers, the hypothesis may be advanced that, while in the nonunion enterprise market the absence of an explicit union bargaining constraint on pay differentials may indeed permit a greater degree of differentiation in pay by experience, the very fact that the jobs in question have been set up and rewarded

Table 7.1
Trainee wage differentials in large-scale unionized employment: selected occupations in four major collective bargaining agreements

Occupation	Year	Experienced/maximum job rate ($/hr)	Ratio, starting to maximum job rate	Duration of differential (months)	Parties to agreement
Machinist (craft)	1974	$7.43	0.83	30	Boeing Co./IAM
Arc welder	1974	$6.34	0.87	20	Boeing Co./IAM
Operator, drill press	1974	$5.74	0.89	10	Boeing Co./IAM
Motorperson (underground)	1980	$9.80	0.91	3	Bituminous Coal Operators/UMW
Baker	1974	$4.45	0.92	na	Martin Marietta/UAW
Lineperson, section	1978	$6.41	0.82	72	Western Union/telegraph workers
Telegraph operator	1978	$5.94	0.82	60	Western Union/telegraph workers

Sources: U.S. Bureau of Labor Statistics, Wage Chronologies, *Bulletins* 1884, 1895, 1927, 2062.

along the favorable lines of the primary segment rather than being assigned to the low pay and instability of secondary status suggests that the incumbent work force possesses bargaining power in an *implicit* sense. The type of the technology (intensive in capital or expensive materials) or the product (perishable or price inelastic in demand) may enable the incumbent work force to threaten tacit sanctions on the employer (for example, by noncooperation or by sabotage) should any attempt be made to beat its job rewards down to the levels of the competitive secondary segment. Under such conditions, employers will then imitate the job rewards of their unionized counterparts rather than lose the required acquiescence of the work force and risk unionization, with all the loss of flexibility and operational control which that entails. Part of this "threat effect" may then be an imitation of detailed pay and employment practices in the unionized segment, including their wage-experience differentials.

In the nonmanual context it must be recognized that salary administration in large firms commonly adopts procedures similar to those governing wage determination (job evaluation, specified ranges in pay for particular occupations, and so on). The scope for both personal rates and growth in earnings with experience is greater than at the manual level. At the same time, the low starting salaries of trainees such as articled law clerks are to be found in professional rather than large-scale primary employment. Average salaries in the bottom rung jobs to which trainees are generally assigned in technical and professional occupations were found in a 1976 survey to lie between \$4.60 (equivalent hourly) for engineering technicians and \$7.04 for engineers (U.S. Department of Labor 1976a).[11] As in the case of manual skills, trainee labor may cost the employer significantly more than its immediate economic worth in white-collar occupations where skills are transferable.

Further evidence is certainly required to validate the argument empirically, in particular evidence on the relative compensation (earnings and, ideally, fringe benefits) of trainee and experienced workers within specific enterprise markets.[12] It does, however, appear that in enterprise markets the experience differential in pay is constrained, when collective bargaining is involved, to levels well below those likely to prevail in productivity in occupations requiring costly training in transferable skills. The wage profile during training typically resembles (or is even flatter than) $w_1(t)$ in figure 7.1, which for a costly skill implies a large and long-lived gap between it and the net output curve $y(t)$.[13]

Implications of Wage Rigidity

The presence of limited flexibility in the wage-experience differential means that the firm that provides training in costly transferable skills will have to finance the training, in part or whole, itself. Nothing, however, requires the firm to provide the training in the first place. This section analyzes the allocation of training activities between the company and external agents, notably the state and the private school system.

Provision Apart from Employment

Formal training for knowledge and skills does indeed take place to a considerable extent apart from employment. For comprehensive data on the issue we have to go back to a 1963 survey of the ways in which the subgraduate labor force had learned its vocational and job skills (U.S. Department of Labor 1964).[14] Occupational breakdowns are available only for large detailed occupations (those with a significant incidence of formal training and employment of 100,000 or more). The occupational categories in table 7.2 were selected for high frequency of employment in large enterprises and high degrees of transferability of skills between plants and employers, insofar as the latter can be judged from general impression. Training times, as estimated by job analysis, are substantial, and costs therefore likely to be large for all but clerical occupations.

In 1963 half or more of the workers in these fourteen occupational categories had received some formal training related to their job tasks. Such training was provided overwhelmingly by the state, through vocational courses in high schools and junior colleges, and through training in the armed forces, or by private schools (special schools, technical institutes, and correspondence schools). Company-based training, including courses at company schools and apprenticeship, rarely accounted for as much as one-fifth of available training. Thus rarely did firms provide the principal source of formal training for transferable skills in enterprise markets. The wage structure may be determined by other than competitive considerations, but the responses of employers to such an exogenously imposed wage structure can still reflect maximizing behavior. The provision of what is potentially the most expensive part of job training fell by and large to other agents—to the state school system mostly for basic clerical skills, to the military for

such jobs as airplane mechanics and bakers, and generally to private
vocational schools for lower professional and technical occupations as
well as for office machine operators and welders.

The removal of training from the domain of the enterprise is by and
large necessary and sufficient for the removal of the firm from a significant role in its finance. On the one hand, formal training within
the firm, whether in company schools or apprenticeship programs,
involves an intensification in costs to the firm, since trainee output is
likely to be low or zero when the training is part of paid employment.[15]
On the other, training conducted at outside institutions receives but
little financial assistance from employers. In state training the case is
clear. The same applies to courses taken at proprietary schools before
persons obtain employment in enterprise markets. Moreover, while
large firms do often make available to their employees financial assistance if they take such courses, aid is by and large restricted to tuition
rebates (the takeup of which is notoriously low) and does not generally
include the payment of wages during time spent in formal training
(OECD 1976). The finance of such training falls primarily to the trainee,
along with whatever aid can be obtained from government programs
such as veterans' assistance (U.S. Federal Trade Commission 1976).

If the wage-experience differential were as flexible in practice as it
is in competitive theory, to what extent would such training take place
at outside institutions? Certainly considerations of efficiency in learning
will imply some optimal division of training activities between the
classroom and the job, according to such factors as relative speed,
depth, and cost intensity. In practice, some blend of classroom teaching
and practical work experience, with an increasing ratio (as training
progresses) of time spent on the job to time spent in practice or with
the books will usually provide the most efficient method of training.
The factor of efficiency may therefore call for a degree of formalization
of training, but that does not necessarily require the removal of that
formal component from the domain of the enterprise. Indeed, given
the advantages that can accrue to maintaining a close link between the
job and the school, the efficiency factor will in many cases suggest that
formal training could best be done in a company-based school rather
than an outside institution. Yet courses in company schools are comparatively rare, being overshadowed in particular by the training activities of proprietary schools.

The potential efficiency of company-based training may frequently
be foiled by the inflexibility of the age-experience relationship. As a

Table 7.2
Formal training for selected occupations: courses previously received by 1963 subgraduate labor force

Occupation for which course designed		Training time required (SVP, years)[b]	Share of employees with formal training for occupation	All courses received			
				Number of courses (1,000s)	Percentage provided by[a]		
					State[c]	Private school[d]	Company[e]
Professional/technical	Accountant/auditor	5.0	61.2%	473	40.5%	57.3%	2.3%
	Engineer	4.6	70.4	529	34.5	59.2	6.2
	Draftsperson	2.7	77.4	839	33.7	58.7	7.6
	Technician (nonmedical)	1.7	54.2	999	31.0	57.4	11.1
Supervision/sales	Personnel	—	—	245	11.3	26.2	60.9
	Insurance agent, broker	1.2	51.5	121	11.6	33.0	55.4
Clerical	Bookkeeper	0.4	64.4	705	83.5	14.6	1.8
	Office machine operator	0.2	58.9	445	14.6	67.1	18.2
	Secretary, typist, stenographer	0.6	85.5	3,303	80.1	19.0	0.6
	Telephone operator	0.6	32.5	141	14.8	23.9	61.3

Manual						
Machinist	3.3	56.1	732	34.2	24.1	41.6
Baker	1.5	21.6	305	68.7	18.7	12.6
Lineperson (utility)	2.2	55.0	260	28.3	9.4	62.4
Mechanic, aviation	2.8	43.4	777	72.5	17.9	9.6
Welder/flamecutter	0.6	41.3	637	27.9	49.2	22.8
All occupations[f]		30.2	35,300	53.6	31.4	14.8

Sources: U.S. Department of Labor (1964, tables 4, 11); Scoville (1966).

a. Totals within occupations diverge from 100 percent due to rounding error and other sources.

b. Specific vocational preparation, as estimated from job analysis for the *Dictionary of Occupational Titles* as "the amount of time required to learn the techniques, acquire information, and develop the facility needed for average performance in a specific job-worker situation," subsequent to requisite general educational development (U.S. Department of Labor, 1966, p. A-5).

c. High schools, junior colleges, and armed forces.

d. Special schools, technical institutes, and correspondence schools.

e. Company school and apprenticeship.

f. Total for all persons surveyed (including those in occupations not reported in this table).

result the firm refuses to provide the training that it could conduct more efficiently itself. The possibility of efficiency losses from the removal of formal training to outside agents receives indirect support from the controversy that has surrounded the operations of many proprietary schools (U.S. Federal Trade Commission 1976) and from the extremely high costs incurred for training in the military (Hanushek 1973).

Direct Company Provision

Thus large employers in noncraft occupations where training is relatively costly or skills are highly transferable, or both, have generally required that any formal training be provided by outside agencies rather than by themselves. Yet, this finding notwithstanding, direct company provision accounts for a significant minority of courses of formal training for the occupations detailed in table 7.2. With the exception of occupations in the professional and technical categories, company-provided courses accounted for at least one-third of courses taken from private sector agents (excluding state schools and the military) in eight out of the other eleven occupational categories. The actual importance of company sponsorship is even understated somewhat by these figures. On-the-job training of a transferable nature is not included for these occupations, nor for such occupations as coal mining, which require little formal training in the first place. Even among courses of formal training, fully 26 percent of courses taken were never used on the job, and it is to be expected that courses taken in private schools figure more prominently in the unused category than those provided by companies. Thus the question arises: What factors would induce and permit employers to provide a significant amount of training in costly and transferable skills if to provide the training is also to finance it?[17] Three factors can be advanced to provide a rational basis for such behavior.

Market Power

There exists a degree of employer power in product and labor markets that can make it profitable to provide and finance some training in transferable skills. In theory competitive forces allow the poaching firm to eliminate any rival that finances training in general skills because of the inability of the latter to maintain a presence in the product market when its relative costs rise as the result of its outlays on training. Added to this is the inability of the training firm to retain trained labor should it need to hold down the pay of experienced workers to recoup its outlays on training. Yet not all product markets are so competitive on price that employers possess no leeway to incur significant training costs without going out of business.[18] In addition the well-known limitations on mobility in labor markets may allow the firm some scope to reduce the pay of experienced workers without experiencing attrition rates of unmanageable proportions.

The firm that faces a degree of wage inelasticity in the supply of labor will find it not only feasible but also profitable to meet its labor requirements by paying lower wages to its experienced workers and spending some of the savings on training new labor, relying on the unwillingness of trained workers to desert en masse when their wages fall below "market" levels.[19] The lower the wage elasticity of supply (the more the experienced workers are tied to the firm) and the lower the costs of training, the greater the willingness of the employer to provide training it must finance itself.[20] At the same time the existence of a narrow trainee wage differential will, by increasing the per capita cost of training, reduce the appeal of training as a way for the firm to augment the stock of transferable skills at its disposal.

Market power thus not only permits the firm to invest in transferable skills without facing bankruptcy but also provides a limited incentive to do so. It is striking that the degree of company provision (and therefore finance) is generally much lower for the nonmanual than for the manual occupations detailed in table 7.2. The lesser degree of employer provision may reflect more fluid and competitive conditions in the markets for nonmanual labor that make it more profitable to insist on pre-employment training, thus limit the firm's investment in training.

Moreover, if there is less wage rigidity in nonmanual occupations, the opposite effect is expected: a higher degree of employer provision than in manual occupations. The relatively high incidence of company training activities in the manual area may relate as well to two other distinctive attributes of manual employment. In particular, for a firm to require prior formal training at a proprietary school in the manual area as a condition of hire might be to incur one, and perhaps two, significant liabilities: deficient labor supply and "occupationally minded" trainees.[21]

Outside Schooling and Trainee Labor Supply
The willingness of potential employees to invest in pre-employment schooling depends upon the returns they can expect, particularly higher

earnings once experienced; their ability to do so depends upon their access to financing to get them through the initial period of low or zero earnings. Each of these considerations will usually be less favorable in the manual than in the nonmanual area. In the nonmanual area the pay of qualified experienced workers tends to be at the very least strongly influenced by the balance of supply and demand in the relevant occupational marketplace—modified of course in the case of professions by the restrictions on access developed by professional organizations. The pay of experienced workers under such conditions will generally be high enough to induce a sufficient supply of persons to take the prior training and enter the occupation.[22] In the case of manual labor the supply of trainees usually exceeds the demand in craft internal markets, with the high earnings of craft workers serving as an incentive. In enterprise markets, however, experienced manual workers in any one occupation generally form just one element of industrial unions alongside a variety of other occupations. In conditions where the skilled or experienced membership constitutes a minority of the local's membership or where the plant's average wage level lies below the norm in the external market, the earnings of experienced workers may not be sufficient to provide the firm with an adequate supply of pre-trained applicants. Then, failing provision by state schools or the military, the company will have to fall back on developing the required skills itself.

Unequal ability to pay for pre-employment schooling reinforces these tendencies. Trainee finance for a period of low or zero earnings comes in the first place from parental contributions and accumulated savings. Each of these sources is likely to be much smaller for persons training for manual occupations than for nonmanual ones, given the difference in earnings between the occupations and the tendency for the manual training slots to be recruited from among children of manual workers. Again, failing state intervention—and public support is invariably made available more widely and generously for nonmanual than for manual occupational preparation—the supply of labor to the firm may be jeopardized by any requirement of pre-employment formal training beyond the high school level.

There is another potentially important dimension to the danger of inadequacy of labor supply when employers require pre-employment formal training of their new hires. In many cases the employer requires a quality of training, in terms of up-to-date and relevant techniques, beyond that provided in outside schools, with their less than direct links to current production techniques. This is perhaps less true of proprietary schools, whose incentive is to provide trainees with the skills actually in demand, than of the state schools and the military.

In the case study of shipyard welding, a company policy requiring of trainees prior training in welding techniques could have reduced the burden of formal training on the firm. The firm knew that trainees who had already taken a welding course at a trade school took on average only one-third as long as wholly inexperienced welders to pass the practical test of welding proficiency required of all newly hired welders by U.S. Coast Guard regulations. The savings to the company would have amounted to $1,000 out of the $1,800 which it cost to place a wholly inexperienced welder into production (and the $5,900 which it cost to bring the latter up to experienced worker proficiency). The reduction in training costs is modest but by no means negligible for a company that searched continuously for ways to reduce its investment in welder training. Such a policy would, however, have been frustrated by its drastic effects upon trainee labor supply. The local metropolitan area lacked a proprietary school that could teach the skills needed, while the local vocational high schools did not respond effectively to company efforts to get them to teach their students suitable welding techniques. Moreover the low rewards offered by the firm to experienced welders meant that few candidate trainees would have been willing, even if able, to make the sacrifices involved in traveling to a suitable proprietary school in a different city. Finally, it was recognized that the range of welding techniques taught in such schools exceeded in breadth, but failed to match in depth, the needs of the shipyard job. Such a mismatch carried the implication not only of higher training costs (to all parties) but also, and more seriously from the employer's standpoint, of the second potential drawback of training at outside schools, the development of a "trade" mentality in the welder trainee.

Occupational versus Employer Orientations
A contrast may be drawn between the principles governing vocational preparation in craft and enterprise markets. The objective of the craft or professional groups that regulate the craft market is to assure their members of an occupational education, with a thorough grounding in the principles and practices of their work. Such objectives are realized only partially in practice by manual craft unions, with their dependence on employer willingness to take on apprentices and provide them with the desired quality of training. However, the objective of firms that

regulate enterprise markets, with or without the explicit collaboration of unions, is to reduce worker preparation to the bare minimum of training required for functioning in the various jobs of the hierarchy. This minimum will not, for most production and office work, require general and theoretical knowledge beyond that obtained in general education; nor will it require a knowledge of general principles or techniques. A training broader and deeper than the needs of the current job is not only costly in terms of resources but also potentially dangerous in that it may serve to widen the horizons of the employee beyond those of current employment, developing secondary and potentially rival affiliations to the occupation in question. The values of the occupation often include such "professional" objectives as breadth of knowledge, self-reliance, and quality of work—values that at the manual level conflict directly with the productivist and hierarchical norms of management.

Training outside the company threatens just such an outcome. Even if the policy of the outside school is to tailor its training as closely as possible to the requirements of potential employers, training in excess of the needs of any one employer is inevitable. Production techniques will vary from firm to firm, and the school will generally have to cater to the needs of other employers as well. Similarly, as trainees can rarely be certain of who will be their future employer, they will be disposed to undertake preparation beyond that likely to be required by any one employer. A broader preparation not only makes it objectively easier for a trained worker to transfer skills to another employer but also, by fostering a sense of occupational identity and independence, makes it more likely that the person will avail him or herself of any opportunities that arise to do so. In practice the methods of any school must contain an element of occupational socialization. Both the systematization of knowledge and technique and its presentation by a distinct category of teachers tend to foster a degree of interest in the knowledge and skill for its own sake, not just for its instrumental value in getting a job. In times of large-scale unemployment, such intrinsic orientations may be distinctly secondary, particularly at the less advantaged end of the labor market, but they are not likely to be wholly absent. However weak this occupational consciousness when compared to that of professional occupations, it will still prove unwelcome to the enterprise. When the formal training remains within the company's jurisdiction, as at a company school, the narrowness of training and the dominance of production-oriented norms can be maintained directly and effectively by the firm. No such direct controls are available when the training is provided at an outside school, public or private. The firm has therefore some incentive to provide some training in transferable skills itself, particularly for the manual production workers whose willingness to work and orientation to the firm are least reliable from the standpoint of the employer (Edwards 1976). In this respect the firm has an incentive to locate as much of the training as possible on the job rather than in a company school. Informal training given on the job minimizes the development of trainee norms at variance with those of production and loyalty to the firm.

In the case of shipyard welding such considerations weighed heavily in favor of the company providing the initial formal training rather than leaving it to an outside agent. In so doing, the cost might appear as a formidable disincentive, but the company's options were more varied than appears at first sight. There is the possibility of imposing upon persons taking initial welder training in the company school the status of candidate rather than employee, and thus, taking them onto the payroll only when they have passed, or are clearly about to pass, the test that qualifies them for production work. In other words, the company provides pre-employment formal training. The excess supply of applicants for trainee vacancies, reflecting the high job rewards available at the inexperienced end of a compressed wage-experience profile, suggested that the prospects facing a policy of "zero pay in school" were indeed favorable. Indeed one-half of a sample of former trainees interviewed subsequently on the job stated that such a policy would not have deterred them, so great was their desire for the training or their need for a job.[23] Senior welders recalled that the company had made the training available on an unpaid basis only when they had been trainees three or more decades earlier. The policy had actually been revived for a spell in the late 1960s, in the form of a well-publicized offer to the interested public of free training in welding after regular working hours, an offer made with the expectation that a substantial proportion of those who passed the test would be attracted into regular employment. A savings in cost of up to $1,300 per person trained would have accrued to the firm, depending on the degree to which the attrition rate exceeded that prevailing under normal policies.

Since the records of the experiment had been discarded, the reason for its early cancellation must be pieced together from the recollections of the officials involved. The first difficulty mentioned was the attrition rate, as a relatively low number of trainees continued on to employee status. However, it would take a very large increase in attrition to cancel the benefit to the firm of reduced wage costs, so this is not likely to have provided the primary reason. Considerations of flexibility and control provide the more plausible reason for cancellation. "Are you a shipyard or a school?" responded the manager of training to questions about the experiment. "[For pre-employment training] you've got to be accredited, have certified instructors, a job for the trainee when he comes down. Right now we train them only when we need them. Also the guy who would set up that kind of school wouldn't want to respond to production in the same way the school does now."

Full company control over the welding school minimized any tendency of the "schooling" to develop occupational rather than employer orientations. The welding school was in fact organized like a production facility, capable of qualifying large numbers of trainees for production in the shortest times possible. The six to eight weeks spent by trainees in the school consisted almost exclusively of repetitive basic welding tasks in a series of increasingly difficult positions. The training was deliberately made to approximate closely the conditions of subsequent production work in terms of tasks, discipline, and working conditions. "The school just teaches them to go backwards and forward with the wire (electrode) like dodos out of an institution" was the succinct description offered by one welding supervisor. The absence of theoretical classes in the "curriculum" of the welding school may simply reflect the firm's interest in minimizing the costs of training by getting the trainee into production as rapidly as possible. This explanation is, however, far from clear-cut. Several experienced observers of the situation maintained that the lack of any introduction to the electrical, metallurgical, and calorific principles involved in welding made for a slower rate of learning in subsequent production work.[24] The proposition could not be evaluated with the data available, but it does suggest a second motive for the avoidance of classwork: to foster a company rather than a trade mentality in trainees. It is quite possible that the employer preferred to absorb an increase in the costs of welder training than introduce theoretical considerations into the initial formal training.

Employer-based training in transferable skills therefore reflects some mixture of three factors: a degree of market power vis-à-vis the experienced work force, an unwillingness or inability on the past of trainees to undertake and finance the training themselves, and the firm's interest in molding the skills and attitudes of its work force in directions suitable to corporate rather than occupational objectives. The strength of these influences will prove highly variable across enterprise markets; the overall incentive provided to pay for transferable training is, however, often heavily restricted by the costs implied under wage rigidity.

Company Provision: Adjustments in Training and Personnel Policy

Among the companies that provide and finance training in costly transferable skills an important distinction can be made according to the position a company holds in the product market and its corporate personnel policies. On the one hand, there are large corporations whose products sell in concentrated markets, sometimes referred to as "core" firms. The internal markets erected in such firms typically offer high job rewards for given labor quality.[25] Such firms have sufficient market power to be able to invest in transferable skills without having to fear competition in the product market from rivals who lure away trained workers. Moreover the personnel policies of these firms frequently include a liberal provision of opportunities to acquire valuable skills and advance within the firm's hierarchy of jobs. They offer such desirable options to their work forces not only because they can afford to, or just because they are prodded by unions, but also because to some extent they will thereby procure the benefit of attracting and retaining labor power of high quality.[26] The policies of the Polaroid corporation, as outlined by Edwards (1979), fit to some extent this description.

The willingness of even these primary segment firms to provide and finance costly transferable training as part of a progressive personnel policy is, however, subject to definite bounds. The concern to foster corporate rather than occupational attitudes in the work force is, if anything, more pressing among such firms than in other employment. The secondary magnitude of company-sponsored training in the occupations of table 7.2 reveals the limits of corporate activities in this area.[27] Moreover the personnel policies of leading large corporations typically restrict the training to persons of proven loyalty, in the sense that training opportunities emerge along successive steps of career paths within the firm. Both seniority and a commitment to the employer are required to move along these paths and acquire the training. Traits such as interest in and willingness to pay for the training are not in themselves sufficient for its acquisition.

At the other extreme of the spectrum of labor market segmentation there are the "periphery" firms whose products are subject to strong price competition from domestic or foreign suppliers. Job rewards for experienced workers are typically unattractive, with high quit rates as a result. If the core employer metes out training opportunities with care, the peripheral employer has little choice but to train in whatever volume is needed to offset high turnover and resist depletion of its stock of skills. However, the very marginality of such firms in both product and labor markets will, if they have no choice but to employ costly transferable skills, make training expenses a serious problem. The result is that, unlike the careful shaping of training opportunities toward corporate interests which characterizes the core employer, in the periphery there is an intensive search for ways to reduce the access of workers to training to the bare minimum consistent with the needs of the firm. On the training side, job and training content may be made extremely narrow both to reduce the cost of each dose of training and, if the transferability of the skill can thereby be reduced, to increase the firm's hold over the trainees in whom it has invested. On the personnel side, the firm may structure job rewards so as to discourage turnover; select workers with a propensity to become long-term employees and without an orientation to the occupation in question; and mold attitudes of trainees and workers in such directions through the socialization content of training and work experience.

The shipyard involved in the case study falls emphatically into the second category of firm. Wages for experienced welders were widely recognized as low, while the plant, operating in a product market characterized by intense competition from foreign yards, survived only by dint of powerful government subsidy. Consequently, both the training and the personnel adjustments were pursued with vigor. On the training side, besides the minimization of formal and theoretical content, the training of novice welders was reduced in scope twice below the dual qualifications (in vertical and overhead work) for which welders were usually tested before moving from the school into production—once by omitting the qualification in overhead welding and once by turning to the new and more rapidly learned semiautomatic (MIG) welding technique. In each case the motives were to speed up the growth of the labor force, to reduce training outlays, and to increase the firm's hold over its trainees. The latter consideration was illustrated by the remark of the manager responsible for recruitment: "the MIG-only policy may lower turnover and pay for itself that way . . . it gives the guy less marketability, he can't peddle it so easily."[28] Each experiment was, however, short lived. The narrowly trained welders were found frequently to be without suitable work and were therefore soon returned to the school to obtain the missing basic qualifications. Similarly, further up the scale of experience, upgrade training in the welding of pipe and aluminum, an item widely sought after among welders both for its intrinsic interest and for its value in the external market, was restricted to a small minority of the work force. Only 8 percent of welders possessed any pipe or aluminum qualifications, and within this group specialization had been increased in recent years. Thus the design of training had been reduced to the minimum levels, consistent with the requirements of the production system.

A tendency toward the truncation of training in directions that make it less transferable between enterprises has also been observed in the context of the company training of computer programmers (Osterman 1982). Its truncation represents an attempt to raise productivity during training toward the exogenously constrained wage-experience profile, thereby limiting the firm's investment. The gap between the curves of pay and product is reduced in such cases by the adjustment of product toward pay, which is the reverse of orthodox analysis. However, in the shipyard case the gap still remained substantial.

Personnel policy was also adjusted to reduce the cost of welder training. A policy of selecting persons likely to stay in the firm's employment after receiving training was pursued both for initial and for upgrade training. At the point of intake into the enterprise, the large excess supply of labor permitted the firm much scope for choice. It responded by devoting resources intermittently to the detailed screening of applicants. The trait sought in applicants was not, however, ability as welders but rather retainability as employees. From this standpoint signs of ability and interest in welding were, if anything, looked on with disfavor, as suggestive of the undesired orientation toward the trade rather than to the company and the job. The ambiguity of the procedure is caught in the comments of one interviewer: "you want people who want to weld . . . well, not exactly . . . you want people who want a job, 40 hours work for 40 hours pay . . . the ones who are interested in welding know they can travel with a trade, they've got a salable skill." The intrinsic difficulty of screening for retainability limited the benefits of the activity. The rate of attrition within the first twelve months of employment was still as high as 47 percent for an intensively screened intake, a reduction indeed from the 61 percent that characterized a prior lightly screened intake but still a long way from providing a solution to the firm's problems in welder training.

A similar procedure was followed when it came to the allocation of upgrade training in the highly prized techniques of pipe and aluminum welding. The records of prospective pipe welders were screened in detail for signs of a propensity to quit. "The department does look for the ones who'll take the training with them," stated an official in the welding department. "They look at the number of jobs he's held, and type of work he's done. They wouldn't give it to an ironworker. It's the career types they're after." Again, any sign of a craft orientation, including even the expression of interest in acquiring the further qualifications, would debar access to the training. "If they are pushing, I get suspicious," remarked an official with influence over the selection of welders for pipe training. "They want as many qualifications as they can get to go outside (the company) with." As the ability and willingness to pay for such training is rendered irrelevant to its allocation by wage rigidity, the best thing that the interested and astute welder could therefore do to acquire the training was to signal company loyalty as strongly as possible and keep any craft orientation strictly hidden from view.

The selection of prospectively firm-oriented persons for both initial and upgrade training constituted the entire response of personnel policy to the burden of welder training. Further possible adjustments, including the allocation of variety in work experience on similar criteria, the erection of substantial career prospects for experienced welders, and the parallel pursuit of worker socialization in the values of the firm were neglected as a result of, or effectively debarred by, the cost of administration, the low wage status of the firm, the cyclicality of the market for ships, the tradition of class hostility in the yard, and the shortcomings of the plant's management structure. The upshot was a system of training distinctly unsatisfactory for all parties. The firm incurred a high cost for each dose of training. It was required by the size of turnover to give so many doses that the cost of welder training amounted to 28 percent of the total labor cost (production plus training) of operating the welding function.[29] Although some trainees were pleased that they were learning a useful skill at rates of pay at least comparable with those available to inexperienced labor in the external market, many objected in interview to the limited depth and breadth of the training, the lack of any educational component, and the difficulty of acquiring exposure to the full range of welding skills in use in the shipyard. From the standpoint of national skill development, the ad hoc, rushed, and generally circumscribed nature of the training provides but a poor version of what a foundation training in welding and metal-working might be.

Conclusion

The internal labor markets of large corporations are marked by a form of wage rigidity to which little attention has hitherto been paid: that concerning the pay of trainee and experienced workers in particular occupations. Trainees are indeed typically paid less than qualified workers. Often this is true however only because trainees enter at the lower end of the wage range in particular jobs. In any case the gap between their pay and that of their more experienced peers is typically small and rapidly eroded. In some instances the narrowness of the pay differential undoubtedly reflects the narrowness of the difference in productivity which might from an orthodox standpoint be expected to lie behind it. If the job is straightforward and the training takes but little time, then the firm can afford to pay trainees well. The difficulty with such an interpretation lies in the fact that compressed wage-experience profiles are observed even when jobs are not straightforward nor training times short. For such workers as manual welders, machinists, typists, technicians, and draftspersons, the skills and knowledge involved take a significant time to develop. A sustained period of low productivity during training means that the employer can no longer afford to pay the trainee close to what is paid to the experienced worker. Consequently, the narrowness of the wage differential must be attributed to other causes. The outstanding candidate is the wage policy of trade unions which, in seeking both to infuse into pay structures the concepts of equity prevalent among their members and to protect the bargaining power of the worker collectivity from erosion under the competition of cheap labor, have pushed with success for the raising of trainee relative to experienced wages.

   The consequence is that trainee labor becomes expensive to the firm. As most of the skills in question have a relatively high transferability to other employers, the firm reacts to this exogenously imposed wage structure by altering the provision of training from what would prevail under wage flexibility. Concerning quantity, fewer training places are offered, the balance being shifted toward pre-employment schooling and recruitment from outside. Concerning quality, each place comes with less training, in the sense of shorter duration, greater informality, and increased employer specificity. Concerning access, the corporation makes available the subsidized training places only to the most trainable and potentially loyal condidates, thereby ruling youth labor out of consideration. The unifying element in these changes in the provision of industrial training is the reduced availability of company-based formal training, for which participants will have to be paid at regular rates while producing little or nothing—in favor of pre-employment schooling, for which no wages have to be paid, and on-the-job training, for which wages do have to be paid but which provides some output in return. In either event the educational potential of the workplace is curtailed rather than developed.

Neither the extent of these alterations in training provision nor the social and economic damage caused by them can be readily assessed from information currently available. There is every reason to expect, on a priori grounds, that, for costly transferable skills, the provision of training will fall short in both quantity and quality of socially desirable levels. Evidence of deficient provision might be expected to show up in skill shortages, such as the unfilled vacancies for craftworkers that characterized cyclical peaks in Britain in the postwar period (GB NEDO 1977). Yet a series of attempts to detect quantitative skill shortages in the United States have generally come up with little evidence of such phenomena; although in the relatively rare times and locations where they are observed, it is indeed skills of the costly transferable type, such as those of machinists, toolmakers and maintenance mechanics, that are involved.[30] Although it may appear that there is no cause for concern, it is worth the complementary finding of the same studies: given strictly limited provision of formal training, such overt skill shortages are avoided only by extensive job subdivision and employee upgrading, that is, by the wholesale utilization of informally and narrowly trained workers. In effect such responses on the part of employers serve to mask rather than resolve skill shortages.

In order to assess the damage caused by distorted training provision, a clearer picture is needed of the relationship between the quality of the vocational preparation of the work force and the economic performance of the firm, the industry, and the country. The link between training and productivity in particularly difficult to pin down empirically. However, studies of industry data for Britain and Germany are consistent with a positive relationship between work force qualifications, particularly at the intermediate craft and technical level, and productivity

(Prais 1981). Certainly among advanced economies there are several—notably Germany, Sweden, France, and, to some extent, Japan—whose performance has surpassed that of the United States in the postwar period. The various systems of vocational preparation in these countries are characterized by thoroughgoing state intervention in pursuit of a level and quality of training provision superior to that spontaneously provided by the private sector, to which the task has been left by and large in the United States. In contrast to the situation in West Germany and Sweden, where it is the goal—and indeed almost the achievement—of public policy to provide workers with a foundation in the knowledge and skills relevant to their occupations, the rarity with which workers in the United States receive formal training may well damage not only their development as individuals but also the success of the enterprises in which they work. The informality of job training, often depicted as a strength of U.S. industry, may in fact be its curse.

A final question concerns the role of increased wage flexibility in state policy toward industrial training. In particular, would a lowering of entry and trainee wage rates suffice to improve the provision of company training without need for further intervention? (We recognize the lack of policy instruments suited to reducing the cost of trainee labor to the employer but assume that, if pay differentials within enterprises cannot directly be widened, then at least wage subsidies to entry-level jobs and training activities can attain the desired objectives.)

Lower trainee wage costs may indeed prove part of a suitable policy for industrial training, by helping to acquire the cooperation of firms in the provision of more and better training for costly transferable skills. However, by themselves they are far from sufficient to ensure such an outcome. There is first the difficulty that, as long as trainees are paid more than they produce, the firm's willingness to train is reduced by the prospect of future quits. Consequently, lower trainee payroll costs can be expected to increase the quantity of training by much more than its quality, as it is high quality that both raises the cost of each dose of training and makes the ex-trainee particularly attractive to other employers. The second difficulty follows directly. Faced with the availability of cheap trainee labor, employers have an incentive to exploit trainees for intensive production work, to the detriment of their training and the security of adult workers. The active opposition of trade unions to the policy can therefore be anticipated. To ensure that the space created for improved industrial training is actually taken up as intended and to avoid trade union hostility, any policy of reducing trainee payroll costs must be complemented by a system of effective state regulation of training provision at the workplace. It is only when employers are required to train youths and raise trainees to mandated standards that a policy of lower trainee costs can expect to avoid strong resistance from unions and to have any chance of being achieved through changes in the pay structures of collective bargaining agreements.[31]

Notes

I thank Paul Osterman, Rick Edwards, Oliver Hart, Heinz Hollenstein, Ian Jones, S. J. Prais, Keith Snell, Steve Tolliday, and Jonathan Zeitlin for comments on drafts of this chapter or related work.

1. Training costs (i.e., opportunity costs incurred by both employers and trainees) have been estimated, using the job training requirements of the *Dictionary of Occupational Titles* (U.S. Department of Labor 1966), for the 1963 U.S. labor force as follows ($1963): craft and supervisory, $8,900; operative, $2,700; clerical, $1,200; laboring, $1,020 (Ryan 1977, table III-13). The estimates for the operative and clerical categories are representative of training costs for the production and office jobs of enterprise internal markets.

2. It will be assumed that the design of jobs and training in enterprise internal markets reflects managerial pursuit of subdivision to the fullest degree consistent with the constraints imposed by the technique and scale of production but unconstrained by the collective restrictions upon "deskilling" imposed by some craft and professional groups (Slichter 1941, ch. 7) or by a rising supply price on the part of individual workers faced with more repetitive and boring work (Scoville 1969). Some (limited) evidence of managerial determination to press the subdivision of labor to high levels along Smithian lines is provided by Davis, Canter, and Hoffman (1955); evidence of the productivity enhancing effects of "job enrichment" experiments (Lawler 1969) underlines the point and suggests that subdivision may be pressed in the interests of workplace control beyond levels most conducive to least cost production. The constraints that might be imposed on subdivision at the margin by worker preferences for broader and more interesting work tasks is taken as relevant more to the sorting of workers between small and large plants, with their differing degrees of task specialization, than to the content of jobs in the latter.

3. Thus in the engineering (i.e., metalworking) and shipbuilding industries of Britain, organized largely by unions with strong craft orientations, the skills of both the machinist and the welder commonly form part of the portfolio of techniques mastered by the skilled production worker. The decision to organize the new skill of welding on an apprenticeable craft (rather than a trainable semiskilled) basis in British shipbuilding in the 1930s is analyzed in Lorenz (1980).

4. Trainee output in measurable, that is, in physical terms at least. As trainee output will even then consist generally of one or more intermediate products, there remains the problem of its valuation.

5. The proportion of young male workers participating in any kind of formal training rose in one (NLS) sample from 13.8 percent at ages 18–19 to 21.0 percent at ages 24–25. (Antos and Mellow 1979, table 6.1).

6. "Unions have generally tended to increase the ratio of apprenticeship earnings to those of journeymen or semiskilled workers. Thus the pattern-makers of Chicago . . . have raised the beginning rate for apprentices from 22.5 percent of the journeyman's rate (in 1941) to 40 percent (in 1953)" (Slichter et al. 1960, p. 84). Craft union strategy is analyzed by Rottenburg (1961). The situation in the United States in the recent period can be illustrated from the findings of the 1970 census. Apprentices, confined to a handful of trades in construction, metalworking, and printing, in no instance constituted more than 5 percent of the total membership of the relevant occupation; their median varied between 22 and 24 years, while median annual earnings amounted in all cases but one to between 70 and 73 percent of experienced earnings (U.S. Census of Population, PC(2)-7A, *Occupational Characteristics*, table 1.).

7. I am grateful to Oliver Hart for bringing this issue to the fore.

8. The agreements are drawn from those *Wage Chronologies* published since 1975 in which bonuses or incentives form a negligible part of the payment system.

9. As the payment system involved no incentive or bonus payments, earnings were dominated by base rates. The relative base rates of trainee and experienced welders provide therefore a good guide to the wage-experience relationship.

10. The importance of considerations of equity within the internal wage structure comes out in another, more fundamental, respect in the shipyard context. The need to train welders in large numbers in the first place arose largely from the inadequacy of the job rewards offered to experienced welders in relation to those available in the external market. The increase in the pay of experienced welders which might have eliminated the difficulty at source was, however, blocked by the impossibility of paying welders more than other shipyard trades, given the importance of horizontal equity (in this case, equality of pay) to the experienced work force as a whole, and by the still greater increase in overall production costs which would have followed if the cost of training welders had been essentially eliminated by increasing the pay of experienced workers in all trades. This constraint placed on the wage-experience differential from an upward direction by considerations of equitable payment may be presumed the least generalizable aspect of the shipyard example.

11. Calculated from monthly salaries on the assumption of a 38-hour workweek. Actual starting salaries will tend to fall somewhat below these figures to the extent that trainees are grouped at the lower end of the range of salaries within each job category.

12. Supportive evidence is provided by an earlier case study of on-the-job training for a costly transferable skill—sewing machine operation. The degree of progression in earnings during a 70-week learning period was well below

that in output, with the result that the firm incurred net costs of training estimated at 17 percent of trainee earnings (Thomas et al. 1969).

13. It might be thought that the decline during the last decade in the earnings of young as compared to those of middle-aged workers, interpreted as the result of intensified competition for jobs among the members of a demographic "bulge" (Welch 1979), contradicts the postulate of inflexibility in the wage-experience differential. In certainly does so at the level of the labor market as a whole; that does not in itself establish a similar conclusion, however, for the differential within enterprise markets. Indeed, if young entrants are restricted initially to a secondary segment that operates on classically fluid and competitive lines, then a reduction in their earnings would come as no surprise—but neither would it carry the implication that when, after a few years have elapsed and the same workers compete for access to the training opportunities of the primary segment, the excess supply of labor to such structured markets, where wages are set by bargaining behavior, will reduce the entry and trainee wage and lead to a larger use of trainee labor. Indeed, given the logic of internal markets, such an outcome would hardly be expected, but rather an intensified use of nonprice rationing of the increasingly sought-after opportunities to enter training slots, together with a growing dispersion of earnings within the "bulge" cohorts.

14. Consequently, for the older cohorts in the survey the data covers training undertaken as far back as the 1930s. The degree to which the results of the 1963 survey have since dated may be seen from the fact that computer programming failed then to pass the test for inclusion in the occupational breakdowns, that is, employment of 100,000 or more. The need for an updated survey to provide information about changes in occupations and methods of training (in addition to the effects of such public programs as MDTA and CETA) has by now become very pressing indeed.

15. Again comprehensive data is hard to come by. A 1960s survey of skilled and technical workers in the metalworking sector did, however, find that, for three out of every four courses of formal training received, either part or all of time spent in training was paid for by the employer (Kincaid 1966, p. 36). As courses taken at outside schools under tuition rebate schemes are included, the incidence of company payment for time spent training will be even greater than this for courses taken in company schools.

16. The criticisms leveled at many proprietary (including correspondence) schools by the FTC report include extensive overcharging, deceptive and expensive sales promotion, high attrition rates, and indifference to the quality of provision. Economists who have studied such schools are, however, impressed by the increases in earnings achieved by those who complete their courses (Freeman 1974).

17. The costs borne by employers for training in company schools cannot be taken to be trivial. The average time spent on all past courses in company schools by those who had taken such courses varied between four and ten months for the three categories of male and female workers interviewed by the National Longitudinal Surveys; the intensity of such training for the only

group reporting this aspect (young men) averaged 21 hours per week (Ohio State University 1973). As already noted, such training is usually provided on company time.

18. It is noteworthy that, of the four occupations in which employers provide half or more of the courses of formal training listed in table 7.1, two (telephone operators and utility linepersons) are employed predominantly in public utilities, industries whose system of public regulation sets prices so as to guarantee a stipulated rate of return on capital and therefore permits the cost of formal training to be passed along to the consumer.

19. In the shipyard example, the inelasticity of supply that permitted the firm to pay substandard wages to experienced labor without inciting a mass exodus was present among the senior experienced welders, whose quit rate was as low (0.1 percent monthly) as that of recently hired experienced welders was high (5.7 percent).

20. This conclusion is derived algebraically by Ian Jones and Heinz Hollenstein (1982). In their analysis, when wage rigidity is absent, the firm comes to finance training in transferable skills only in a small way, because of increasing per capita training costs as the scale of the training increases.

21. There is also the potentially important, but essentially unverifiable, possibility that the intrinsic technical transferability of skills is lower in manual than in nonmanual occupations because of a lower degree of standardization across employers in the materials, equipment, and products involved in the work.

22. The dynamic maladjustments that have been observed in such markets do not alter the conclusion (Freeman 1971).

23. There is no basis for assuming that the half who would have been deterred contained more able or retainable trainees on average; indeed there are reasons of an informational kind for expecting precisely the opposite.

24. "There are five essentials to welding," insisted an instructor in the school, formerly a senior production welder himself, "current, wire, arc length, travel speed and angle—and the relations between them have to be taught. The beginner doesn't get this, although it only takes one lesson to do it. The beginner doesn't know why, and knowing why helps production. Say you blow through the plate. Who knows to change the wire size as well as to turn down the heat (amperage)—the Beginner or the Apprentice?" These words echo those of an academic observer who cited welding as a rare example of a skill resistant to "rationalization" and the elimination of intellectual requirements. Friedmann (1955, p. 211) observed that in welding "it is hard for the machine to replace the journeyman's hand" but in arguing that "intellectual qualities are so necessary for this work" underestimated the interest of employers in turning out production welders without any education in the principles of their work.

25. See Oster (1979) for a discussion of the industrial correlates of labor market segmentation.

26. Sadowski (1982) takes the argument further in positing that firms invest in transferable skills to improve their reputation in the labor market, thereby

paradoxically reducing the propensity to quit despite augmenting the opportunity to do so. It would, however, be a rash employer that relied on goodwill to retain the skills that it had financed without providing the complementary financial incentives to stay.

27. Nor does the 1963 survey show signs of any increase in the relative importance of company training over time. Its share of all courses of formal training received (for all occupations) was actually lower (8.9 percent) in the 35–44 year old cohort than in the 45–64 year old one (10.8 percent; data based upon survey worksheets kindly supplied by the U.S. Department of Labor).

28. The remark recalls the comment of an observer of job training in London before 1914: "a certain type of firm, indeed, attempts to keep each of its boys and men at a single thing in order to increase its hold over them" (Dearle 1914, p. 146).

29. The "cost" of training is measured with reference to the (unavailable) alternative of employing a fully experienced welding work force at the prevailing rate of pay.

30. NMC (1954); Horowitz and Hernnstadt (1969); Franke and Sobel (1970); U.S. Department of Labor (1971); and Ginzberg (1979, p. 121).

31. The alternative forms taken by state intervention in advanced economies are analyzed in Ryan (1981, sec. 3). The West German system, which, with its combination of enterprise provision and state regulation, might be considered most relevant to U.S. conditions, is specifically discussed in OECD (1979, 1980) and Sadowski (1981). In West Germany all workers between 16 and 18 years of age must by law be treated as apprentices by their employers; are given a prescribed two- or three-year course systematic formal training (including technical education) for a recognized occupation; and are tested at the end of their time for proficiency in the skill involved. Employers are encouraged to take on these young workers by the relatively low "allowances" that they pay as part of the special nonemployee status of the apprentice. In recent years the state has threatened to impose a payroll tax in order to increase the provision of apprenticeship. The opposition of trade unions to "cheap labor" is reduced by the state's insistence that youths be trained first and used for production second—with examinations, inspections, and decertification as weapons to enforce such a policy. As a result in 1976 over 85 percent of the relevant age bracket in the labor force received the desired foundation training (OECD 1980, p. 74).

References

Antos, J. R., and W. Mellow. 1979. *The Youth Labor Market: A Dynamic Overview.* BLS Staff Paper No. 11. U.S. Department of Labor, Washington, D.C.

Becker, G. S. 1964. *Human Capital.* New York: National Bureau of Economic Research

Davis, L. E., Canter, R. R., and J. F. Hoffman. 1955. "Current Job Design Criteria." *Journal of Industrial Engineering* 6 (March):5–8.

Dearle, N. B. 1914. *Industrial Training.* London: King and Son.

Doeringer, P. B., and M. J. Piore. 1971. *Internal Labor Markets and Manpower Analysis.* Lexington, Mass.: D. C. Heath.

Edwards, R. C. 1976. "Individual Traits and Organizational Incentives: What Makes a 'Good' Worker?" *Journal of Human Resources* 11:51–68.

Edwards, R. C. 1979. *Contested Terrain.* New York: Basic Books.

Feldstein, M. S. 1973. "The Economics of the New Unemployment." *The Public Interest* 33 (Fall).

Franke, W., and I. Sobel. 1970. *The Shortage of Skilled and Technical Workers.* Lexington, Mass.: D.C. Heath.

Freeman, R. B. 1971. *The Market for College Trained Manpower.* Cambridge: Harvard University Press.

Freeman, R. B., 1974. "Occupational Training in Proprietary Schools and Technical Institutes." *Review of Economics and Statistics* 56 (August):310–318.

Friedmann, G. 1955. *Industrial Society.* New York: Free Press.

Ginzberg, E. 1979. *Good Jobs, Bad Jobs, No Jobs.* Cambridge: Harvard University Press.

Hanushek, E. A. 1973. "The High Cost of Graduate Education in the Military." *Public Policy* 21 (Fall):525–552.

Horowitz, M. A., and I. L. Herrnstadt. 1969. "The Training of Tool and Die Makers." Mimeograph. Boston: Northeastern University.

Jones, I., and H. Hollenstein. 1982. "The Provision of Training by Firms: A Summary of Results to Date." Mimeograph. London: National Institute of Economic and Social Research.

Kincaid, H. V. 1966. *The Scope of Industrial Training in Selected Skilled and Technical Occupations.* Standford, Calif.: Stanford Research Institute.

Lawler, E. E. 1969. "Job Design and Employer Motivation." *Personnel Psychology* 22:426–435.

Lorenz, E. 1980. "The Extension of Welding in the 1930s and the Employers' 'Welding Scheme.' " Mimeograph. Cambridge, England: Faculty of Economics, University of Cambridge.

Mincer, J. 1962. "On-the-Job Training: Costs, Returns and Some Implications." *Journal of Political Economy* Pt. 2, supplement, 70 (October):50–79.

National Manpower Council. 1954. *A Policy for Skilled Manpower.* New York: Columbia University Press.

Oatey, M. (1970). "The Economics of Training with Respect to the Firm." *British Journal of Industrial Relations* 8 (March):1–21.

OECD. 1976. Center for Educational Research and Innovation, *Developments in Educational Leave of Absence*. Paris.

OECD. 1979. *Policies for Apprenticeship*. Paris.

OECD. 1980. Manpower and Social Affairs Committee. "Review of Youth Employment Policies in the Federal Republic of Germany." Mimeograph. Paris.

Ohio State University, Center for Human Resource Research, National Longitudinal Study. *Code Books*. 1973.

Oster, G. 1978. "A Factor Analytic Test of the Theory of the Dual Economy." *Review of Economic Studies* **61** (December):33–39.

Osterman, P. 1980. *Getting Started: the Youth Labor Market*. Cambridge, Mass.: The MIT Press.

Osterman, P. 1982. "Employment Structures within Firms." *British Journal of Industrial Relations* **20** (November):349–361.

Piore, M. J. 1968. "On-the-Job Training and Adjustment to Technological Change." *Journal of Human Resources* **3** (Fall):435–449.

Prais, S. J. 1981. "Vocational Qualifications on the Labor Force in Britain and Germany. *National Institute Economic Review* **98** (November):47–59.

Rosen, S. 1972. "Learning and Experience in the Labour Market." *Journal of Human Resources* **7** (Summer):326–342.

Rottenberg, S. 1961. "The Irrelevance of Union Apprentice/Journeyman Ratios." *Journal of Business* **34** (July):384–386.

Ryan, P. 1977. "Job Training." Unpublished Ph.D. dissertation. Harvard University, Cambridge.

Ryan, P. 1980. "The Costs of Job Training for a Transferable Skill." *British Journal of Industrial Relations* **18** (November):334–351.

Ryan, P. 1981. "Human Resources, Job Training and Industrial Restructuring in OECD Countries." Paper presented to Experts Meeting on Changes in Work Patterns: Educational Implications. OECD/CERI, Paris, November.

Sadowski, D. 1981. "Finance and Governance of the German Apprenticeship System." *Journal of Institutional and Theoretical Economics* **137** (July):234–251.

Sadowski, D. 1982. "Corporate Training Investment Decisions." In G. Mensch and R. Nichaus (eds.), *Manpower Planning and Technological Change*. New York: Plenum.

Scoville, J. G. 1966. "Education and Training Requirements for Occupations." *Review of Economics and Statistics* (November):387–393.

Scoville, J. G. 1969. "A Theory of Jobs and Training." *Industrial Relations* **9** (October):36–53.

Slichter, S. H. 1941. *Union Policies and Industrial Management*. Washington, D.C.: Brookings.

Slichter, S. H., J. J. Healy, and E. R. Livernash. 1960. *The Impact of Collective Bargaining on Management.* Washington, D.C.: Brookings.

Stone, K. 1973. "The Origins of Job Structures in the Steel Industry." *Radical America* 7 (November–December):19–66.

Strauss, G. 1965. "Apprenticeship: An Evaluation of the Need." In A. M. Ross (ed.), *Employment Policy and the Labor Market.* Berkeley: University of California Press, pp. 299–332.

Thomas, B., J. Moxham, and J. A. G. Jones. 1969. "A Cost-Benefit Analysis of Industrial Training." *British Journal of Industrial Relations* 7 (July):231–264.

Thurow, L. C. 1969. *Poverty and Discrimination.* Washington D. C.: Brookings.

Tillery, W. L. 1972. "Seniority Administration in Major Agreements." *Monthly Labor Review* (December):36–39.

U.K., National Economic Development Office. 1977. *Engineering Craftsmen: Shortages and Related Problems.* London: HMSO.

U.S. Department of Labor. 1964. Manpower Administration, Office of Manpower, Automation and Training. *Formal Occupational Training of Adult Workers.* Manpower/Automation Research Monograph No. 2. Washington, D.C.: GPO.

U.S. Department of Labor. 1966. Bureau of Employment Security. *Selected Characteristics of Occupations (Physical Demands, Working Conditions, Training Time)—A Supplement to the Dictionary of Occupational Titles, 3rd ed.* Washington, D.C.: GPO.

U.S. Department of Labor. 1969. Bureau of Labor Statistics, *Major Collective Bargaining Agreements: Training and Retraining Provisions.* Bulletin 1425-7. Washington, D.C.: GPO.

U.S. Department of Labor. 1971. Bureau of Labor Statistics. *Occupational Manpower and Training Needs.* Bulletin 1701.

U.S. Department of Labor. 1976a. Bureau of Labor Statistics. *National Survey of Professional, Administrative, Technical and Clerical Pay.* Bulletin 1931 (March 1976) Washington, D.C.: GPO.

U.S. Department of Labor. 1976b. Bureau of Labor Statistics. *Wage Chronology, Boeing Co. (Washington Plants) and Machinists, 1936–77.* Bulletin 1895. Washington, D.C.: GPO.

U.S. Federal Trade Commission. 1976. Bureau of Consumer Protection. *Proprietary, Vocational and Home Study Schools.* Staff Report. Washington, D.C.

Welch, F. 1979. "Effects of Cohort Size on Earnings: The Baby Boom Babies' Financial Bust." *Journal of Political Economy* 87 (August):S65–S97.

8

The Search for a Societal Effect in the Production of Company Hierarchy: A Comparison of France and Germany

Marc Maurice,
François Sellier, and
Jean-Jacques Silvestre

The research reported here was designed to explain important and significant differences between France and Germany in company organization, workers' training, the wage scale or wage "laws," and the system of industrial relations. In order to explain these differences, we conducted in-depth studies of twelve firms in France and Germany. These firms were carefully matched to be comparable in terms of size, product, and technology.[1]

The first significant difference between the two countries is the size of the wage dispersion in industry. In the aggregate the coefficient of variation of individual wages of male workers is nearly twice as high in France (55 percent) as in Germany (33 percent). Another significant difference is that variations in wage differentials go hand in hand with variations in job structures, especially as far as the number of nonmanual workers in the industrial labor force is concerned. For example, in the companies observed, French nonmanual workers are relatively better paid and significantly more numerous. Numerical differences are accounted for primarily by white-collar workers and middle management, including foremen.[2]

These observations are open to various types of interpretation, and their analysis can orient comparative research along very different lines. There are two diametrically opposed directions. In the first the differences observed between countries are the result of comparable agents acting in accordance with a universal rationality but in different cultural environments or under different institutional constraints. It is tempting, for example, to apply the neoclassical model of the labor market to both countries and to identify the constraints imposed by institutions or cultural habits that either orient foreseeable adjustments specific to each country or else that condition the rationality of companies and workers.[3] The same type of universalistic approach can be found in some comparative research on organizations.[4] Indeed results obtained in this field are of two types. In the first, researchers claim to test the existence of technological determinism on the structure of organizations; that is, for a given type of technology there exists a rational type of organization. The differences in company organization in the two countries are then attributed to uneven technological development in the production units. In the second type, one admits that for a given type of technology differences between countries exist; these differences are then explained by company *environment*, which is an indirect way of applying a rationality without questioning its universal character.

Universalistic approaches have several characteristics in common which considerably limit the heuristic interest of comparative research. First, they tend to consider the *deviations observed as residual factors* that can be explained by the specific characteristics of the countries being compared. Deviations are thus necessarily marginal when compared with the basic structures of the societies under consideration. In this way such approaches tend to explain *national effects* (on wages, job structures, the supply and output of education) rather than bringing to light different types of societal coherence. These effects are then considered to be contingent by nature: they will disappear as soon as the rigidities justifying their existence have themselves disappeared. Even more basic is the fact that such universalistic approaches assume the invariability in societies of two components in the basic model: the nature of the social agents, be they institutions (companies, trade unions, or the educational system) or social categories (workers, managers, craftsmen, or employees); and the model of rationality behind the actions of these agents. Only the strategies used and the environmental constraints change.

The method we have used corresponds to another orientation. It tends to consider that the chain of command, job qualifications, job structures, and the division of labor are all interacting social phenomena. Consequently, a certain coherence exists among them that is relatively specific to each type of society. The institutions where they can be observed are themselves relatively specific manifestations of the way social relations are organized. For example, a school or a company is supposed to deal with relatively universal techniques used to reach goals considered common to all countries, and yet schools and companies are never the same from one country to the next. Our hypothesis is that the influence a society exerts on institutions, organizations, and agents is so vital that neither the management of technical questions nor the way goals are reached can really be compared. In each country different forms and processes of socialization exist. Therefore an international comparison of management systems can only be relevant if these systems are related to all the particular social relations that make up a society.

Now social relations neither develop nor do they combine in the same way in two different types of societies. In our research strong statistical evidence points to three particular types of relevant social relations: the educational relation (which binds individuals to a society through the educational and vocational training system), the organizational relation (which binds individuals to a society through the division of labor), and the industrial relation (which binds individuals to a society through systems that establish social identity and economic opposition, i.e., management, workers, and their organizations). The constants in such an analysis are the types of social relations that can be found everywhere but whose modalities and combinations can vary. For us, the analysis of an observable phenomenon in a company must lead to the discovery of significant social relations concerning the phenomenon and that helps to shape the company itself.

A Look at the Historical Development of Agents

The nature and workings of educational, organizational, and industrial relations can be observed at a given moment. But at the moment when the observation is being made, these relations have been operative for a long time. This justifies our taking a look at history. This is not to say that a historical description can replace a basic explanation. However, inasmuch as institutions and agents have been shaped by specific social relations, it is indispensable to look at their historical development. This is evident as far as educational systems, the formation of social classes, and the structuring of companies and trade unions are concerned. Let us look in particular at the development of industrial relations, closely tied to the development of social classes.

Class relations did not develop in the same way in two different societies. This in any case appears to be true of France and Germany.

The French urban working class came into being very slowly between 1830 and 1950. It drew upon very heterogeneous types of people—rural day laborers and salaried workers; urban craftsmen and rural immigrants ended up living alongside workers already in the cities and towns. Moreover there was very early on a large percentage of female workers, not only in industries that traditionally used female labor—textiles, clothing and food—but also in other branches where labor shortages helped them to overcome the opposition of male workers. The number of white-collar workers in relation to the industrial labor force rose only slightly during the period of industrialization.

The development of the German working class is almost exactly the opposite. Growth was sudden and massive; the working class more than doubled in a quarter of a century.[5] Growth occurred despite a high rate of emigration—to America in particular—in a population that was expanding rapidly: from 1850 to 1900 it grew from 35 to 56 million (i.e., 60 percent), whereas the French population during the same period grew only 14 percent (from 36 to 41 million).

These quantitative differences could not but have qualitative effects, even if the latter are difficult to measure. The first consequence of this rapid growth is the homogeneity of the German working class. The French working class grew slowly; like geological strata, layers of peasants and craftsmen were added from the city and the country. The latent hostility that existed in the countryside between farm workers and rural craftsmen's assistants was probably carried over to the city.[6]

The French working class moreover came into being earlier than the German one, at a time when the population was living at subsistence level, particularly as far as food was concerned.[7] Beginning in 1871, food prices began to drop considerably. Food imported from abroad and improved farming techniques solved the problem of hunger.[8] Thus the German working class came into being at a time when poor city dwellers no longer ran the risk of starving to death. It was also a time of political change, and the German working class was rapidly able to form a single party and hence trade unions.

A second cause of differences in homogeneity between the two working classes is that downward mobility of artisans was no doubt lower in Germany than in France. As can be seen in table 8.1, the total number of artisans in Germany remained fairly stable even as the proportion of artisans, as opposed to manual workers, dropped by over half (from 45 to 20 percent) between 1882 and 1907. In France, on the other hand, the proportion of artisans compared with manual workers dropped by only one-third between 1876 and 1906 (thirty years), yet in absolute figures there was 1 percent less artisans each year, which represented a loss of one-third of the total over a thirty-year period.

This is a well-known phenomenon in economic demography: changes in structure can produce very different social consequences (especially

Table 8.1
Active population in industry in France (1876–1906) and in Germany (1882–1907) (in thousands)

	France			Germany		
	1876	1906	Annual variation rate	1882	1907	Annual variation rate
Manual or blue-collar workers	3,150	3,385	+0.25	4,096	8,500	+3.0
Artisans or white-collar workers	193	220	+0.45	99	696	+8.1
Percentage of artisans/ white-collar workers among manual wage earners						
Employers	1,126	780	−1.2	1,861	1,729	−0.28

Sources: For Germany, *Statistisches Jahrbuch 1880* and E. Lederer, *Die Privatangestellten in der modernen Wirtschaft*, Mohr, Tubingen, 1912. For France, J. C. Toutain, "La population active de la France de 1700 à 1959," *Cahiers de science économique appliquée*, Série A.F. no. 3, 1963, p. 130, tables 75, 76, 77.

as far as downward mobility is concerned) depending on whether the population as a whole is growing or is stable. Indeed when burgeoning industries produce a growing share of the market supply, it is obviously easier for a given number of artisans to stay in business, because the total population, and hence demand, is growing. We therefore deduce that the French working class was formed in a more heterogeneous and proletarianizing fashion than in Germany.

The greater homogeneity of the German working class seems to us to be one explanation for what can be called "strong worker status." This underlies the notion of *Arbeiterschaft* used by German sociologists when stressing the development of a working-class identity.[9]

Table 8.1 also shows the sharp difference between white-collar workers in industry in the two countries. At the beginning of the period under consideration, this category was relatively more developed in France than in Germany, and it grew almost twice as fast as that of manual workers (annual growth rate of 0.45 as against 0.25). In Germany, on the other hand, the number of white-collar workers in industry increased sevenfold over this twenty-five-year period. The same phenomenon of rapid, massive growth is therefore observable as for manual workers. There appear to be similar consequences (the rise of class consciousness and of conscious opposition to employers), even though the occupational diversity of the group gave rise to various associations and even though it never created a closely related political party and union as the workers did.

In France, on the contrary, the slow progress made by this category kept alive the image of the industrial white-collar worker as the boss's "right-hand man." Union activity first began in the public sector and in the tertiary sector, reaching management in 1936. It would thus seem that the form taken by industrialization in the two countries created specificities in the development and nature of wage earners' collective agents: greater homogeneity of the working class and a stronger sense of identity among white-collar workers in Germany.

The effects of the mode of industrialization on employers are better known: very early on in Germany cartels brought about a strong structuring of employer organizations, conferring an authority on its members that was never attained in France. The weight of the state before 1914 and then of the army during World War I not only forced German employers to recognize labor representatives, but it also oriented companies toward types of collegiate boards. In both instances company legitimacy was strengthened.[10]

One can therefore say that the agents and the social relations among agents developed differently in these two countries; industrial relations did not have the same content and did not bring about the same consequences.

This historical preamble helps us understand the sequence of developments. We shall, first, examine how and in which ways the socialization of workers takes place in each country under the influence of the educational and vocational training systems. We shall review the educational relation and the process of stratification by job qualifications.

Second, we shall examine the organizational relation: how organizations grow out of the stratification of job qualifications or what we shall call the "qualification space"; the functional and managerial division of labor, social compartmentalization (blue-collar–white-collar workers, management, and nonmanagement); and the ways of passing from one category to the next.

Third, we shall examine the ways in which modes of stratification and organization interact with social relations within the company: wage structure and wage claims, and relations of conflict.

To conclude, we shall see in more detail why the type of relations that exist between a company and society is the only way to understand how social relations come into being, function, and change in each country.

The Educational Relation: Forms of Socialization of Workers and Industrial Qualifications

The results presented here deal with the relations established in each country between the educational system, worker mobility and distribution in various job categories, and qualifications. Such an analysis of the relations between forms of worker socialization and labor market stratification assumes that one can answer these closely related questions: What are the processes by which worker mobility takes place, and how do the categories that reflect this mobility develop? What are the characteristics of workers in the different strata of the labor market, and what relations of continuity or discontinuity develop between these?

Before presenting these results, we should comment on the method used. The fact that we had to present a synthesis of a number of basic results obliges us to isolate the functioning of the educational systems and the study of types of mobility in the industrial labor market.[11] We will, nonetheless, propose a tentative synthesis of the types of industrial qualifications and the stratification of the labor market in the two countries at the close of this section.

Stratification of Educational Systems: The Relation between General Education and Vocational Training

The first structural difference between the two countries is the way in which the general education system is related to the vocational training system, as well as the type of worker categories produced by a weeding-out process based on scholastic performance and social background in the two educational systems. The articulation between general education and vocational education depends on the way in which pupils are oriented upon leaving primary school at age 11.

In Germany pupils can enter one of two basic types of school: the first type concerns the general secondary school (the *Gymnasium*) which leads to the baccalaureate (*Arbitur*).[12] There is a highly selective process of admission, considering the proportion of young people entering this system and their family background. The second type is the extended primary school (the *Hauptschule*), which provides basic vocational education. A large majority of pupils from widely different social and educational backgrounds are oriented toward these schools. A third type of school (the *Realschule*), situated between the other two types, has remained compartmentalized, and of marginal importance at least till the end of the sixties, compared to schools preparing students for the baccalaureate (type 1).

In France, on the other hand, the majority of pupils enter the general secondary school system (type 1), open to young people from a broad gamut of social and educational backgrounds (with a large number from working-class backgrounds). This secondary school system is heterogeneous, with at least two subtypes, one of which is comparable to type 3 in Germany. In this case the educational process is highly selective when one considers how few students actually pass the baccalaureate and the type of baccalaureate they pass. Nonetheless, the type 1 school is considered the most attractive, and around it the educational system and the relations between the educational system and society are structured. Schools similar to the extended primary school in Germany (type 2) are less prevalent in France; students generally come from less privileged homes, so the orientation toward vocational training is more residual than central.[13]

The German system favors the development of mass vocational education that is at once efficient and independent of the general education system, and where genuine social competition exists. Vocational education consists of company training combined with school learning.[14] As a "socialization space," the apprenticeship system has two basic characteristics.

It is heterogeneous and competitive given the types of companies it takes place in, the types of trades learned, and the social and educational backgrounds of the apprentices.[15] At the same time it promotes homogeneity because of the type of qualifications acquired (a few "basic trades") and the uniformity of social and occupational relations developed during company training. These relations produce a unifying effect, primarily because of the quantitative, social, and occupational importance (as well as the homogeneity) of the group of foremen who are responsible for training apprentices.

These competitive and homogenizing aspects of apprenticeships are important insofar as they apply to adolescents from predominantly working-class backgrounds, although a large number are sons of white-collar workers, middle, or top-level management. This conditions two basic traits in the vocational education system: strong vertical integration and its power to weed out the students and exercise social control. Indeed, the majority of workers who succeed in obtaining occupational diplomas of intermediate or high level (a foreman's diploma, a technician's or graduated engineer's diploma) do so after having been trained as an apprentice.[16] In 1970 this was the case for all those with a foreman's diploma, for 73 percent with a technician's diploma, and for 63 percent with a graduated engineer's diploma. One should also note that workers from nonpeasant or nonworking-class backgrounds stand a much better chance of getting a higher occupational degree than young men from working-class or peasant backgrounds. These two elements of continuity and discontinuity are essential if one is to understand the homogeneity of the German vocational education system and its independence from the general education system. They also help us understand how the two levels of the vocational education system mutually strengthen one another in terms of their effectiveness and power of attraction to create a mass of graduates of all types.

In France, one must look to the secondary school system to find most of the structural traits that characterize vocational education in Germany. The principal traits, both common and distinctive, of a large majority of future workers can be traced to the competitive process whereby students rise in the hierarchy according to their level of education: the primary school certificate, the BEPC, taken around age 14, and the first and second baccalaureate examinations. Higher education and the *Grandes Ecoles* (which are the most prestigious and most vocational part) merely continue the stratification process begun in secondary school. Vocational education is residual, and students enter the system either because of their lower-class background or, when they come from a higher class, by the fact that they failed at various stages in secondary school. This mode of production has two effects on the structure of vocational education. First, the students' social background is more homogeneous than in Germany.[17] Second, levels of elementary education (the certificate of basic vocational training) and intermediate and high levels (diploma of vocational training and the technician's diploma) are highly compartmentalized and recruitment is practically independent. Recruitment depends entirely upon the orientation pupils receive in the general education system.[18] Such compartmentalization prevents the creation of a reinforcing mechanism between the two levels of the vocational education system similar to that in Germany.

Having briefly described the main distinguishing traits and functioning of the two educational systems, we should like to make two remarks about the methods used.

We should like to draw attention to the fact that the order of presentation of structural traits we used in no way implies cause and effect. In Germany, for example, the quality and autonomy of the vocational education system, in terms of its effectiveness and social tolerance, legitimate the early selectivity of the general secondary school system of which they are also the product. As for France, the strength and attractiveness of the general secondary school system are a cultural phenomenon, but they are also the result of the fact that the vocational education system is incapable of reaching a size and gaining the kind of recognition that would legitimize its autonomy and its social and occupational drawing power.[19] It is therefore the coherence of selection and orientation processes that is important in the understanding of how these processes come into being and are perpetuated.

The second remark has to do with the supply of qualifications in the two countries. A comparison of educational characteristics of the active male population shows, as could be expected, important differences which we have summarized in table 8.2. The higher level of vocational training in the German labor force is striking if one looks first at the group with an elementary education (11, 11a, and 21 in France; 11, 21, and 21a in Germany) and then at the group with intermediate-, high-, or university-level education (12, 12a, 22, and 3 in France and 12, 22, and 3 in Germany). The structure of the second group is particularly revealing as to the prevailing situation in each country.

In Germany the dominant subgroup is comprised of those with a nonuniversity-level vocational education. In France this group is only a small minority compared with those with intermediate high- or university-level education in categories 12 and 12a.[20] Similar differences can be observed when one looks at age groups, with the exception of the oldest workers, where differences are more pronounced.[21] In our opinion this is important because it calls attention to the historical origins of the two educational systems and to types of manpower from which industrial labor was drawn in both countries.

If we refer to the state of supply of qualifications, we in no way intend to assimilate it to a stock of human capital nor to treat the processes producing it as labor investments. There are two reasons for this. The first, as we pointed out, is that the supply of skills reveals structures in which the orientation of individual strategies is inseparable

Table 8.2
General and vocational education of active males (national level in 1970)

France		Germany	
No vocational diploma	**69.5**	**No vocational diploma**	**27.0**
(11) Without a diploma	32.0	(11) General primary education	25.0
(11a) Primary school certificate	28.0	(12) General secondary education	2.0
(12) BEPC and first baccalaureate	6.5		
(12a) Second baccalaureate and *propédeutique*	3.0		
Vocational diplomas not acquired in higher institutions of learning	**27.0**	**Vocational diplomas not acquired in higher institutions of learning**	**68.5**
(21) Certificate of professional aptitude	22.5	(21) Manual worker's apprenticeship diploma	36.5
(22) High or intermediate level vocational diploma	4.5	(21a) Office worker's apprentriceship diploma	10.5
		(22) High or intermediate level vocational diploma	21.5
Diplomas from institutions of higher education	**3.5**	**Diplomas from institutions of higher education**	**4.5**
Total	**100.0**	**Total**	**100.0**

Sources: For France, *Enquéte formation, qualification professionnelle* (INSEE 1970). For Germany, *Survey of occupational employment, education, and careers* (Employment and Labor Market Institute, Nuremberg, 1970).
Note: Category 11 can be related to 11 and 11a in France, and category 12 to 12 and 12a.

from the various strata or types of education that produce them. The second is that it also shows the use to which industry and companies put these types of training, their conception of the qualification associated with each type of training, and the types of labor mobility associated with each. This is what we would like to examine now.

Worker Mobility and the Establishment of the Industrial Labor Market

The labor markets in France and Germany differ with respect to labor mobility in the following way: the industrial labor market in Germany seems at once more self-contained in relation to the rest of the economy and more homogeneous in its internal functioning. These characteristics arise from two types of mobility. The first is horizontal mobility, in which former apprentices are integrated at the outset into a broader industrial labor market, even though they did their training in a specific company.[22] The second is vertical between blue-collar and white-collar jobs, as the result of a highly developed system of continuing adult occupational training. Indeed it is during the first half of their career, and usually a few years after finishing their apprenticeship, that practically everyone, be he a foreman, a technician, or a graduated engineer, obtains the diploma he needs to rise to an intermediate- or high-level white-collar worker job. Such diplomas constitute a test of technical skill, but as we have seen, they also constitute a form of social control underlying the hierarchy of blue-collar and white-collar categories.

As with apprenticeships, additional training is done in close conjunction with the industry, but advancement does not necessarily depend upon the internal market of a particular company.[23] This is validated and guaranteed by the industrial training system, or more precisely by its system of diplomas. Companies encourage it by their recognition of the hierarchy it produces. The relation between worker mobility, companies, and training systems helps to produce two basic characteristics of industrial workers taken as a group: its central position in the production of the industrial work force and its stability, homogeneity, and autonomy in relation to other categories of workers.

In France we find two types of mobility which, by contrast to the German situation, produce what we shall call an open-ended, unstable, and Balkanized industrial labor market. First, worker mobility from the industrial labor market to the nonindustrial labor market is greater, and generally speaking there is a more active exchange between these two zones of the labor market. Second, there is mobility between levels of qualification (unskilled and semiskilled workers, manual and non-manual workers). This mobility depends much more on company management and organization than on the possession of formal qualifications. For example, a worker's position in the hierarchy—his salary and socioprofessional category—depend much more on seniority in France than in Germany.[24]

In France it is not necessary to have an occupational diploma corresponding to a job category to get that job; most of those who change job categories, especially from blue to white collar, usually have only an elementary-level diploma (CAP or CEP).[25] Obtaining a diploma during one's working life career is also much rarer in France than in Germany. In those rare instances where an occupational diploma is obtained after initial general education, it is very often an elementary-level diploma (CAP).[26] Promotion after obtaining a diploma depends very much on whether the company was involved in the worker's decision to undertake further training.

We thus find a very different kind of relation between the company, the educational system, and worker mobility in France. It affects the workings of the industrial labor market in two ways. The more direct involvement of companies in determining access to different job categories and in the recognition of skill levels (even when workers already have diplomas) contributes to the continued or even engenders weakness of the vocational training system, its powers of stratification and of the "supply" of diploma holders it produces.[27] As a result each organization has to assume many of the functions of social and professional control involved in the allocation of workers to the main job categories. The small part played by professional diplomas in job allocation creates a type of mobility where assessment of a worker's potential is more important than recognition of professional qualifications. Although this system of "self-taught" workers encourages social and occupational mobility, it also gives rise to unstable occupational categories and weak internal cohesion.[28] This is especially true of manual workers in industry, who as a group are particularly "open" to the self-employed and to nonmanual and nonindustrial jobs. Moreover this group is shaped by the structuring power of organizations.

Two Types of Stratification of the Industrial Labor Market:
A "Qualification Space" and an "Organization Space"

A preliminary synthesis of those results can be based on the continuities and discontinuities that characterize each market and the types of parameters, or "spaces," in which blue- and white-collar qualifications are defined.

The preceding analysis brought to light two types of industrial qualifications and two types of "spaces" in which these qualifications are defined. In Germany we find qualifications that are specific in relation to the rest of society but whose generality and unity contribute to the construction of a "qualification space." In France we find industrial qualifications that on the whole are relatively unspecific but dependent upon the "organizational space" in which they are formed.

The German qualification space involves a continuum of occupational qualifications. The highest of these appear as an extension of blue-collar worker qualifications. There is also a set of occupational and social continuities and discontinuities that reinforces the identity and homogeneity of each qualification, distinguishing the levels of the hierarchy and reinforcing control over conditions that create them (see table 8.3).[29]

The French "organizational space" corresponds to different articulation between, on the one hand, a continuum of hierarchically structured general diplomas that give rise to general (nonspecific) qualifications, to poorly structured mobility paths, and, on the other, discontinuities that are marked by the importance attached to certain jobs within the job system, by the relative nature of social professional definitions of the groups that are formed, and by the instability and heterogeneity of these groups.[30]

This opposition between qualification and organization spaces synthesizes the preceding results. Two essential dimensions are missing if we are to progress from this type of partial coherence to the societal analysis implied in our approach: the direct study of organizational relations and of the mechanisms of social regulation and the conflict in the two societies.

The Organizational Relation: Cooperation and Hierarchy

In the German situation industry's institutional power is particularly evident in the preponderant role it plays in conceiving and organizing

Table 8.3
Occupational and general education by broad categories of wage earners (1970 national data)

Diplomas	Manual[a]	Nonmanual	Management[b]	Nonmanagement[c]
France				
Without a diploma (general or vocational)	44.0 (29.0)	9.0	5.0	13.0
Primary school certificate	26.0 (25.0)	26.0	11.0	31.0
Certificate of basic vocational training	26.0 (40.0)	26.0	9.0	25.0
General secondary school diploma	2.0 (2.0)	20.0	23.0	17.0
Vocational diploma (intermediate or high)	2.0 (4.0)	11.0	11.0	12.0
University diploma	0 (0)	13.0	41.0	2.0
Total	100.0	100.0	100.0	100.0
Germany				
Without a diploma	36.0 (13.0)	9.0	6.0	10.0
Worker apprenticeship diploma	57.0 (76.0)	16.0	4.0	20.0
White-collar worker apprenticeship	0 (0)	28.0	33.0	25.0
Vocational diploma (intermediate or high)	7.0	39.0	38.0	40.0
Higher education diploma	0 (0)	8.0	19.0	4.0
Total	100.0	100.0	100.0	100.0

Sources: For France, *Enquête formation, qualification professionnelle* (INSEE 1970). For Germany, *Survey of occupational employment, education, and careers* (Employment and Labor Market Institute, Nuremberg, 1970).
a. Results in parentheses are for skilled workers.
b. This category corresponds in France to the definition of INSEE (National Institute of Statistics and Economic Studies). In Germany the persons concerned fall into a slightly broader category than wage earners; they are classified as "unclassified wage bracket."
c. Administrative, technical, and commercial white-collar workers; their supervisors and those of production and maintenance.

occupational training. In contrast, French companies seem to enjoy greater freedom in defining and organizing jobs and their job hierarchy. Their relatively greater role in the socialization of the labor force is no doubt a reflection of their weak institutional link with the system of vocational education which is itself more autonomous.

This comparison spotlights the interaction specific to each country between the educational system and the production system (industry, companies), and it underscores the coherence between two types of social factors: socialization and organization. In fact a study of the "organizational relation" (the link between individuals and society through the division of labor and work organization in the company) is also a study of the "educational relation." The concept of an "organizational relation" lends special status to an analysis of the enterprise, revealing both its ties with society and social relations within a company, be they functional relations of cooperation in work or hierarchical relations that express the company's system of power and authority.

We shall examine both the horizontal and vertical dimensions of the organizational relation, relations of cooperation to the work system, and hierarchical relations linked to the company's stratification system.

The Work System and Cooperation

There are two ways in which a company can design its work system: it can use its own criteria to define jobs, to which workers then have to adapt, or it can take into consideration workers' qualifications and organize tasks to fit their capabilities and skills. In the first case job definition determines the worker's "profile"; in the second, the worker's qualifications shape the content of the job. Obviously, these two types of company behavior are never so completely distinct in practice. But they reflect the tendencies we observed in French and German companies.[31]

Indeed one is more likely to encounter the first case in situations where vocational training is so limited and rare that the company is led to develop its work organization in such a way that subordinate tasks needing only short training on-the-job are quite separate from planning and organizational tasks, which of course devalues the first with respect to the second. The company will be interested in a worker's "potential," his capacity to adapt to work processes and norms, and seniority will be the best indicator of success on the job.

The second type of company behavior is found when vocational training is the general rule and its social value is recognized. The company is led to organize work according to occupational norms. Such a work system tends to be based on a more homogeneous qualificational space where the distinction between tasks to be executed and planning tasks tends to correspond to complementary capacities rather than to hierarchical functions.

Taking the multiskilled worker as an example, because multiple skills is one indication of the degree and nature of a worker's qualifications, we can characterize the relational capacity of each work system and draw attention to its specific significance in each country.

In the German labor market a situation favorable to the development of multiple skills already exists because there is a limited number of basic trades in most industries and a large number of workers with similar training, so companies have to deal with a group of relatively homogeneous qualifications.[32,33] But the way German companies conceive their work organization and the division of tasks is no less decisive. A great deal of autonomy is left to production units (consisting of workers, gangers, and foremen) in job definition and the way tasks are carried out. Jobs correspond to groups of complementary tasks which the foreman can organize at will to fit the qualifications of his workers. By being assigned to different jobs, a worker gets the equivalent of in-service training.[34] The multiple skills acquired resemble a qualificational process rather than a mode of organization and compensate in some ways for the deskilling of the technical division of work.[35] In this sense a promotion usually takes the form of improvement in the original job category rather than a step up in a hierarchy.

The way multiple skills are deployed, insofar as they are based on a broad job definition, also helps to develop the relational capacity of the work system. Less division of labor indeed implies closer cooperation, not only between members of a production unit but also between the unit and the technical department above it. As they are based on complementary capacities, work relations thus tend to become functional rather than hierarchical.

In the French firms we observed the use of multiple skills was very different. In terms of organization, multiple skills tend to be a response to management problems such as absenteeism or fluctuations in production. Because of these economic considerations the use of multiple skills reproduces rather than modifies the technical division of work. A worker is considered multiskilled if he has had experience on several jobs, which he can take on alternately even though his job qualification does not change. It is worth noting that the main obstacle to more widespread use of multiple skills is that the men themselves object to doing a job with a higher rating than the one they usually do. This observation pinpoints an essential aspect of the work system: its dependence on an administrative management that is relatively autonomous in relation to technical management (involved in production). In this case job descriptions and job assignments are no longer the domain of those directly responsible for production but of the personnel department, which is close to general management. One can also observe another type of dependence relation in production in the way operational tasks are distinguished from those of work organization. What may appear as a universal principle of organization ever since Taylor takes on new meaning, when placed in the preceding context. As the part played by the technical departments in determining production tasks increases, autonomy in production is reduced.[36] Consequently, the involvement of administrative management in job structures and the priority given to work organization over production weakens the relational capacity of the work system. Work that has been fragmented and deskilled does not promote relations of cooperation. Nor do such relations develop better when jobs are assigned by administrative decision; this tends to isolate each worker in a chain of command that corresponds more to an organizational space than to a qualification space. The development of technical and administrative control functions inherent in this system goes hand in hand with a preponderance of hierarchical relations over relations of cooperation.

The preceding considerations indicate one of the dimensions of the "organizational relation" implied in each work system by the way operational tasks to be executed are distributed and organized as well as organizational and conceptual tasks. The greater the distinction made between these tasks, the less relations of cooperation develop. But the organizational relation cannot be reduced to the functional demands of the work system; it is also an indication of the company's stratification system, and especially of its managerial structure.

The System of Stratification and Hierarchy

Our approach leads us to ask what contributes in each country to the definition of statuses and their arrangement in a hierarchy rather than to measure their respective degrees of congruency, which assumes a priori that categories of statuses in one country can be compared with those of another country. This implies that a company's internal stratification cannot be independent from the social conditions that produced it.

One has only to evoke the debates that took place in the 1920s in Germany on the social definition of employees (*Angestellte*) or, more recently in France, debates on "the new working class" or on managerial staff to grasp the social specificity of these categories. To be a worker or a manager does not mean the same thing in each country because the dividing line between blue- and white-collar workers does not correspond to the same types of social relations. Therefore one can hardly state that stratification within the company corresponds solely to the functional demands of a technology that are the same everywhere or to the demands of a so-called "universal" management science.

This is the conclusion arising from our observation of French and German companies. Some idea of a company's stratification can be had from the way jobs are structured: for technologies and categories of comparable size, job distribution varies considerably from one country to the other. In short, there are comparatively more blue-collar workers in German companies and comparatively more white-collar workers in corresponding French companies. To be more precise, in France the greater proportions of clerical staff, technicians, and middle management (foremen, shop and office supervisors), account for the difference. This empirical observation relates back to the historical development of each type of social actor discussed in the introduction. However, it is important to identify the *processes* behind the relative stability of the dividing lines between categories. Two of them seem particularly significant: the line between blue-collar and white-collar workers and that between management and nonmanagement.

The Dividing Line between Blue- and White-Collar Workers
While recognizing that differences between blue- and white-collar workers are diminishing, their relative persistence still poses a problem.[37] The dividing line will be all the sharper when skills are based on specific training, provided of course that the company recognizes these in its work organization and the distribution of tasks. This is more likely to happen if training in schools and companies is complementary. The interaction between forms of socialization and the division of labor implied in the preceding remarks allows us to account for the processes that create the different demarcations in France and Germany.

Indeed it is in Germany that the division between blue- and white-collar workers (whose sociohistorical significance was examined earlier) is the most significant, that is, where job categories and educational levels correspond more closely, and especially where the status of manual worker is more strongly supported by the social importance of apprenticeships. Indeed one can judge the importance of apprenticeships in the educational system by the fact that they involve a broad segment of the population, evidenced by the social origins of the apprentices, who come from both working-class and nonworking-class backgrounds.[38] But the company itself reinforces the status of manual worker by the type of work organization it institutes. As we have seen, the work system tends to lend more importance to operational than to organizational tasks, giving the production unit (workers, gangers, and foremen) more freedom to distribute tasks. Such a system results in a certain professionalization of workers' jobs, which sustains and enhances their competence. But a stronger occupational identity is created when a group is relatively self-contained. Thus in terms of (intrageneration) mobility, skilled workers in Germany are more stable than their French counterparts but are less dependent on a particular company.[39] Another characteristic of the German workers' stability is the relatively higher rate of *social reproduction*.[40] Thus the dividing line between blue collar and white collar no dount owes its relative permanence to a situation where the high status of manual work goes hand in hand with a strong sense of working-class identity.[41]

In France a very different situation developed. Instead of the categorical stability of German workers, one finds relative instability. There is not as high a degree of professionalization among French workers; this can be tied to the residual nature of vocational training and to lesser autonomy given to subordinates by the type of work organization. A worker will be more likely to acquire qualification through mobility in the company's *organizational space* (a change of categories or status) than through progression in the same *work space*, evidenced by the comparatively greater seniority of the skilled than the unskilled, and among clerical staff and middle management compared with manual workers generally. This goes along with the greater prestige of office jobs, whose functions are to oversee, plan, or administrate operational and production tasks. Such a system can only encourage the development and attractiveness of white-collar grades or of management functions that enjoy higher status. Thus the mobility from blue to white collar, which is more frequent here, tends to lower the status of the blue-collar worker.[42] Promotion is seen negatively as a breakaway from one's original status and positively as a step up the hierarchy of jobs and functions.

The Dividing Line between Management and Nonmanagement

Promotion to management is the other component of a company's system of stratification, but here too its significance differs in France and in Germany.

In general, where technico-productive functions predominate over administrative and conceptual functions, there is greater autonomy of the work force, and production management becomes a more autonomous and homogeneous category. Because the basic production unit (workers, group leaders, and foremen) experiences less autonomy, the distinction between staff and line becomes less important. Likewise, in a work system that legitimizes occupational norms, authority tends to be based on one's technical ability rather than on authority delegated from above. Because relations between superiors and subordinates will be based more on ability than on hierarchy, differences in status will be less pronounced.

The German *Meister* is a case in point: his technical competence is sanctioned by a socially recognized diploma, which puts him in the same qualification space as the skilled worker, though at a higher level, and with a broad span of control.[43] German foremen are less numerous than their French counterparts and have more men under them (see table 8.4). This is the concept of *Arbeiterschaft* which, according to Popitz, covers the worker-foreman relationship: there is only a slight difference between workers and technical management which is comprised of graduated engineers, for they fall into the same qualificational space.[44] Graduated engineers receive an education that is oriented more toward applied technology than a university-trained engineer, and their social background is more modest. All this makes them feel closer to the workers than to university graduates.

The middle-management characteristics observed here apply equally well to all levels of management: promotion into management corresponds more to increased technical competence recognized by the company than to a change of status decided on by management. This is one of the basic traits of company stratification: there is a strong tendency to link the level of training with the job level. The result is a relatively homogeneous management, and a degree of continuity between management and nonmanagement. In most cases, irrespective of the level

Table 8.4
Average number of workers per supervisor

	Unit production	Mass production	Continuous production
French establishments (1)	10.0	16	4.5
German establishments (2)	25.0	45	6.0
Ratio (2 : 1)	2.5	2.8	1.3

Source: Survey of French and German companies by the Laboratoire d'Economie et de Sociologie du Travail (LEST), Aix-en-Provence.

of training reached later on, this homogeneity is related to a technical competence whose basic point of reference is the manual apprenticeship. Among top management in industry only 19.4 percent have university degrees (as opposed to 41 percent in France).[45] The majority have nonuniversity occupational education, that is, further education after apprenticeships but on a fairly high level (*Technikschule-ingenieurschule*). Only a minority of top management is hired on the basis of diplomas to exercise executive functions (*Leitende Angetellte*).[46] The relative continuity between management and other categories reflects both occupational mobility based on a progressive development of qualifications and on less sharp social and occupational distinctions made between management and nonmanagement.[47] This holds true particularly for technical middle management, but it often applies to top management (those who hold an L.A. function) as well, for many start out as workers or apprentices.[48]

The dividing line between managers and nonmanagers in French companies is drawn more often according to organizational rather than to professional criteria. In this respect the movement into management represents a discontinuity. Whereas in Germany managers and nonmanagers have relatively similar types of education and a continuity of qualification, in France one finds a greater professional diversity among management even though their presence in the organizational hierarchy might provide a symbolic unity. The case of production supervisors (foremen) is particularly revealing. Although the French foreman usually starts off as a worker, like his German counterpart, conditions for promotion are not the same. His position is not supported by an occupational diploma; it is given to him by the company, which bases its choice on his capacity to lead men and give orders. Moving into a supervisory job thus represents a break rather than continuity:

it means that he is entering management (albeit at the lowest level) rather than developing a higher level of training. The French foreman's functions are also different from those of the German *Meister*, for he does not play the same role in the work system. Production norms are more precisely laid down by the technical departments, and the foreman has to ensure they are met. He will also inform the personnel department of all the aspects of administrative management over which he has no control. His authority, which has only weak professional justification, is based on rank; as he is at the lowest level of the hierarchy, he has little scope for decision making. This is particularly evident when questions of personnel management come up or when there are claims or labor disputes. The foreman may exercise authority, but he has no power.[49] The higher foreman-to-worker ratio in France could indicate the importance of (technical and social) control functions in a work system where operatives have little autonomy and where labor disputes can be solved only at the top.

Though one cannot make broad generalizations for all of French management, these traits are nonetheless the most basic: becoming a manager corresponds to a promotion up the status hierarchy rather than the attainment of greater technical ability. Therefore access to a management position and internal mobility within the category will generally result from the way the company functions and from socialization in accordance with its organizational norms. Attachment to the company tends to become one of the principal criteria for stratification, as evidenced by the greater average length of service; French managers have more seniority compared with their German counterparts.[50] In this sense all the managers, including those who were graduated from a *Grand Ecole*, are considered by the company to be "self-taught": success in the company depends on their degree of integration. Though socialization is similar for all managers, there are in fact significant discontinuities within the category. These are the result of the importance given to managers who have graduated from higher education institutions (usually the *Grandes Ecoles*) over others whom the company calls "self-taught men" (a category which to all intents and purposes does not exist in Germany).[51] This discontinuity in education is also reflected in differences in career and in rank. Even though graduates often start out as technical managers in charge of production or research, within a few years they will take over management functions at the highest levels. The "self-taught men," on the contrary, reach their ceiling much more quickly at an intermediate level, having made their career in the production or technical divisions, or more often in the administrative or sales departments.[52]

Work and Stratification

The preceding analysis highlights significant differences between the work system and the stratification system peculiar to each country and interactions between the two systems. In each country we have observed a structural and functional coherence between work organization and differentiation of jobs and status. What we have called the "organizational relation" is precisely the result of this interaction. We should remember that this relation can vary from country to country for the same technology depending on the emphasis a company puts on co-operation and hierarchical relations: stratification merely expresses the state of these social relations.

In this respect a comparison of German and French companies reveals independence between the nature of the professional structures of technico-productive tasks and the degree of functional and hierarchical differentiation between functions of authority and technical competence. When work organization is based on a homogeneous qualification space common to all the technico-productive categories (workers, foremen, technicians, or production engineers), the functions of authority and technical competence are less distinct from production tasks. Similarly, authority and competence will be more interdependent. The result of such a process is that the middle-management categories will be less developed, inasmuch as their function, in the reverse situation, will be the technical, administrative, and social control of "productive" workers who have a low degree of autonomy. Indeed in this last instance the logic of organization tends to dominate that of qualification. Whereas a more homogeneous distribution of skill limits hierarchical differentiation and encourages decentralized authority, an increase in the number of technical and administrative controls strengthens hierarchy and concentrates authority. This is the reason for the development of middle management and a higher density of top-level management with executive functions.[53]

In sum, in each case the "organizational relation" reveals a certain balance between the distribution of conceptual and operational functions, of authority and technical competence. This balance between functions goes hand in hand with a more or less sharp division of work and uneven distribution of skill. In another sense this idea of balance also reflects the forms of social control and conflict that arise in a company, and consequently the social relations of subordination and domination that are directly expressed in the social division of work and in the corresponding economic relation.

The Industrial Relation: Wages, Claims, and Labor Disputes

The preceding examination of the development of stratification and organizational phenomena raises the question of how work relations are institutionalized. Indeed socialization processes at school and at work are so different in each country that one can expect to see differences in the way companies function, as seen in their system of industrial relations. There should be some form of interaction among occupational status, the agents involved, the organization of the work system, the development of labor disputes and the way they are settled.

In general, class relations are determined by the workers' dependence on the company, that is, the "wage relation." Such dependence can, however, vary considerably in degree and type so that, despite numerous formal analogies, systems of industrial relations often cover very different social relations. This is the case of the educational and organizational relations which, though they may be examined separately, can only be explained by their mutual interaction and coherence. We shall now examine one aspect of this interaction and coherence by looking in succession at wage structures, the localization of negotiations, and the handling of company claims.

Wage Structures

As we mentioned earlier, the starting point of this research was an attempt to explain the systematic differences in earnings differentials between skilled and unskilled workers, blue-collar and white-collar workers, and between management and nonmanagement grades. These differentials were in every case greater in France than in Germany: the findings we made in companies confirm the results of wage-structure studies undertaken by the Statistical Office of the European Communities.[54]

Explaining these differences in terms of human capital and a supply-demand, or "price-productivity," mechanism is made difficult by the fact that nonworker categories (especially white-collar workers and middle management, including foremen) are relatively better paid and considerably more numerous in France than in Germany. If one were to explain these higher wages by the fact these types of people are relatively harder to find in France than in Germany, one would have to suppose that productivity is extremely high; however, there is little to substantiate such a hypothesis. It is therefore necessary to look for other types of relations and in particular to ask whether the pronounced structural differences examined earlier do not play a role in this phenomenon. Thus we leave the one-dimensional frame of analysis offered by the market for the problematics of construction of social spaces: stratification according to job categories or to qualifications is no longer the sole result of adjustments induced by the agents' productivity. This stratification is the end result of a process whereby individuals are oriented toward categories and are kept there.

Thus an examination of statistics on wage differentials reveals two striking facts: the role of age and length of service, on the one hand, and of the position of nonmanual workers, on the other. A subsidiary consideration is that authority functions, particularly for foremen, also have a differentiating effect, though to a lesser degree.

Examining all workers in industry, one can see that the effect of a worker's age on his income is twice as high in France as in Germany. The difference between the two countries is even more pronounced if we measure the influence of length of service in the company. In France skilled workers have markedly longer service than unskilled workers, and their seniority is a vital factor in their qualification. In Germany this is not an essential criterion for skilled workers and their length of service is frequently shorter than that of unskilled workers. As for the ratio between average salaries of manual and nonmanual workers the average is higher in France (1.8 percent) than in Germany (1.35 percent). Age, length of service, and status (manual or nonmanual) are thus given more value in France than in Germany. Our hypotheses allow us to provide an explanation that is confirmed by other observations.

One of the most striking contrasts in attitudes as to the factors determining wages is the emphasis put on efficiency and performance (*Leistung*) in Germany and on seniority in France. In Germany unions and employers agree that on principle seniority should not be taken into consideration, even though in practice it sometimes is, whereas *Leistung* is considered essential at all levels and for all jobs. In France it is common knowledge that trade unions generally refuse to accept productivity over length of service as a criterion, even if they, too, do not always practice what they preach. As for employers and personnel managers, their attitude does not differ in practice very much from that of the unions.

These attitudes are most certainly linked to the nature of and the importance given to vocational education in these countries. In Germany the fact that employers recognize the value of apprenticeship and post-apprenticeship diplomas makes this education a basic criterion of skill, and to a large extent, of a worker's efficiency. Being classified in a given wage range depends more on what diplomas one has than on the job one does. On the other hand, the fact that diplomas are given scant recognition in France means that belonging to a company for a long time is the decisive factor in promotion.

In Germany there is a standard way to acquire qualifications, so men are less dependent on one company, and the labor market is more homogeneous, a factor that promotes greater wage uniformity. In France the stratification effect of organization is stronger than the unifying effect of the market. The low level of professional organization of workers increases their dependence on the company and makes seniority the principal criterion in creating the hierarchy, at least among manual workers.

Differences between manual and nonmanual workers also can be traced, in our opinion, to the very different educational systems. In Germany apprenticeship training is not restricted to manual workers; corresponding apprenticeships exist for white-collar workers. What is more, a good many nonmanual workers in the technico-productive sector got their basic training as apprentices. One can therefore speak of a greater professional homogeneity in the case of many technicians and graduate engineers of the same qualificational space.

In France, on the contrary, poor levels of professional organization for both blue- and white-collar workers are linked to the traditionally inferior technical and vocational education as compared with general education. Diplomas are the same for a white-collar worker and a blue-collar worker, if the latter has one. Indeed the general education system eliminates more manual workers earlier, so it would seem that wage differentials between blue-collar workers and white-collar workers reflect the different statuses of the two educational systems.

These remarks may seem surprising, especially when one remembers that the social gap between blue- and white-collar workers is without doubt more evident in Germany than in France. In France the long-established social security system and the recent monthly pay system tend to give uniform status to all employees. On the contrary, in Germany the social identity of each category in relation to the other is much more apparent in institutions.[55] It is therefore in the country with the biggest institutional and social heterogeneity that wage differentials are the lowest (and that economic equality is the greatest), and vice versa. To explain this anomaly, it is perhaps useful to recall the historical development of these social agents: German white-collar workers felt the impact of industrialization on their work much earlier than their French counterparts and developed their union movement with the idea of maintaining an institutional specificity in relation to workers.

Where Negotiations Take Place and How Claims Are Handled

Just as wage relations reveal certain aspects of social relations, so too does the level at which negotiations and claims take place and the way claims are handled in companies.

Where Negotiations Take Place

When an observer looks at institutions to determine where negotiations take place, he gets a very misleading impression. At first glance he is struck by the fact that German trade unions have neither a legal place nor a negotiation role in companies whereas in France, at least since a law was passed in December 1978, union locals have been given legal recognition in companies and, since the 1971 collective bargaining law, the right to negotiate at this level.

But in fact negotiation occurs on a much higher level in French unions than in German unions. The most important negotiations do not take place on the company nor on the branch level but on the *confederate* ("interprofessional") level. In Germany they take place on the level of a branch of industry or a region. And even though employer and union organizations choose an industrial branch or a region for tactical reasons, it is nonetheless rare that negotiations actually take place on a *confederate* level. Paradoxically, if collective bargaining has developed considerably in France since the 1960s between the central employers' organization and the major union confederations, it has essentially been to reach nationwide agreements that affect industry and commerce as a whole. Examples of such agreements are a progressive reduction in the number of work hours, uniform status for blue- and white-collar workers (monthly paychecks), job protection (procedures for redundancy and for protecting those who are made redundant, guaranteed income for workers before they reach the full retirement age, and measures to improve working conditions. Some of these agreements were expressly designed to avoid negotiations and disputes within the company, especially on job questions, to raise the level at which negotiations take place; and to neutralize the union's influence. Though they were collective agreements, they tend to have as much impact as a law. What happens then in France is that there is an obvious desire to place negotiations on the highest level in order to avoid disputes on the company level. By and large employer organizations are afraid that unions will use agreements signed on a higher level to negotiate on the company level.

In Germany, on the contrary, it is the trade unions that seem to fear bargaining by works councils on questions that have already been settled in the collective agreements they have signed: such negotiations are authorized on the condition that a special "opening" clause exist in the collective agreement. If unions are wary of this way of opening negotiations, it is because they want protection against the works council, over which they might have no control. In most cases, however, they do in fact control the councils so that negotiations on the company level, by the *Betriebsvereinbarungen*, are common practice.

One is struck by the fact that in general German unions accept the principle of an action or a negotiation with no labor strife in a company, whereas French unions strongly reject it.

Yet it is equally striking that German unions have increasingly taken their disputes to the national level, in particular during the debates on the co-management law whereas negotiations led by French unions on this level have been by and large peaceful and fruitful.

This difference in attitudes toward negotiations on a company level seems to us to be related to the status of companies and trade unions in each society. In Germany there is mutual recognition of the company and the union, which are looked on as basic institutions in an industrial society. This recognition appeared early on when collective bargaining began to develop, whereas the system of collective agreements became powerful in France only in the 1950s. The German attitude also reflects the powerful status of the worker and his organizations as well as the prestige of private enterprise and its social role in German society, which has its practical applications in the vocational education system. French companies have not become involved in such a system.

The Way Claims Are Handled

We have already pointed to the greater dependence of the skilled worker on the company in France, a dependence that is shown in the greater differential in seniority between skilled and unskilled workers, compared with Germany. We have also noted the importance of seniority in determining French wages. These characteristics are related to the fact that promotions are given to workers not so much because they have reached a level of qualification or acquired a diploma as because they are progressively assigned to better-paying jobs, in a semiautomatic career process. A worker's salary is determined primarily by the coefficient given to the job he is doing and by the content and requirements of the job, which are set by administrative decision. In this situation regulating wages is equivalent to regulating job assignments in a company. Such regulation must be centralized since the organization chart and job evaluation are rigidly determined and depend on a central decision. It is inconceivable that a foreman or a shop manager would reclassify a job just to promote someone. In most cases promotion depends on the existence of a vacancy. In companies where the turnover for skilled jobs is low, a comparison of seniorities and merits of those in line for promotion requires a centralized decision, especially since competing individuals belong to different departments or workshops. This way of determining promotions did not develop by chance. It is linked to the fact that individual qualifications can only become a criterion for status through the mediation of a centralized work organization.

The German foreman's power over work organization, for example, is based on the fact that a job assignment does not automatically affect status or wages. Status and wages are more directly based on ability, independent of the job. The example of multiskilled workers in both countries clearly shows the different weight given to judgment of an individual's qualities and his job assignment. In France a person who is completely multiskilled is dangerous in the eyes of personnel management: if he is doing a job with a coefficient higher than his usual one, this gives him an almost automatic right to a pay rise or in any case immediately constitutes the basis for a claim. In Germany the fact of being multiskilled only opens up the possibility of increased ability which, if it is noticed by the foreman, might give rise to a promotion.

Under these circumstances job assignments in France must be the prerogative of management and must necessarily be centralized. In Germany not only is centralization nonexistent or limited, but job assignments are no longer the exclusive prerogative of management. In a company the management has to agree with the workers' council on matters of hiring, changing jobs, and regrouping teams (Article 95 of the Works Constitution Act).[56] In general, the sphere of operational tasks is relatively independent of management. This autonomy is seen in combination at this level of technical management and social management. In France, on the contrary, questions of social management (whatever affects the status of personnel, including the work sphere and its practical organization) tend to rise to the top. The institutions and functions of German "codetermination," inasmuch as they affect work organization and the concrete, daily determination of worker status, appear to be the result of the relative autonomy of the work sphere in relation to the administrative and executive spheres of the company. For it is obvious that the mere existence of an institution cannot be an explanation in itself, because there is no guarantee that it will actually function. For the past thirty years French companies have been busy establishing institutions of cooperation one on top of the other without really changing the way they function. On the contrary, it would seem that shop floor level codetermination, which is combined with a system of "shop stewards" who are often placed in "supervisory groups" in the various shops, owes its effectiveness to the "relational capacities" in the qualification space comprising workers, supervisors, and graduated engineers (by isolating them to a certain degree from top-level management).

The preceding remarks show that different behavior patterns exist in union and company relations, which are tied to the nature of work relations in the two countries. When an action is underway, a greater distinction is made in Germany between political and technical (or concrete) spheres, whereas in France both spheres are often merged. The fact that disputes tend to rise to the top is a reflection of the absence of any clear functional demarcation. In our opinion this is due to the lower degree of autonomy in work and to the lesser importance of technical aspects of production, as compared with the company's administrative functions, be they job preparation functions, new investment, commercial, or most important personnel functions. It would seem that many decisions are taken in France without consulting production managers, whereas in Germany a production engineer or even a foreman is consulted on such questions as where to install a new machine, the form of a new product, a new production method, or a new way to organize work.

In Germany this characteristic seems to us to be related to the strength of worker status and its influence, via apprenticeships, *on all the qualification space*, from the skilled worker to the graduated engineer. It is also related to what can be called the double legitimacy of the company and the union in society.

Thus the nature of the enterprise and its industrial relations cannot be studied independent of other basic social relations, which like the educational or organizational relations express the different dimensions of social control and of the relations between social classes.

Conclusion: The Company and Society

The preceding analysis has brought to light three types of social relations that have proved to be particularly important in the comparison of these two countries. By concentrating perforce on analysis, we have not brought out the interactions between these social relations. Let us note in passing that the way these relations combine is a characteristic that distinguishes the two societies. It can play the role of multiplier of individual differences, though only to a certain extent if one agrees that interactions of social relations correspond to the type of coherence particular to each country. Indeed, although in theory the range of possibilities is considerable, it is much less so when we consider the disparate historical components of particular societies. This is no doubt one of the limits to such an "hypothetical-inductive" approach: its claim to theoretical generalization is based on the assumption that there is a multiplicity of comparable experiences.[57] In this case the interaction among educational, organizational, and industrial relations allows us to determine what may be the invariable and the principal characteristics of each system of coherence. Thus even if one agrees that in any industrial society the differences in general education and vocational education, the ways in which work is divided between operational tasks and conceptual tasks, the nature and localization of disputes between the employer and the union all constitute important elements in the social relation, the combination of these elements is not due to chance. In fact in each society the wage relationship of labor and capital can be taken as a constant that corresponds to that society's own historicity, to its particular development and the makeup and state of social hierarchy.

But what might be only the outline of a social theory takes on added significance in our approach, whose prime characteristic is that it starts with a study of the company in order to study society.[58] This has several implications as far as method and theoretical orientation are concerned.

The choice of the company as an object of study can easily be justified if one considers such institutions in the industrial societies to be central to economic and social relations.[59] This choice also corresponds to the question posed at the outset of our research concerning wage structure in French and German companies.

The "societal effect" approach tends to "socialize" the idea of the company with respect to the social relations that go to make it up. In this sense a company has neither an *interior* nor an *exterior*; it is studied in society. This is a departure from conceptual approaches which take the company in relation to its environment (the economic market, the strategy of competitors or dominant organizations, or the cultural context). The societal effect considers all the (particular) social relations expressed in the company, which it helps to produce or to reproduce. This puts emphasis on the autonomy of the company which in fact is regarded as relative.

Our study of the "historical development of the agents" indicates that analytical categories must themselves be socialized. The French foreman then cannot really be compared with the German *Meister*, nor the top-level manager with the *Leitende Angestellte*, because categories of agents were constituted in different social spaces. Treating worker apprenticeships in Germany as much more central to the educational system only makes sense if one considers apprenticeships as a particular social space, which is inseparable from the company's conception of work organization, and the occupational position of a graduated engineer in relation to the skilled worker. The same approach holds true for a trade union, a company council, or incentive wages. Each institution only makes sense in connection to the nature of social relations on which it is based.

In this sense our approach tends to *conceptualize differences rather than similarities* by pointing up the noncomparable quality of the analytical categories that were a priori considered to be comparable. This is a natural result of our undertaking an international comparison which in fact is used for its heuristic interest. It allows us to highlight the relativity (and variability) of analytical categories and the processes that go to make it up. Societal effects exist only to the extent that the comparison brings to light the particular modes by which different societies express their basic social relations. One can thus admit that in German as well as French companies, the hierarchical phenomenon expresses relations of inequality and domination, but the analysis is improved if one can show how this generally recognized phenomenon comes about and by which processes. The most significant differences are then no longer merely differences in degree but in kind. The phenomenon can no longer be reduced to an economic or organizational parameter, for it expresses all the social relations at work in a company which no doubt constitute the deep-seated structure of its relations with society.

Notes

1. M. Maurice, F. Sellier, and J.-J. Silvestre, in collaboration with J. Dupex, O. de Fontmagne, and C. Marry, as well as M. Brossard, and J. Jaudas. *Production de la hiérarchie dans l'enterprise, recherche d'un effet sociétal: Allemagne-France* (LEST, October 1977). This research was funded by CORDES.

The methods used for the survey are indicated in the report. We would like to recall the following points. Twelve industrial establishments were studied in all, they were in the chemical and engineering industries and in mass production. In each establishment we collected:

1. individual statistics on wage earners, particularly on the management staff,

2. qualitative information during numerous talks with the administration and with wage earners at various levels of the hierarchy (information gathering during 1974, 1975, and 1976). These in-depth studies were accompanied by an analysis of a large quantity of statistics gathered in each company and on the national level.

2. See J.-J. Silvestre, "Les différences de salaire dans l'industrie," *Revue Internationale du Travail* **110** (December 1974):551–553. These microeconomic results were later confirmed on an industrywide level by the Statistical Office of the European Community. In 1972 there were in French industry 27 white-collar workers and middle-management for 100 workers as compared with 20 in Germany. These differences are even greater in large establishments (over 1,000 employees), where the numbers of workers per foreman are, respectively, 16 and 29, and the numbers of nonmanagement nonmanual workers are 33 and 22 per 100.

3. This orientation is found in comparative research on salary structures and particularly in the not very recent work by G. Lydall, *The Structure of Earnings* (Oxford: Clarendon Press, 1966).

4. On this subject, M. Brossard and M. Maurice, "Existe-t-il un modèle universel des structures d'organisation?" *Sociologie du Travail* **16** (1974).

5. For thirty years, from 1876 to 1906, the French working class grew by 10 percent; see the comparisons in A. Sturmthal and J. G. Scoville (eds.), *The International Labor Movement in Transition* (Urbana: University of Illinois Press, 1973), particularly the contributions of P. Losche and F. Sellier.

6. E. Guillaumin, *La vie d'un simple* (Paris: Stock, 1943).

7. In France potato cultivation became common around 1850–1860; see G. Fayolle, *La Vie quotidienne du Périgord* (Paris: Hachette, 1977), p. 208.

8. H. Burgelin, *La Société Allemande, 1871–1968* (Paris: Arthaud, 1969), p. 90.

9. See in particular H. Popitz et al., *Das Gesellschaftsbild der Arbeiter* (Tubingen: Mohr, 1957).

10. M. P. Fogarty, "Codetermination and company structure in Germany," *British Journal of Industrial Relations* (March 1964):79.

11. We would like to draw attention to an essential point of method. Most comparisons of the two countries refer us to statistics on education, employment, and so forth, but these categories are in fact not comparable. There are a great many divergencies and differences as to the nature of the social processes that produce them, so the object of comparisons should be two societal coherences.

12. The statistical observations we base our comments on deal primarily with the functioning of the two educational systems from 1950 to 1970. More recent trends might lead us to revise certain comments. We do not believe that they are pronounced enough to alter the validity of our comparative analysis. We will refer to results on older trends, which entirely confirm our analysis in the absence of a historical study that we could not incorporate in this report. We should add that, except where mentioned otherwise, the statistics we use deal with the active male population.

13. Here are a few statistical indications of the relative importance of types of schools in the two countries during the 1960s. In Germany the extended primary school education is comprised of 75 to 80 percent of the students in that age group, type 1 about 15 percent. In France extended primary education (type 2) is comprised for 40 to 45 percent of the students; 55 to 60 percent of students are in general secondary schools (type 1), divided into two subgroups of equal importance; 35 percent take the baccalaureate examination.

14. Apprenticeships usually take place from the ages of 15 to 18, during which time *all* adolescents not attending school full time are obliged to attend vocational classes one day a week. The great majority of these adolescents combine this schooling with an apprenticeship in a company. Eighty percent of the apprentices are worker apprentices. We refer to this type of apprenticeship here. White-collar worker apprenticeships are socially more selective and attract an equal number of students from the two types of secondary schools and from the elementary schools.

15. We include in this group both foremen in industry and craftsmen who have the *Meister* diploma. This group, whose authority is conferred by the diploma, represents roughly 7 percent of the active male population.

16. About one-third of those who do a worker apprenticeship are included in this group.

17. In France 45 percent of the students who get the CAP (certificate of occupational aptitude) are from peasant or manual work backgrounds; in Germany the proportion is only 25 percent. One also notices in France that only 12

percent of the sons of management or the liberal professions have the CAP. In Germany the percentage for the same categories is 40 percent.

18. Another compartmentalizing factor is evident in the group of workers with an occupational aptitude certificate. Half of these workers were apprentices and half were full-time students in a vocational school. These two types of basic vocational education attract only a small proportion of students by age group (23 percent in France vs. 62 percent in Germany), and there is a high rate of failures and dropouts.

19. For both France and Germany, we should refer to a broader analysis that takes into account the role of the company and the industrial system in the building, or nonbuilding, of this legitimacy and effectiveness of the vocational education systems.

20. There are few graduates of the *Grandes Ecoles*. They hold positions at the top of the hierarchy of both general and vocational types of education as well as privileged positions in industry.
21. Such is the case especially as far as workers with intermediate or high-level occupational diplomas are concerned.

22. It is interesting to note that only 13 percent of apprentices in crafts and 30 percent in industry stay for more than five years in the place where they got their training and that only a small percentage of those who stay are promoted to a category higher than skilled worker. It would seem then that apprenticeships mean two things to companies: they are considered (1) as an often heavy investment in an individual and as a collective investment to train a socio-occupational stratum of skilled workers with general rather than specific qualifications and (2) as a form of socialization that contributes to the stability of workers in that stratum.

23. The statistical evidence available on a national level and the more detailed statistics that we gleaned in the companies we studied show that the vast majority of workers who acquire a high-level occupational diploma during the course of their career change companies.

24. For industrial wage earners as a whole, the effect of seniority on wages is three times higher in France than in Germany. This is also borne out by the relation between average salaries and average seniority by economic sector. In industry generally and in the companies we studied, we also found that in France seniority and sometimes age are more discriminant variables for hierarchical categories: manual workers–skilled workers, and nonmanual and manual workers. Seniority is particularly discriminant for middle management. It is as if in France, much more so than in Germany, the stability of the labor force pushed men toward the top of the classification structure.

27. Observations are based on two results: (1) the trend toward company-based training programs or multicompany-controlled occupational schools and (2) the high integration of *Grandes Ecoles* diplomas into the internal markets of companies, and particularly the strong influence of length of service on

wages, even though the high professional qualifications that go with these diplomas are recognized.

28. It seems that for the two countries in the period from 1965 to 1970, two-way movements in mobility—between manual and self-employed nonmanual workers, skilled and unskilled workers—were stronger in France. The same seems to apply, according to available information, to intergeneration mobility.

29. Skilled manual workers and even manual workers have a diploma at the end of their apprenticeship. With the exception of administrative and commercial personnel who have white-collar apprenticeship diplomas, white-collar workers generally have an intermediate or high-level apprenticeship diploma. University diplomas are very rare, even for management. In France, a minority of manual workers have a CAP diploma, whereas 52 percent of the manual workers and 46 percent of nonmanual workers have a primary school diploma (CAP or CEP). Diploma holders from institutions of higher learning (*Grandes Ecoles*) represent a relatively large group. Date gathered in the companies we studied on management show another difference: wage earners with a primary education are in the majority in Germany.

30. In other words, the orientation and nature of mobility movements go hand in hand with the negative and relative definitions of clerical staff categories. Technicians and foremen are nonmanagement nonmanual workers. Manual workers are defined by their nonpromotion to clerical, technician, or foreman grades and skilled workers by their promotion from unskilled positions.

31. The gap between school and company is in this case of another order, even though the employers' "hold" over the educational system is sometimes criticized. In fact the comparison between the two countries renders the nature of relations between the two institutions relative; their specificity then excludes a term-to-term comparison.

32. Labor statistics allow us to identify a hard core of basic trades; the rest of the industrial trades can be grouped around this hard core. These basic trades also have a high degree of "transferability" from one company to the next. See *Berufswege und Arbeitsmarkt* (Nuremberg: Institut für Arbeitsmarkt und Berufsforschung, 1976), pp. 30–33.

33. One should remember that occupational training in a company is one of the basic characteristics of the vocational system. In 1974, 52 percent of the men with a primary school education had learned a worker's trade through company training.

34. One of the functions of the German foreman (*Meister*) is his training role, specified in his diploma. That is why he is given the responsibility for job definition and job assignments.

35. It has been observed that semiskilled workers have a "surplus" of qualifications that allows them to solve problems that are much more complex than those designated in the usual qualification; see F. Weltz, G. Schmidt, and J. Sass, *Facharbeiter in Industriebetrieb* (Frankfurt: Athenaum Verlag, 1974).

36. The head of a technical department is one of the French companies had this to say: "What we're aiming for is to be able to run these machines as easily as a car." He went on to stress his desire to make the worker's job as simple as possible so the job would require no thought.

37. Nonmanual workers in France and *Angestallte* in Germany.

38. Sixty percent of the men from working-class families followed a worker's apprenticeship; for sons of nonmanual workers, the figure is 44 percent and 35 percent for sons of high-level management and the liberal professions.

39. German skilled workers generally have less seniority than unskilled workers (the contrary is true in France) and a higher rate of intercompany mobility. In particular, most apprentices leave the company soon after they have finished their training, which shows the general value of the training they received.

40. Thus 61 percent of skilled workers are the sons of skilled workers, compared with 46.7 percent in France. This is consistent with the idea of professionalization. Those qualified for an occupation feel less attached to any one company; this can also reinforce the phenomenon of social reproduction.

41. It is worth noting that the social identity of blue-collar workers is as strong as that of white-collar workers. The white-collar worker's sense of social identity can be seen by the fact that the union movement developed earlier and was more autonomous than that in France. This no doubt helped the white-collar worker remain more independent of the employer.

42. Mobility from manual to nonmanual is greater in France than Germany, according to the mobility index calculated for the period 1972–1975: 2.35 as compared with 1.75.

43. In 1970 one out of seven male workers with company training had a *Meister's* diploma; a fair percentage had a job outside industry.

44. See H. Popitz et al., *Das Gesellschaftsbild.*

45. In Germany most university graduates have jobs in government administration, and we know that nonuniversity vocational education is the dominant component in the educational systems.

46. This is more common in the chemical industry than in metallurgy. In the chemical industry, men with doctorates in chemistry are almost automatically given the status of *L.A.* Professional associations are strong in this sector and keep a check on companies.

47. This is encouraged by a training system during employment that is older and better developed than in France.

48. In the companies studied, about 40 percent of top management in industry and 60 percent in metallurgy began their career as workers or did an apprenticeship to become a skilled worker. One should also note that the rate of social reproduction for top-level German management is lower than that in France.

49. The fact that he is often assisted in large companies by a shop technician or an administrative assistant indicates a low level of professionalization. Most

often he is there to transmit technical orders or to collect information for the personnel department. He complains that he is "short-circuited" by personnel representatives in his dealings with management.

50. This is also true of managers with *Grandes Ecoles* diplomas: in our study, those with over ten years in the company represented about 60 percent; their German counterparts represented only about 20 percent. Similarly, national statistics (FASFID in France, 1971, and VDI in Germany, 1974) show that 71 percent of engineers with diplomas in France had been with the company for over 21 years as compared with only 53 percent in Germany.

51. This division within the management category, which makes for a double hierarchy, is very significant; it is interesting to note that the proportion of "self-taught" men is aroung 40 percent and has been rising slightly since 1956 according to UIMM statistics published in 1970.

52. A small number of them obtained a technician's or engineer's diploma after having attended a less prestigious technical school or engineering school. The others, especially in administration, reached the intermediate level of general education in a secondary school. This means that they failed in the competition to reach the university level rather than that they acquired specific knowledge that is recognized professionally.

53. This density corresponds in France to a larger number of top-level managers than the *Leitende Angestellte* alone (who correspond more to the French middle management; they owe their status to the fact that their salary is higher than the highest negotiated rate). But it also reflects a social phenomenon of concentration of top-level diplomas and of being co-opted by peers. This is particularly evident at the level of executive management.

54. Statistical Office of the European Community, *Wage Structures in Industry in 1972* (special publication, yellow series).

55. These include the social security administration; the law governing the establishment of companies; statutes in government administration, which make a distinction between civil servants (*Beamte*), white-collar workers, and blue-collar workers; apprenticeships; and lastly unions.

56. It is important to distinguish codetermination in a workshop (1971 law on establishing companies) from "qualified codetermination" in worker representation on company supervisory boards.

57. Some further research on the LEST project was done in 1976–1977 in Great Britain by Arndt Sorge (International Institute of Management, Berlin) and by Malcolm Warner (The Administration Staff College, Henley-on-Thames). An analysis of company organization in the three countries (Federal Republic of Germany, France, and Great Britain) will be published in the near future.

58. We would like to specify that this research strategy in no way implies an extrapolation of an analysis of companies to that of a society, and vice versa.

On the contrary, it opens up the possibility of integrating macro and micro sociology.

59. We will not raise the question of the postindustrial society here, which deals with the problem of treating social change as a process of historical change, for it goes beyond the scope of our subject.

9   Internal Labor Markets and Paternalism in Rural Areas

Peter B. Doeringer

Conventional wisdom holds that poverty and economic backwardness in rural areas of America mirror the long-term shift of employment out of agriculture, and other primary-products industries, into the manufacturing and service sectors of urban areas. This rural decline is usually traced to factors such as the mechanization of agriculture, the rise of agribusiness, and the decline in mining and rural mill-based industry, all taking place against the backdrop of rising demand for heavy industrial products and sophisticated business and personal services normally produced in urban areas.[1]

Beginning in the 1950s, however, this trend began to change. The rural labor force stabilized while farm employment continued to fall, and by the 1970s nonfarm jobs outnumbered agricultural and related work in many rural areas.[2] Moreover, during the 1970s rates of employment growth in nonmetropolitan areas exceeded those of metropolitan areas.[3] Taken together, these changes appear to signal the beginning of a new turnaround in rural economies based less on agriculture and more on an economy fueled by the growth of manufacturing and service sectors.

Many "theories" have been offered to explain changing patterns of rural development.[4] The lack of locational or other cost advantages needed to attract the industrial and service jobs which could replace traditional sources of employment, the failure of capital markets to finance profitable ventures, and an absence of a "market" for entrepreneurial services are cited as causes of stagnation or decline. Urban areas, it is argued, are able to outbid rural areas in the competition for jobs. Low wages, freedom from trade unions, lower energy costs, and industrial development incentives are frequently mentioned sources of growth, particularly with respect to the rural south.

There have been few direct tests of these explanations of rural development to determine which should be used to shape policy thinking, and more generally, considerable dispute clouds the question of regional development.[5] Moreover there are virtually no in-depth studies of rural economies, or of rural labor markets, that might provide empirical insights into rural labor market processes.[6] What forces control employment levels by establishment and areas? What are the determinants of wages? Who gets hired for which jobs? What are the training, upgrading, and career paths in rural labor markets? How do out-migration and in-migration affect the skill mix of rural areas?

In the absence of facts we are faced with a choice between two competing analytical frameworks for addressing these employment questions. The wage competition/human capital approach argues that employment and earnings are largely the result of competitive adjustments made by employers and workers. The alternative view argues that competition is modified in many important ways by unions, wage regulation, and custom. Unemployment and underemployment may be persistent, and job rationing may be substantial. Discrimination may segregate employment by race, sex, or age and may alter supply and demand relationships in the labor market. Internal labor markets and enterprise-specific training may shape career advancement for many workers. As a result labor markets may become segmented into noncompeting groupings of jobs and workers.[7]

While the nature, causes, and quantitative significance of labor market segmentation have been the subject of extensive debate during the past decade, there is substantial agreement that labor market outcomes vary substantially by type of worker, type of occupation or job, and by type of establishment. Both the debate and the data, however, are strongly influenced by the urban experience, and there is some evidence to suggest that rural labor markets may operate on a very different basis.

Anecdotes from employment and training officials in rural areas, for example, suggest that neither human capital models nor segmentation theories based upon sex, race, or industrial divisions in the labor market are applicable to rural areas. The economic structure of rural areas differs markedly from urban areas, as employment is relatively more concentrated in agriculture and in the production and processing of resource-based goods, in light industry, and in smaller-scale establishments.[8] Labor force participation rates as well as wages tend to be lower in rural than in urban areas suggesting marked supply and demand differences between urban and rural areas.[9] Finally sociologists have documented substantial differences in the social systems, attitudes, and values between urban and rural America.[10] Collectively, these findings suggest that rural labor markets manifest a distinct set of characteristics.

Case Studies of Rural Employers

In order to explore some of the consequences of urban-rural differences in labor markets, and to understand the reasons for recent growth in manufacturing employment in rural areas, a series of case studies were undertaken of the pay, employment, and labor relations practices of rural employers. These studies were designed to develop data on the employment practices of rural manufacturing firms and to determine to what extent they were influenced by the social and economic environment of the rural community.

These studies were conducted in two areas of rural Maine. One area consisted of a group of towns clustered around Dover-Foxcroft, the county seat for Piscataquis County, located some forty miles northwest of Bangor, Maine. The towns in this area included Dexter, Dover-Foxcroft, Guilford, Milo, and Corinna. The second group of towns was in southwestern Maine in an area about forty miles west of Portland consisting of a group of towns—Cornish, Parsonsfield, Hiram, Kezar Falls, and Limington—mainly located in York County. The remainder of this section presents a brief of these two areas to provide the reader with a flavor of the rural environment in which workplace employment practices are developed.

The two groups of towns share many features in common. They are all small, ranging in population in 1970 from 4,178 in Dover-Foxcroft to 686 in Hiram. Commuting distances to urban areas keep them relatively isolated from urban labor markets.[11] The populations in these rural areas are relatively homogeneous. Although there were ethnic differences within these communities, over 99 percent of the population was white and most were native born.

It was not possible to get detailed education data on a town-by-town basis. However, there was a general consensus that the majority of the youth in the towns graduated from high school, but not from college. One survey in 1979 in rural York County, for example, reported that 87 percent of the 20 to 21 year old males and 79 percent of the females had completed high school, although none had yet completed college. Among 22 to 44 year olds, the comparable figures for males were 65 and 18 percent, and for females the figures were 70 and 14 percent, respectively.[12] Census data for rural Piscataquis County, which contains

Table 9.1
Education and work of rural high school graduates, 1980

Activity following graduation	Southwestern Maine area		Dover-Foxcroft area		
	High school 1	High school 2	High school 3	High school 4	Vocational school[b]
Four-year college	20.0	20.0	23.0	22.0	
Two-year college	16.0	5.0	9.0	0	20.0
Other postsecondary education	1.0	17.0	22.0	0	
Military	20.0	10.0	9.0	9.0	8.0
Work		38.0		50.0	
Other[a]	43.0	10.0	37.0	19.0	13.0
Total	100.0	100.0	100.0	100.0	100.0

Source: Follow-up reports obtained from local schools.
a. Homemaker, unemployed, travel, unknown, left labor market.
b. 1979 data.

a number of towns in the sample around Dover-Foxcroft reveals a similar pattern. Almost half the males and over half of the females over twenty-five had completed high school, whereas only 14 percent of the males and 18 percent of the females had completed college.

Interviews with employers, and with local secondary schools, suggest that there are not wide differences in the educational preparation of recent cohorts of young workers who remain in the rural area. Although there are substantial variations among schools, and among different years in the same school, on average about half the graduates go directly to work (see table 9.1).

Construction, services, and government employment have grown in both areas. There were a number of manufacturing plant closings during the early 1970s as a result of declines in the shoe and textile industries. These were more or less offset by new industries locating in these areas, and by a number of manufacturing plants adding to their capacity. In Dover-Foxcroft, for example, three manufacturing firms closed during the early 1970s, and other towns in the area faced either plant closing or layoffs. By the late 1970s several of these factories reopened or expanded under new ownership, and manufacturing became a growth sector. Data on the industrial composition of employment confirm the prevalence of nondurable manufacturing. For example, in rural Piscataquis County 43 percent of employment was in manufacturing, compared with 25 percent for the United States as a whole. The leading employment sector was furniture and lumber products accounting for over one-third of all manufacturing jobs. Textiles accounted for almost another third, and all nondurables comprised almost 60 percent of all manufacturing.

Perhaps the most characteristic feature of these rural economies is that, with some exceptions, manufacturing plants tend to be relatively small and to pay low wages. In some labor market areas there are one or two high-paying employers at most; other areas have none. More common are small- to medium-size firms producing shoes, textiles, or wood products and paying around the minimum wage. In the southwestern Maine area, for example, of the nine manufacturing plants with over 20 employees in 1980, three had less than 50 employees, and all had less than 250 employees.[13]

In addition to this formal employment there is considerable informal economic activity. Workers performing informal economic activities are self-employed. They chop wood, fish, hunt, and do craft work, but much of this work is highly seasonal. The magnitude of informal activity is difficult to assess since the boundary line between hobby, production for home consumption, and paid employment is vague. Often such work is undertaken on a casual basis and is "unreported" in official surveys.

Overall, employment in these areas has been rising during the 1970s, although labor force participation rates tend to be below the national average. These are not ideal indicators of local labor market conditions, however, because the opportunity for self-employment in rural areas, particularly among males, often blurs the dividing line between working and not working. Nevertheless, on balance, there appears to be general evidence of local labor reserves, and most employers have queues of job applicants.

Labor surpluses are also reflected in pay. Anecdotal evidence suggests that pay in these rural areas is generally somewhat below that which is obtainable in nearby urban areas and substantially below that in metropolitan areas in southern New England. This is borne out by one survey of wages in the Dover-Foxcroft area that compared pay in seven occupations with comparable jobs in Bangor and in Portland. With the exception of general clerks, there were pay differentials of 5 to 25 percent relative to Bangor and 14 to 40 percent relative to Portland

Table 9.2
Rural-urban pay differentials, 1972

	Dover-Foxcroft LMA		Dexter–Corona–Newport LMA	
Occupation title	Ratio to Bangor labor market area	Ratio to Portland labor market area	Ratio to Bangor labor market area	Ratio to Portland labor market area
General clerk	0.997	0.973	0.884	0.863
Secretary	0.909	0.833	0.845	0.775
Maintenance workers	0.752	0.607	0.891	0.726
Millwright	0.767	0.695	0.826	0.749
Janitor	0.777	0.721	0.796	0.738

Source: Eastern Maine Development District, "An Economic Adjustment Strategy for Piscataquis County and S. W. Penobscot LMA" (July 1978), table K.

(see table 9.2). Such differentials are larger than would be expected purely on the basis of objective costs of commuting or labor migration.

What appears to set these rural communities apart from urban communities is an economic structure characterized by (1) small firms paying near the minimum wage, (2) the presence of only an occasional large firm paying substantially higher wages, and (3) widespread opportunities for informal employment. In the following sections, these three types of employment situations are examined.

Informal Employment

In rural ares many people seem to work irregularly on their own to sell their product to others. Sometimes these are small service contractors, or they may be seasonal or occasional workers. Many are craft workers who try to produce for retail sale, but who keep for themselves whatever is unsold.

Informal work can be quite remunerative, as in the case of skilled boat builders, but for many it is a form of low-wage earnings that supplements income from other sources. Informal male occupations in this sector include woodcutting, casual construction work, and hunting. Females are more heavily concentrated in small crafts production, often suitable either for commercial sale or home consumption. Many informal jobs are marginal, and the product from such work is sold in highly competitive and uncertain markets.

Informal work is found in urban areas in casual jobs such as day labor, dishwashing, street vending, and urban craft work. Petty crime and illicit activities may also be counted in this category. In rural Maine, however, the illicit component of informal work appears less important, and what is striking is the large number of workers who seem to engage in such work during some part of the year.

Labor Relations and Employment Strategies in Large Firms

In some, but not all, of the rural communities studied there is a single, large, high-wage employer. Often this will be a paper company, but it could occasionally be a large machine shop or even a large electronics plant. These companies have few economic linkages to the local community. They tend to be located in rural areas either because of proximity to some raw material, such as timber, or because there has been a tradition of local ownership. Other than employing labor, providing wage income, and paying taxes, these firms have little direct influence on the locality.

These firms pay high wages (usually two to three times the starting pay in other local companies), have good promotion opportunities and working conditions, and provide the full gamut of fringe benefits. The firms studied were usually unionized and had been experiencing modest growth during the period of the interviews.

Because of the high wages and good working conditions, these firms were considered to be the most desirable places of employment. As a result they had the pick of the local labor force. New employees were typically recruited from a pool of applicants who had indicated their availability for casual or temporary employment with the firm. Workers who performed well as temporary employees would then become eligible for full-time employment. Although these large firms were in a position to be highly selective in drawing from the labor pool, selectivity was based on trial employment experience and had little to do with the age, skill, or educational characteristics of the labor force. In all observable ways, including ability on the job, workers in the larger firms resembled workers in other parts of the rural economy.

Labor relations in the large firms were quite traditional. The rights and responsibilities of labor and management were described in collective bargaining agreements resembling those of unionized manufacturing firms in urban areas. Workers knew what was expected of them in terms of a day's work and relationships between labor and management were relatively formal. During contract negotiations or grievance disputes, both sides perceived themselves as adversaries.

The wage policy of these companies was generally set outside the community, either through collective bargaining or by the policy of a parent corporation. Aside from being able to draw labor from the local community, the wage policies of these firms had no spillover effect on other wages in the locality. Other firms simply conceded labor to the high-wage firms and set their own pay as if these firms did not exist.

With the exception of their isolation, such large firms are similar to those found in many urban areas. Their pay and labor relations practices are indistinguishable from those of many primary sector employers found throughout the economy.

Employment Practices in Small Firms

While there are differences in both informal employment and in large enterprise employment between urban and rural areas, these differences are more one of degree than of major distinctions in the nature of the employment relationship. The employment practices of small firms, however, contrast sharply with similar work situations in urban areas. Small firms, usually those with fewer than 100 employees, constitute the major source of formal employment in the rural labor markets studied. Light manufacturing firms engaged in the production of textiles, furniture, wood products, electronic components, and shoes are of principal interest in this study.

Production workers in small manufacturing firms are generally low paid with wages being at or near the legal minimum. Fringe benefits are rudimentary if they exist at all. Working conditions are often unpleasant, and the pace of work tends to be pressured. Usually the firms are nonunion, or have nonmilitant unions.

Job content and job structures in this sector appear to be like those in similar companies in the secondary labor markets of urban areas. The technology, work organization, and working conditions are similar to those found elsewhere, whether in textiles, shoes, or light fabrication and assembly. Employment is dead end because there are few promotion opportunities.

Despite the apparent similarities in pay, technology, work organization, and working conditions between jobs in the rural economies studied and those in urban areas, labor-management relationships at the workplace differ substantially. In urban areas such low-skilled jobs would be filled by workers who are dissatisfied and alienated from their work; who are uncommitted to their particular employer; and who exhibit high rates of quitting.

In the rural companies surveyed, the reverse tendency exists. Workers often identify with goals and objectives of their companies. They work hard, are loyal and committed to their employers, and are concerned with the quality and quantity of the work they produce. Quit rates appear to be relatively low for the respective industries and many workers who are laid off return to their employers even after substantial periods of separation. In the somewhat larger companies and in those with the poorest working conditions where the amount of dissatisfaction with working conditions is slightly higher, the same patterns of attachment to employer and low turnover appeared to prevail. Moreover, though these firms did not always have such long queues of job applicants, they were readily able to recruit additional labor at the prevailing wage rate. Indeed, several of these firms had experienced periods of quite substantial growth and had been somewhat surprised at the ease with which they could obtain additional labor, particularly female workers.

The picture that emerges in small rural firms is thus one of a work force that receives pay, fringe benefits, and working conditions comparable to those provided by the least attractive employers in urban labor markets but exhibits attitudes and behavior like those found in the most attractive jobs in urban labor markets. Instead of high alienation and high turnover, employees of small firms showed a dedication and commitment to their employers that is most characteristic of employees of high-wage nonunion firms that cultivate and encourage workers to identify with the goals of their firms.

This impression is confirmed by employers in the dependent sector. They characterize their workers as being "good" and willing to put in a full day's work. Interviews with employers were filled with stories of individuals or work teams putting forth special efforts or voluntarily making special sacrifices.

Employers frequently recounted examples of the dedication and willingness to sacrifice found among their workers. Turnover was reported to be very low. Employees frequently were willing to stay late, often without premium pay, to complete a production job or to solve a troublesome production problem. Requests by management to work an extra shift, or to work on weekends, were accepted without complaint.

There was even one example, provided by a union official, of the attitudes of employees during a rare strike. Throughout the strike supervisory employees had continued to operate the factory. Rather than being disturbed that production was continuing in the face of the strike, the main concern of the strikers was that the supervisors would not be able to maintain the quality of the production and that there might be damage to the equipment. There was great relief when the strike was settled, not so much because of the economic implications, but because workers were anxious to preserve the reputation of the company's product.

Employers appear to make reciprocal commitments to their workers. They undertake to rehire workers who have been laid off and to give preferential employment to relatives of incumbent employees. They are familiar with the unemployment insurance system and attempt to ensure that regular employees will have enough work each year to be eligible for unemployment compensation when laid off. Dependent sector employers often aid employees during financial emergencies with loans or time off with pay. While none of these responsibilities is formally codified, and all remain at the discretion of the employer, they are well understood by the work force.

Paternalism as a Source of Worker Contentment

How is this worker commitment to be explained? One possibility lies in the basic traits of the rural labor force. Through values instilled by education and upbringing, it is possible that work attitudes of rural workers are shaped to respond positively to managerial authority. Such an explanation would be consistent with studies by rural sociologists stressing the value placed upon hard work and the respect for authority found in rural areas.[14] On the other hand, these attitudes are not found among workers from identical backgrounds who work in large, high-paying firms. Moreover, when workers transfer from smaller firms to larger, high-paying firms, their attitudes toward management and work appear to conform readily to their new environment. Thus, whatever predisposition toward work and authority may be present in these rural areas, they do not seem to explain the observed patterns of behavior.

A second explanation lies in the work incentives present within a labor surplus economy. Where jobs are scarce, they are more highly valued by workers, and worker behavior is likely to reflect a desire to preserve employment. Because small firms are usually nonunion, there is no contractual obligation to follow due process in discharges and employers retain the right to terminate workers at will. Fear of discharge and subsequent unemployment could well breed dedicated worker attitudes.[15]

. This "valuing the job" explanation is consistent with different worker behaviors observed in large and small rural firms. In the large firms collectively bargained grievance procedures or other types of management commitment to "due process" personnel practices protect workers against arbitrary discharge so that fear of job loss is not likely to emerge with the same force as in small firms. This explantion is also consistent with the high labor turnover found in the secondary sector of urban labor markets, where employment is also low wage and dead end. In urban areas such jobs are generally perceived to be readily available and therefore are less valued than in rural areas. Nevertheless, the level of commitment to dead-end jobs in small rural firms seems extraordinarily high, particularly since it even affects workers for whom informal employment is a realistic alternative. In addition, if the threat of discharge were as effective as this explanation would imply, it is not clear why employers should make any reciprocal commitments to workers beyond providing a job at the minimum wage.

A third explanation comes from the effect of labor relations practices within small firms upon workers' attitudes. A striking feature of labor relations in these firms is the presence of paternalism. Paternalism assumes a number of benign forms in the firms studied. Management knows each worker by his or her first name; there is a generally relaxed atmosphere about social relations in the plant; relatives are given special consideration in employment, and there is often an attempt to tailor job assignments and working hours to the needs of individual workers. These practices contribute positively to working conditions.

Paternalism, however, also affects the economic circumstances and income security of workers, particularly in the areas of fringe benefits and unemployment compensation, by defining the terms on which such benefits are made available. Small rural firms provide little in the way of fringe benefits as a matter of entitlement. Paid vacations, life and health insurance, and the like are rudimentary, at best. Such firms, however, often make fringelike benefits available on a *discretionary* basis to individual employees. For example, if an employee needs to borrow money for home improvements, or to buy a car, or to meet a sudden financial crisis, the employer may make a salary advance or may help with a loan at a local bank. If illness strikes, workers are sometimes continued on the payroll. If there is a sudden emergency or a death in the family, paid leave may be allowed. In addition, employees are often allowed to borrow tools or to use company equipment for personal projects.

Although these benefits cannot be "claimed" as a matter of legal right, they are made available to workers as part of the factory custom. The *quid pro quo* for these benefits is that the worker be loyal and committed to the company. Such unspoken contracts between employers and workers are the foundation of the paternalistic work relationship.

Similar contracts relate to employment security. Paternalistic employers may tend to rotate work assignments during slack periods to allow those most in need to continue to work. Such rotation is also used to ensure that all regular employees receive a sufficient number of days of work a year so that they are eligible for unemployment insurance. This is particularly important because sales in dependent sector firms tend to fluctuate, making it difficult to provide steady, year-round work.

In addition to paternalistic practices affecting the well-being of workers already employed in these small firms, there are intergenerational and kinship elements to paternalism as well. An established work relationship with a dependent sector employer carries an implied commitment by the employer to give hiring preference to the children of employees and often to other relatives as well. It is common to find several members of a family working in the same dependent sector firm, thereby increasing the economic dependence of the family upon the firm and further leveraging the importance of the firm's success to the long-term welfare of the family.

Reciprocity of relations between paternalistic employers and loyal workers creates incentives not only for productivity but for strong attachments of employees to their firms. Most of this attachment comes from the benefits of employment in a paternalistic firm, but paternalism also interacts with the labor market environment.

Just as loyalty is the dominant characteristic of the dependent work relationship, quitting is the strongest indicator of *disloyalty*. Workers who quit their jobs in paternalistic firms face serious consequences for reemployment since quitting is prima facie evidence of a disloyal, and therefore unreliable, worker. As a result workers who quit are likely to be branded as having "wrong" attitudes, and are unlikely to be hired by other dependent sector employers. For such workers the reemployment options are thus limited to prolonged "waiting" for a job in a high-wage firm where "disloyalty" is not a factor in the hiring decision, becoming self-employed, or migrating to some other labor market area.

Paternalism and Labor Force Quality

Inherent in paternalistic employment systems are strong barriers to the exit of workers. These barriers derive, in part, from the discretionary granting of fringe benefits, the provision of income security in conjunction with unemployment insurance, and the preferential hiring of family members. They are further reinforced by the marketwide obstacles to reemployment in other paternalistic firms that are posed by the act of quitting. The general condition of labor surplus in rural economies further enhances the value of jobs in paternalistic firms and, by reducing competition for labor, allows the prejudice against the reemployment of disloyal workers in paternalistic firms to be sustained.

Paternalistic employers are thus able to obtain a rather special labor force, one available at low wages that identifies with the goals of the firm and works hard to accomplish these goals. The ability to obtain labor at low wages derives from the labor surplus conditions prevailing in rural areas where labor supply is relatively elastic at or around the minimum wage. The high productivity and commitment to the firm come from the paternalistic practices of employers and the reciprocal nature of the labor exchange occurring in paternalistic firms.

In addition to low wages, abundant labor, and the productivity benefits that derive from loyalty and commitment, paternalistic employers derive an additional advantage from their employment practices that is often unrecognized—the ability to treat labor as a variable factor of production. This ability to vary the labor force within the paternalistic enterprise through layoffs may at first seem to contradict the idea of a strong attachment between workers and their paternalistic firms. Paternalistic attachments, however, appear to be sustained even in the face of layoffs. The paternalistic employer is expected to try to control the pattern of layoffs so that laid-off workers will receive income from unemployment insurance and that those most in need of income will have the greatest job protection. Similarly, worker loyalty is expected to continue during layoffs so that workers will return to their employers when recalled. In practice, paternalistic firms seem to be able to recall employees from even lengthy layoffs with few losses to other companies.

This freedom to lay off workers without fear of losing them carries further implications for worker productivity. Economic theory tells us that employers should be concerned with labor turnover when they have made enterprise-specific investments in their workers and that such investments should also discourage layoffs. As a result labor becomes a "quasi-fixed" factor of production and may be underutilized during periods of economic slack.[16] The experience of urban employers making such investments is that premium pay or fringe benefit incentives are necessary to discourage labor turnover and to ensure that workers can be successfully recalled. In rural areas, however, paternalism serves as a substitute for such compensation premiums as a deterrent to turnover among workers who have been laid off, and the employment of specifically trained labor can be varied at will in response to fluctuations in demand.

Economists may find elements in this analysis of paternalism that suggest familiar territory—oligopsonistic behavior among paternalistic employers, the market distortions of minimum wages, and the theory of the "collective" firm. While paternalism, as described in this chapter, is clearly an economic process with economic consequences, it would be a mistake to interpret the findings in terms of such concepts.

For example, employers do not collude in the usual sense of either fixing wages or agreeing not to hire one another's labor. Wages are "fixed" by the minimum wage, but employers further augment worker compensation through the giving of discretionary benefits. The absence of labor piracy simply reflects the overall surplus of labor which makes piracy unnecessary and the independent decisions of paternalistic emloyers not to hire disloyal workers. The act of luring a worker from another paternalistic firm, or of hiring a worker who has quit his or her job with such a firm, is unthinkable because it is inconsistent with the worker traits demanded under a paternalistic system.

The idea that workers and managers are participating in some form of collective undertaking comes somewhat closer to capturing the spirit of paternalistic employment relationships, but it must be realized that the common identification of workers and managers with the objectives of the firm are the result of an unequal reciprocal exchange. Managers and owners control both jobs and discretionary benefits. As a result they set the terms of the exchange, and it is to be expected to run in their favor, even if the exchange is conducted in the most benign of ways. The paternalistic relationship is essentially one of dependency where the workers are more dependent on their employers than vice versa.

In this respect paternalistic employment systems are akin to markets governed by the exchange of gifts as well as the exchange of services and money.[17] The employer makes the worker a gift of discretionary benefits while the employee provides the gift of loyalty. The employer's gift, however, is harder for the worker to replace than it is for the employer to find another loyal worker.

Implications

These findings carry implications for understanding internal labor markets, for industrial relations practices, and for economic development. First, they suggest that there is considerable room for organizational discretion even within internal labor markets having similar technologies and producing similar products. These organizational differences may have varied consequences for employee behavior. For example, low-wage firms with dead-end jobs that are organized along paternalistic lines will experience markedly different levels of worker attachment, commitment, and productivity than will those organized according to more antagonistic industrial relations arrangements. High-wage firms, however, also have considerable latitude in their organizational arrangements but are less likely than low-wage firms to experience wide variations in worker attitudes or productivity.

The economic environment facing the internal labor market will also have an influence upon organizational arrangements and performance. This conclusion is supported by the observation that the presence of labor surpluses and underemployment is an important environmental factor in allowing paternalism to be sustained. It is difficult to imagine paternalism having the same effect in an economy with considerable competition among firms for low-paid labor.

It is often argued that the social environment of the community will also have an independent impact on internal labor market structure and performance. Without denying that community factors may be important, it is clear that the style of workplace labor relations has a more significant effect. There is limited evidence from the studies that workers from rural communities, regardless of any predisposition toward authority or a strong work ethic, adapt readily to different plant level industrial relations environment. For example, similar workers from the same community working in different plants show markedly different work attitudes and behavior, depending on the industrial relations practices in the plant. Moreover, in those instances where the same worker moves from one industrial relations environment to another, a similar malleability in behavior has been observed. Workers who move from paternalistic plants to larger, high-wage plants, usually as a result of major layoffs or plant closings, readily adapt their attitudes to the new industrial environment. Therefore, when problems of worker attitude, motivation, and turnover are encountered by employers, they are not necessarily immutable and may be subject to remedy through changes in personnel practices.

Third, the growth of employment in the rural areas studied seems to hinge upon an employment system that benefits employers through (1) wage rates that are as low or lower than those for labor anywhere in the country, (2) employee attitudes toward hard work, loyalty, and high-quality work that can be traced to paternalistic practices, and (3) the ability to treat labor as a varible cost through judicious use of paternalistic practices with respect to layoff and recall, flexible work assignments, and the incentives provided by jobs in a labor surplus economy. Labor surplus without paternalism will not guarantee a high-quality labor force, and paternalism cannot coexist with labor market competition.

The conclusion that a major attraction of rural areas is the presence of "bargain" labor is consistent with the observed growth in employment among paternalistic firms. A development policy stressing employment growth must therefore recognize the importance of "bargain" labor, particularly as it relates to worker productivity and commitment. This suggests that the expansion of rural employment may entail the preservation of paternalistic ties and the lack of competition in local labor markets. The alternative, that of pursuing a more competitive labor market strategy, is likely to undermine paternalism and low pay in particular local markets. This implies a trade-off between employment growth and pay levels that has the potential of undermining cost advantages which made for rural growth in the first place.

Notes

The author is grateful for comments provided by Susan Hudson-Wilson, Michael Manove, Heath Paley, and Paul Osterman and for the preliminary ideas developed in Peter B. Doeringer et al., "Rural Labor Markets and Rural Economic Development," *New England Journal of Employment and Training* 1 (Winter 1981):6–14.

1. The Carter Administration, *Small Community and Rural Development Policy*, (Washington, D.C.: The White House, December 20, 1979) p. 1.

2. Ibid., p. 2.

3. See Thomas E. Till, "The Rise of the Factory in Rural America: Changes in Manufacturing Employment in Non-metropolitan Areas," prepared for the Future of Rural America Project, Farmers Home Administration, U.S. Department of Agriculture, September 1, 1979.

4. See William Alonso and John Friedmann, *Regional Policy, Readings in Theory and Applications* (Cambridge: The MIT Press, 1975); Douglass C. North, "Location Theory and Regional Economic Growth," *Journal of Political Economy* **58** (June 1955):243–258; George Borts, "The Equalization of Returns and Regional Economic Growth," *The American Economic Review* (June 1960):319–347; and Peter Kilby, *Entrepreneurship and Economic Development* (New York: The Free Press, 1971).

5. See Bennett Harrison and Barry Bluestone, *The Deindustrialization of America* (New York: Basic Books, 1982).

6. Most studies of rural areas either rely solely on survey data or are oriented toward sociological concerns. See, for example, J. H. Copp, "Rural Sociology and Rural Development," *Rural Sociology* 37:515–533, E. Matthews, *Neighbor and Kin: Life in a Tennessee Ridge Community* (Nashville: Vanderbilt University Press, 1965); Louis Plock, "A Study of Health Related Factors: Bucksport, Orland, Verona, Maine 1973, A Preliminary Report," Misc. Rep. No. 238, U.S. Department of Agriculture, Resources and Economics, University of Maine, Orono; Arthur J. Vidich and Joseph Bensman, *Small Town in Mass Society: Class, Power and Religion in a Rural Community* (Princeton: Princeton University Press, 1958); and Rungeling et al., *Employment, Income and Welfare in the Rural South* (New York: Praeger Special Studies, 1977).

7. Peter Doeringer and Michael Piore, *Internal Labor Markets and Manpower Analysis* Lexington, Mass.: D.C. Heath, 1971); and Marcia Freedman, *Labor Markets: Segments and Shelters*, Conservation of Human Resource Series (Allanheld, Osmun, and Co., Montclair, N.J., 1976). For a critique of the dual theory, see Glen Cain, "The Challenge of Dual and Radical Theories of the Labor Market to Orthodox Theory: A Survey," *Journal of Economic Literature* **14** (December 1976):1215–1257.

8. According to the Bureau of the Census employment distribution in urban and rural areas by industry is as follows:

	Urban		Rural	
	1960	1970	1960	1970
Agriculture, forestry, fisheries	1.11	1.02	22.16	12.04
Mining	0.63	0.56	2.07	1.64
Construction	5.51	5.37	6.97	7.84

(table continued)

	Urban		Rural	
	1960	1970	1960	1970
Durable goods mfgr.	15.91	15.25	13.26	15.61
Nondur. goods mfgr.	11.41	10.02	10.88	12.29
Transportation, commerce, public utilities	7.48	7.10	5.28	5.75
Wholesale and retail	24.95	21.13	14.52	16.82
Finance, insurance, and real estate	4.95	5.73	2.03	2.78
Services	22.59	35.69	16.48	27.98
Public administration	5.46	5.91	3.56	4.18
Total	100.00	100.00	100.00	100.00

Source: Bureau of the Census, U.S. Department of Commerce, *Census of the Population*: General Social and Economic Characteristics, U.S. Summary (1970, table 103; 1960, table 91).

9. Unemployment rates for small areas do not provide an accurate picture of labor market surplus. A somewhat more reliable indicator is the labor force participation rate (LFPR).

LFPR for males in Piscataquis County manifest comparable patterns over age groups as do those for the nation. But in nearly every age category the county has lower rates. The female rates are again comparable in pattern but are lower for nearly all age categories. In 1970 labor force participation was as follows:

	Male		Female	
Age	U.S.	Piscataquis County	U.S.	Piscataquis County
16–17	47.5	13.6	34.9	17.8
18–19	69.9	60.7	53.7	47.5
20–24	86.6	92.8	57.8	47.0
25–34	96.6	95.5	45.0	39.8
35–44	97.0	94.6	51.1	60.5
45–64	88.7	88.6	48.7	46.6
65+	26.8	18.1	59.7	7.8

Sources: For United States, Employment and Training Administration, U.S. Department of Labor; *1979 Employment and Training Report of the President* (Washington, D.C.: GPO), table A-2, p. 236. For Piscataquis County, Bureau of the Census, U.S. Department of Commerce, *Census of the Population*, vol. 1, 1970, table 121.

10. See, for example: Gerald Somers et al., "Industrial Invasion of Non-Metropolitan America: A Quarter Century of Experience," Department of Rural Sociology, University of Wisconsin, Madison, 1974; Olaf F. Larson, "Values and

Beliefs of Rural People," in Thomas R. Ford, ed., *Rural U.S.A.: Persistence and Change*; and Paul H. Landig, *Rural Life in Process*.

11. York County Employment and Training Agency, Project Rural; "Transportation and Commuting Patterns: Facts and Issues for Policy Makers" (Mimeographed, March 1980), derived from table 3-B.

12. York County Employment and Training Agency, Project Rural; "Urban Demographics: A Planning Package for Government and Industry" (Mimeographed, n.d.), derived from tables 3-3 and 3-4.

13. Maine Department of Manpower Affairs, Bureau of Employment Security, Manpower Research Division, *Annual Planning Information for York County, Fiscal Year 1981*, April 1980, table 23.

14. See, for example, Vidich and Bensman, *Small Town in Mass Society*, and Larson, "Values and Beliefs of Rural People."

15. See Steven Stoft, "Cheat-Threat Theory: Techniques for Modeling Involuntary Unemployment," Discussion Paper 82, Boston University, Economics Department.

16. See Gary Becker, *Human Capital* (New York: Columbia University Press, 1964); Walter Y. Oi, "Labor as a Quasi-fixed Factor," *The Journal of Political Economy* **70** (December 1962):538–555.

17. See George A. Akenlof, "Labor Contracts as Partial Gift Exchange" (Mimeographed, University of California, Berkeley, September 1980).

Index

P_{ITQ}